WORLD WAR II
There at 18—Told at 81

Grenades, Guitars, Guts & Glory

To: Karen,

With Best Wishes

Ronald Ray

2019

By SGT Ronold Ray

With Gina Ray

First published by Dog Ear Publishing
4010 W. 86th Street, Ste H
Indianapolis, IN 46268
www.dogearpublishing.net

dog ear
PUBLISHING

ISBN: 978-159858-706-7

This book is printed on acid-free paper.

Printed in the United States of America

There at 18

Told at 81

*This book is gratefully dedicated to every person,
from the beginning of this Great Nation to the present,
who has put his or her life on the line fighting for the
freedom we now enjoy, and for those who continue to
sacrifice for this cause. May future generations always be
willing to pay the price in order to protect and live in a free land.*

In gratitude to my daughter Gina, for taking my manuscript and dedicating many hours to editing and for probing my mind for details long dormant.

CONTENTS

Introduction

I had just finished an exceptionally good day at the shop and was on my way home. Wanda, my wife, had called and told me supper was about ready. She was preparing her specialty— southern fried chicken, creamed potatoes, green beans, tossed salad, fresh baked bread and for dessert, a hot cherry pie topped with liberal scoops of vanilla ice cream. As I jumped into *Clunke*r, my old, rattletrap—a light green 1952 Ford pickup, I was thinking, "You couldn't beat a day like today with a stick!"

Driving two blocks east on Second Street, I slowed down to turn right on Gary. I noticed that the pecan trees on the huge corner lot were ready for harvesting. I continued on to the stop sign on Fourth and Gary. Then, I pulled into *Cabell's Minute Mart* to get a half gallon of Gandy's ice cream and to see if Larry or Gina might be waiting to hitch a ride with me. Sometimes they would walk to the store and wait, so they could ride in the bed of ol' Clunker to our house, which was only a couple of blocks away. However, today it was obvious that they were doing something else.

When I was almost home, I was startled by what I saw—the flurry of orange and red colors swirling in the yard. Japanese flags were flittering all around the place, and my mind went berserk!

For a moment, I flashed back to Okinawa. I could hear the shells exploding and smell the stench of decaying bodies, and I could hear a voice frantically calling for a medic. My thoughts changed so drastically and suddenly . . . for a fleeting moment, I was reliving the war.

Fortunately, this lasted only a second or two, and I realized that the Japanese flags I had collected and stored away, were now being used to play a game called *War.* Our backyard was usually Grand Central Station in the neighborhood crawling with kids, and today was no exception. Our four-foot cinder-tile fence was just perfect for a fort, and believe me, every kid in the neighborhood, including ours, was either inside defending or in the adjacent yards attacking. They were having the time of their lives!

What a contrast to what I was seeing and what I was remembering as my thoughts raced back in time. Here I sat in ol' Clunker as I watched all these children, ranging from five to twelve years old, run with those flags and scream with delight!

They were having so much fun and did not have the faintest idea of what war is really about, while at the same time I was envisioning the real thing.

It was just one of those times when the only thing I could do was to ask God to deliver each child from ever having to play the *real* game of war.

He will judge between the nations and
will settle disputes for many people.
They will beat their swords into plowshares and
their spears into pruning hooks.
Nation will not take up sword against nation,
nor will they train for war anymore.
Isaiah 2:4-5

Although I was scared to death,
I raised my billy club and was ready to crack
this guy over the head if he kept coming!

Raring to Go!

"First of all, young man, you're a farm boy, and we need you to help plant, cultivate, and harvest crops more than we need you in the service at this time. You'll be called soon enough. I was in World War I, so don't be in such a hurry to go to war. You'll understand what I mean someday if you ever have to go into combat," explained the chairman of the draft board.

The year was 1944. I wanted to quit school and join the Navy. My parents, who already had three sons in the military, were not about to sign the papers for me to enlist. Instead, they insisted I finish school and wait to be drafted. As soon as I graduated from Novice High School, I ran down to see the chairman and eagerly told him that I was ready to serve. I could not believe my ears. Instead of encouraging me, he was *actually* discouraging me!

My best high school buddies Gerald Henson, Milton Terrell, Frank Sartor and I had planned to join the military with hopes of staying together. However, there was one minor problem. I wanted to join the Navy, and they wanted to join the Army Air Corps. Finally, we all were eighteen years old and could have joined the service without our parents' consents. But, since we could never agree on which branch, our time expired. Then, *Uncle Sam* decided for us.

The big day rolled around on September 7 of that year when we joined other Coleman County draftees at the Coleman Bus Station. Full of enthusiasm and the spirit of patriotism, we were ready to conquer the world as we headed off to San Antonio to be inducted into the Armed Services! We were on our way to start a new life—one that would take each of us in different directions, yet toward the same goal. It would be the last time all my buddies and I would ever be together again.

After we arrived, we jumped off the bus at the Fort Sam Houston Induction Center. A sergeant warmly greeted us, "Grab a cot in one of those tents for tonight. The chow hall is over there and the latrine is down there. Good luck." Then, he disappeared.

The following morning after breakfast, the fun began. While I stood in what seemed like an endless line to be processed, a sailor announced over the public address system, "The Navy needs 125 more men. If you want to join the Navy, fall out now and form a line on the other side of the room."

Man, I grabbed my stuff and ran to join the stampede! I could not believe my eyes. To my surprise, Gerald and Milton were already standing in line! *Never* had they talked about joining the Navy. After I completed the lengthy procedure of having my orders verified, arranging to have my clothing sent back home and finishing all the recruiting requirements before the induction into the military, it was my turn for the final interview.

Since I did not savvy the different ranks, it was only later did I realize my interviewer was a full chicken colonel. He said, "So, you want to be a sailor?"

"Yes, sir!" I proudly answered as I stuck my chest out and stood as tall as I could while thinking I was *already* in the Navy.

"Well, we'll add about twenty-pounds to your weight, put a ninety-pound pack on your back and you'll make a darn good soldier," he said as he stamped **ARMY** on all my induction papers. As soon as he pointed to the Army line, my Navy career was history.

While we were in San Antonio awaiting our shipping orders, my first assignment was to pull guard duty. I had only been in the Army for a few days, and I did not have the *slightest* idea of what I was supposed to do. The first part was not bad at all. My job was to take nonviolent prisoners to the mess hall and bring them back to the guardhouse after their meals. It was easy. The prisoners told me *how*, *when*, and *what* to do. No problem!

The second part of guard duty was somewhat different. I patrolled the barracks where the black soldiers were quartered. Segregation was practiced in World War II. The lush green lawns were perfectly manicured and signs were posted—*Keep Off the Grass.* However, some soldiers delighted in pitching a blanket under a shade tree to catch a nap or to roll the dice. I protected the grounds by ordering violators off.

After midnight, I stopped anyone who was leaving or returning to the barracks. Most of the time it was quiet except for when the cornfield adjacent to the barracks gave up its lovers. Around 11:45 p.m., I could hear voices as the girlfriends scrambled to catch the last bus of the evening back to San Antonio.

One time shortly after midnight, a car pulled up to the curb and a giant of a man got out. He was in one big hurry. Barreling down the gravel road, he headed straight toward me!

My instructions were to call out, "Halt," from a safe distance. If the person did not comply, I was to repeat the command. After calling out twice to this guy, he just kept coming and was not showing any sign of stopping. If a person failed to heed the third command, the order was to take action to stop him.

Very little time elapsed between the second and third command. On the third command, I raised my weapon, and was ready for action. I would have given a dollar to have a picture of what happened.

Although I was scared to death, I raised my billy club and was ready to crack this guy over the head if he kept coming! A high-ranking sergeant, he apparently was not accustomed to being challenged, especially next to his quarters. At some point, the sergeant realized I was not out there just gazing at the stars looking for the *Big Dipper*.

However, this realization came almost too late. The next few frames would have made a great cartoon as he came skating right up to me. The loose gravel from the road was flying all around and over me as he skidded to a halt. The sergeant was mortified, and I could see the whites of his eyes. After asking me *why* he was being stopped, I told him that I was just doing my job. When he asked for permission to go inside his barrack to go to bed, I was very quick to grant his request!

It did cross my mind more than once, "Now, *why* am I stopping these people and *what* am I supposed to do after I stop them?" No one ever told me that. Well, I soon learned during basic training.

Raring to Go!

T. J. Haney, Lowell Ray, Ronold Ray, Milton Terrell, Lavan Gotcher, and Gerald Henson

Gerald Henson

Frank Sartor

**Ronold Ray
and
Milton Terrell**

When I find you harebrained idiots,
I'm going to kick your tent down with you inside!

Basic Training

Each day we flocked to the bulletin board to see if our names were on the list. We were anxious and jittery to find out what our assignments would be. It seemed as if the Army was manufacturing jobs just to keep us busy, but the troops were getting restless.

Gerald and Milton had already left, each on separate trains. What was the deal? This was not our plan! Gerald, Milton and I had spent most of the summer working in the fields together including the wheat harvest in the Texas Panhandle. We had discussed our futures countless times and had definitely agreed that we would always be together during our military stint. For sure, we would be looking out for each other. We were in this thru thick and thin.

However, after staying ten days in San Antonio, my orders came down. The following day, I boarded a troop train and Frank was left behind still waiting to hear where his future would take him. What happened? He was supposed to be with us, too.

Although I had my orders, I still did not have any idea where I was going. All I knew—my friends were gone, and I did not know a soul. And, I was now on a troop train rolling down the track, heading north to some unknown destination. For all I knew, I might wake up in Canada. Then, my mind began to play some unfamiliar tricks on me.

It seemed as if I were rolling down a steep riverbank, desperately grabbing for *something* to hold on to, but everything was slipping thru my fingers. The reality of all the plans we had made and dreamed of for months was jerked right out from under us. And, it was just beginning to sink in. I was trying to cope with the idea of *when* I would see my friends again or if, in fact, I had seen them for the last time.

After twenty-four hours of traveling at a snail's pace, stopping on sidetracks and having too much time to think, we arrived to Camp Joseph T. Robinson in Little Rock, Arkansas. On my third day in camp, I was standing in the chow line thinking how dramatically my life had changed. Suddenly, someone yelled, "Snake! Run for your life." Then, quick as a flash, two strong arms grabbed me from behind and proceeded to squeeze the living daylights out of me. After being held for only a second, I turned around and discovered my fun-loving buddy, Milton.

The following day during an orientation class in a huge auditorium, Milton was marching with his company to exit the building when someone grabbed him. Stunned, Gerald had been sitting on the front row when he spotted Milton as he marched right past him. That's when Gerald jumped up and chased Milton to let him know which company he was in. The celebration really kicked off when Milton told Gerald that I was also in camp. As it turned out, we were all in the same battalion, but assigned to different companies.

Although we each trained in different rifle companies, we were able to visit at night. How great to be together again! Unfortunately, Frank did not make it to our camp. However, I heard thru the grapevine that he had been shipped to Fort Hood.

During basic training, KP duty (kitchen patrol) was one task dreaded by most of us. Having to get up as early as 4:00 a.m. was a problem, but the Army had a solution. Instead of waking everyone at that inconvenient hour, a white towel was tied to the foot of each soldier's bed who was scheduled for KP. Then, an orderly would quietly wake those without disturbing the rest.

Well, I had a great solution, too! When it was my turn, I decided to wait until everyone had gone to sleep before moving the towel from my bed to the foot of another bed to get a little extra shut-eye. But, when the guard came in and gently shook my buddy to report to the mess hall, an argument ensued. Of course, my buddy claimed he was not on KP duty for that day, and to put it mildly, he was rather upset. He pled with the guard to check the roster for that day and find out who was *really* supposed to be on duty. However, the guard's order was simply to wake the soldiers with the white towels tied to their beds.

Being no stranger to training recruits, the guard had heard all the excuses before and did not want to hear them again. Therefore, my buddy had to get up and report to the mess sergeant. And, for me? Well, I didn't think it was so funny when my friend threatened to kick my tail up between my shoulder blades! However, I was quick to let him know that he deserved it, and I was just getting even.

I vehemently reminded him of the *hotfoot* he had given me, and believe me, it was not your everyday run-of-the-mill hotfoot! He had taken it a step too far. Here I was, taking a little nap and somewhere in his mind, he thought that shoving three matches in-between the upper part and the sole of my shoe and setting them on fire would be a good way to spend his time.

When I had to report to the mess sergeant, he was not the least bit interested in hearing *why* I had moved the towel to another soldier's bed. In fact, he was very adamant that he would do the talking, and I would do the listening. He was not impressed at all with what I had to say. "Ray, do you know what a double dip is?" The mess sergeant asked in an agitated tone.

"Of course," I answered. "It's a double helping of ice cream." Without missing a beat, he snapped, "Wrong! It means I want to see you at four o'clock for the next two mornings; I have some potatoes that need peeling!"

Most of the draftees in September of 1944 were just out of high school or were older men who were married with families. Most of the older men, who were training in my company, were twenty-eight years old. The eligible men, who were younger than twenty-eight years of age, had already been drafted.

Anyway, there was an older fellow from Alabama named, Private Wright. Very colorful and friendly, hard drinking and quite a storyteller, Wright was full of pranks. He had one thing he especially loved to pull on me.

Wright would go into Little Rock every time he could get a Saturday pass, buy a bottle of whiskey and drink all but a few drops. Then, he would save those precious last drops for good ol' Private Ray. Since I was a non-drinker, he usually had *special* plans for me.

We were billeted in one of the many thrown-together-overnight-barracks, which housed approximately twenty-five troops each. The length of the building faced the company street and had two doors, which opened onto the street. Each door was positioned at opposite ends of the building, and my bed was next to one of the doors.

On Saturday nights, when Wright came in from his night out on the town, he took great pleasure in finishing off the bottle by pouring the remaining whiskey right into my eyes. What a shock to my nervous system! As I opened my eyelids to my eyeballs drowning in whiskey, I could see red in more ways than one. And, I can assure you that payback time was sudden and certain! Wright did not get to sleep off his hangovers on Sunday mornings.

One Friday afternoon, we came in from the rifle range and went to mail call. There, we noticed an announcement posted on the bulletin board: *Free Saturday.* Well, some of the guys got all excited and scurried around to get ready to go home. They decided that they could go home and be back by Monday morning for roll call, so they took off without a pass.

It was not necessary to show a pass in order to leave the camp. We had never had a free Saturday before. Very soon, we learned that it never happens in basic training. *Free*, in Army lingo did not mean we were free to do as we pleased.

Imagine our shock when we had to fall out at the regular time in the dark hours for roll call on Saturday morning! There were so many missing soldiers that we could not even begin to answer for our buddies. In addition, the Army had their way of doing things— like having us move to the other side of the street when they called our name, was one of them.

The free Saturday turned out to be a day to move all the beds to one end of our barracks, scrub the floor with sand soap and a GI brush, and let the wooden floor dry; then, we moved all the beds to the other end of the barracks and repeated the same procedure. In addition, we had to do a multitude of other details.

By mid-afternoon after we had finished our job, we were told we could have a pass provided our rifle and uniform passed inspection. Soon, I was on my way with my friends Gerald and Milton to Little Rock. For country boys, the tall buildings were like magnets, drawing us inside to inspect their wares. One thing I could not get enough of was the soft ice cream which was new to me. A small cup was only a nickel and a large cup was a dime. What a deal!

The narrow streets were jam-packed with soldiers. There were so many people on the street that we had to fight our way thru the crowd. As I was pushing my way, I failed to see an officer who was standing by and consequently, I failed to salute him. Gerald and Milton experienced the same fate. As it turned out, the Army had set this trap. There were some MPs working with the officer and writing up the ones that failed to salute.

One of the MPs would take *non-salutes* back to stand in line and wait for the MP with the pen and paper to write the citations. I was green and did not know the ropes, and like a dummy, I stayed in the line until the *pencilman* issued me a citation— ditto for Gerald and Milton. The guys, in the know, would just fade away into the crowd after the MP left the line to catch another criminal.

Well, I forgot to tell First Sergeant Jenkins about being caught, and when he found out, the fat was in the fire. He was furious! He wanted to know why I did not come to tell him about my little problem. I replied, "Where I come from, people don't squeal on each other or confess to anything." I don't think he *liked* my answer. After a few kind words, he told me that twenty-six soldiers in our company had gone home on the free Saturday and their lot would be two weeks of company punishment. He also told me to be prepared to make it twenty-seven soldiers!

Prior to basic training, I had been working sixteen hours a day in the wheat harvest, so extra marching and extra KP was not so bad. At least twenty-seven of us knew how to march by the end of two weeks, and in KP, we could have all we wanted to eat. What could be better for a growing boy?

I was somewhat surprised to learn that Gerald and Milton were only restricted to their company boundaries for one week. Big deal! About the only place we could go was to the PX and our buddies could do that for us.

After that, Jenkins, kept an *evil eye* on me, but by a twist of fate, I did get the last laugh. One cold, misty day, we were out on the rifle range and our rifles and clothing became filthy. Most of us wanted to go into Little Rock later, but our rifle and uniform had to pass inspection before getting passes.

One of my buddies was on latrine detail that day, so he had all day to clean his rifle. He was already dressed and ready for his pass when we came in for the day. So, he went right up to the Orderly Room to have his rifle inspected, got his pass and was on his way. I asked him, "Who is doing the inspections?" He replied, "Corporal Hash."

What a break! Hash was such a laid-back guy, which was rarely found in corporals. He was trying to form a band and was hoping for a chance to perform at the USO shows after we finished basic training. All at once, I had a great idea! I grabbed my towel, soap and necessary things to get ready to go into town. My buddies were busy cleaning their rifles, and they told me I was out of my mind to take a shower before cleaning my rifle. I told them to "do their thing and let me do my own thinkin'."

Hash had me pumped-up so much that I was living in the fantasy world. Oh, yes, when basic training was over, I would be doing one of the things I loved best. I would just be running around having a good old time and entertaining the troops with Hash! So, I had no inhibitions whatsoever in taking another person's rifle up for Hash to inspect.

Shortly, I came back from the shower, dressed and was ready for uniform inspection. My buddies really thought I was off my rocker when I took the clean rifle out of the rack and headed to inspection. However, I did take time to memorize the serial number before marching up to the Orderly Room. Well, I just walked right in without knocking as if I owned the joint and nearly had a heart attack when I saw Jenkins sitting behind that desk!

He jumped up and bellowed, "Soldier . . . Get out of here and report like you have been taught!"

Horrified, I said, *"Yes, Sir!"* And, I was out the door in a split second!

Now, I must tell you that Jenkins, a veteran combat soldier, was a big burly, no nonsense kind of top kick. It was not necessary to wear a hearing aid whenever he spoke. His fair complexion easily turned redder than an overripe tomato when he was angry.

This time, I knocked on the door, marched up to his desk and spoke up, "Pvt. Ray. Serial number 38281678, reporting, Sir!" Jenkins wanted to know what I wanted, and I told him that I wanted a pass to go into Little Rock. He took the rifle and asked me to recite the serial number. I rattled it off without a slip. Thank goodness, he did not look in the record book to see if that was the rifle issued to me.

At this point, I began to see a funny side of this incident. Jenkins had just told me he did not like my attitude. However, I knew something he had failed to discover; he did not know the rifle I gave him for inspection was issued to another soldier and that it had already passed inspection once that evening.

Since I knew this, he was the one under the gun now. If the rifle failed inspection, I would know this guy really had it in for me. He took the rifle apart and carefully examined everything he could think of, put it back together and said, "Ray, I don't think much of your attitude as you are probably aware, but I have to say one thing for sure. You do know how to clean a rifle."

Jenkins wrote out my pass. I went back to the barracks and suggested to my buddies to stop cleaning their rifles and take the one that had passed inspection twice. I told them that all they needed to do was to pass the uniform inspection, and they would get their pass to Little Rock. None of them would take the chance. After squawking and flapping my arms around like a chicken, I left them cleaning their rifles and caught a bus to town.

I decided that Jenkins was a fair-minded man and was just trying to get us ready for combat. As for Hash, his plans for becoming a famous singer and bandleader to entertain the troops never materialized. I suppose he was just a *wannabe* like the rest of us.

Most of the things, which were done in the Army involving personnel, were done alphabetically. I have often wondered how many more hours I had to stand in line than the ones whose last names began with an *A*. Of course, the ones whose last names began with *Z* were really discriminated against. Being an *R* is how I got to know Private Hector Rivas.

Growing up on a farm in Coleman County and attending school in nearby Novice, there were no minority students; so I had never been around a Mexican. Rivas, who was older than most of us, was married with four children, lived in Fort Worth, Texas and was a brickmason by trade. He was a proud man and very *macho*. During that time, Mexicans were not accepted or integrated into society as they are today.

Rivas was in the same boat with most of the older men. Leaving wives, children, obligations and many other things behind was extremely difficult for them. My age group, being fresh out of high school, did not have the worries that the older men had. Therefore, Rivas did not enter into discussions or pranks, and everyone knew not to push him. In time, Rivas warmed-up to me, but I was about the only *gringo* that he did. He became my first Mexican friend after we discovered that we had much more in common than being in the Army.

I grew up on music, and came from a musical family where nine out of twelve family members played instruments. Music was in my blood. I was lost without an instrument and on my first payday, I went to a pawnshop and purchased a guitar. Being the only one in the barracks with an instrument, I was certainly willing to share it with other soldiers.

One day, when there were just two or three of us in the barracks, Rivas wanted to know if he could play my guitar. Of course, I granted him his wish, and to my amazement, he was quite the singer and guitar player. Most of his singing was in Spanish, but music has a way of transcending languages and has a tendency to bring people together. Music certainly strengthened our friendship. However, I could never get him to play if there were more than a half dozen guys in the room.

Although Rivas did not like playing for an audience, he did not mind performing for an audience. During training, he was very athletic and was not intimidated by anyone. In fact, he loved the competition—for instance, when we practiced hand-to-hand combat in the sawdust pits. The pits were round and about twelve feet across. The sawdust was about a foot below ground level and three or four feet deep, so we had to step down into the pit. This made it more challenging to throw our opponents out.

The favorite game was to put five men in the pit—three against two to see which team could throw the other team out. Rivas would challenge any three men to come in against the two of us. We never did lose. We would hurl our opponents out, which was mostly Rivas's doing, and then he would challenge me. I never once was able to throw him out of the pit. His arms and legs were as hard as the bricks he laid back home, and he frequently kidded me that my little baby muscles would never be able to make the twenty-five-mile-march.

Our training ended two weeks earlier than scheduled and that march came much sooner than we had anticipated. On December 16, during the bitter, cold weather, the German army made an immense surprise counterattack against the U. S. First Army, by driving 18-miles inside Belgium—known as the Battle of the Bulge. The outcome of World War II was questionable and our military was in desperate need of supplies, equipment, and additional soldiers in order to stem the tide of the German army.

On December 25, we were served the traditional Christmas dinner. Our instructions were to have our full field packs ready; we would leave at midnight and live in a bivouac area for seven days. When this phase of our training was completed, the twenty-five-mile-march would follow, and this would end basic training. Then, new orders would be forthcoming.

Arkansas had an unusually cold, wet and harsh winter that year. Ice covered the limbs of trees and any weed or grass that could support the weight. Light rain fell intermittently, adding more ice to the trees and vegetation. Leaving shortly after midnight, we slogged along until morning and stopped only for breakfast. We trained for about a week under simulated combat conditions.

The first night, the *Lucky R Duo*, Ray and Rivas, caught a detail to clean a machine gun or a mortar and to protect it from the weather by applying a light coat of oil. Rivas grabbed a mortar, and we very quickly cleaned, oiled and set it in a dry place inside the equipment tent. According to the lieutenant, we did not have to stay and help clean the other weapons. When we finished, we went to our pup tents and crawled into our sleeping bags with hopes of warming-up and getting some shut-eye.

The lieutenant left the equipment tent for a short time, and when he returned to inspect the weapons, the detail had split. Most of the machine guns and mortars were still dirty. The lieutenant was hotter than a Fourth of July firecracker. He found Corporal Duthie and ordered him to find the *runaways* and get the weapons cleaned and report back to him. Since the Lucky R's had finished their job before the rest of the detail arrived, Duthie did not know and could not find out who had cleaned the mortar.

Duthie then changed the rule and decided that everyone assigned to the detail needed to help until the job was finished. In addition, the search was on! Duthie was livid and could be heard kicking the ice off the grass and cussing from a mile away! He kept hollering, "When I find you harebrained idiots, I'm going to kick your tent down with you inside. You had better come out *now*!" At last, someone remembered who the Mexican was—Rivas's goose was cooked.

Since we slept in our clothes, Rivas only had to pull on his boots to go join the detail. I was sleeping in a different tent from Rivas, and my tent mate was really getting nervous when Duthie discovered Rivas was one of the two missing men. I was starting to put my shoes on when I heard Duthie ask Rivas who helped him clean the mortar.

With relief, I quietly eased back in my blanket when I heard Rivas say, *"I seen this guy before. I never know his name."* I sure was glad that we had become friends, and we certainly had a good laugh the first time we were out of Duthie's sight.

After surviving the miserable, freezing weather and training, it was time for the twenty-five-mile-march. By then, all of us were dog-tired and wondered if we could even make the night trip back to our barracks. As we trudged thru the slush with field packs on our backs while carrying our nine-pound rifles, the drizzling rain and ice formed on our woolen overcoats as well. The wet coats added additional weight to an already heavy load. But, one of the secrets in making the march was to keep our feet dry.

We were wearing good quality high-topped leather-soled shoes with leghorns, and if the shoes were waterproofed properly, it was possible to escape having wet socks. Some of us carried dirty, dried socks in our coat pockets in case of an emergency. When we traveled long distances by foot, blisters sometimes became a problem and holey or wet socks increased the chances of getting one. It was also reported that we traveled more like thirty-miles, but it seemed like fifty-miles. However, knowing how many miles we covered was not determined by the marchers.

The twenty-eight year old soldiers began to drop out first. Most of them understood nothing bad would happen to them for failing to complete the march, but they knew extra details would be applied before they shipped out. Nevertheless, some soldiers were considered *goldbrickers* and took the easy way out—they just sat down and waited for the ambulance to rescue them.

The older macho men hung in there as long as they could, and Rivas was one of them. Mile after mile, up hills and down hills, we traversed; the steep hills were difficult going up, but more hazardous coming down. The danger was caused when a soldier would either slip or lose control of his speed and run over soldiers in front, which would cause a pileup.

Singing some of the old Army marching songs in cadences, helped to occupy our minds. Songs like, "The Sergeant's got the Seven-Year Itch" is one we chanted. However, the night became very difficult both physically and mentally. We knew that we could take the easy way out, but it was important to most of us to know we could do it rather than always wonder if we could have finished the course. Some soldiers were exhausted before starting, and some just did not have the stamina to go all the way and had to fall out.

Buddies tried to help their friends by carrying their rifles in order to give them a breather. Of course, we joked and encouraged one another as we moved along. In time, Rivas began to lag behind. He began to stagger and wobble, and it was noticeable that he was struggling with each step that he took. I offered to carry his rifle for a while, but he would not accept help. He was determined to make it on his own, and he was the one person I wanted to see cross over that finish line. However, he just could not do it. Hector Rivas was shocked and his pride was hurt when he could not finish the big one, and I felt bad for him.

Looking back, I realize how much easier basic training was for an eighteen-year-old. Although Milton, Gerald, and I were in different companies, all three of us had successfully made it back to our barracks. There were a number of soldiers in my company that did not, but the ones who survived were treated like kings.

Until we shipped out, we pulled no details, were given preference in the chow line, and received passes to Little Rock. In addition, we did not have to lift a finger in cleaning the barracks for the next bunch of recruits. Living the *Life of Riley* was great for about a week as we waited for orders.

Last *Hoorah* Together

Gerald Henson and Ronold Ray

Gerald Henson and Milton Terrell

As I stood at the door while waiting for my ride,
I was strengthened by her encouragement.

New Orders

The New Year, 1945, rang in loud and clear with the Battle of the Bulge raging out of control! The German army had overrun many of our positions and most of our battalion was flown immediately to the war in Europe to stop the Germans from driving deeper into Belgium. The remaining twenty-six of us were sent to the West Coast. Although we were disappointed for not getting a furlough at the end of basic training to go home for the holidays as we had anticipated, things seemed to work out after all.

My Novice buddies and I were on the same shipping roster, and we could not believe it when we read our orders. Gerald, Milton and I were being sent to the West Coast and were given a ten-day delay en route to get from Little Rock to Fort Ord, California. We were to travel by train and our selected route would be through Abilene, Texas. What a break, since we lived only thirty-five miles from there! We figured that we could stop for a few days and still make it to Fort Ord on time. However, what happened next was almost unbelievable.

We arrived in Abilene bright and early one morning with our duffel bags crammed full of our stuff; those bags must have weighed at least fifty pounds each. In addition, Gerald and I had our guitars to haul. When we got off the train, Milton asked the ticket agent at the depot if he knew where the bus station was located.

The agent said that it was nearby and quickly made a phone call to check and see when the next bus was leaving for Novice. During the war, civilians were more than eager to help those who wore a U.S. military uniform. As it turned out, the bus was leaving immediately. We skedaddled with all our junk and made it to the bus station just in the nick of time!

We were so excited to have made the bus connection in Abilene that we could not believe the next stroke of good luck. As we were nearing the Coleman County line, all at once Milton noticed the Novice school bus heading toward us. This was the bus we had ridden for years, and we knew that it would turn around at the county line. Gerald yelled for the bus driver to stop and let us out, while I ran to the front door and got ready to jump off to flag down the school bus. It was split second timing, but we pulled it off like real soldiers.

After we boarded the school bus, we were able to visit with friends as the bus driver continued to pick up more students. What a surprise for a couple of kids when they saw their big brothers getting off the bus as they were getting on. Imagine the feelings of our parents when we just showed up!

Since there were no telephones on any of the farms, and we had no way to notify our parents to pick us up, it is amazing how perfect the timing was and how the school bus delivered each of us to our homes. It seems to me that we had a little help from a higher power. Our parents were aware that we were getting off the train in Abilene, because we had sent telegrams. However, we had no way of communicating to them the exact time to meet us at the Novice Bus Station.

Milton was the first to be dropped off and then Gerald was next. When I got off the bus, my three youngest siblings, Lowell, Opal and Ed were waiting to get on. What a moment! They could not believe their eyes and were so excited that I was home that they wanted to skip school. However, the bus stop was quite a distance from our house, and they did not have time to run back and ask Mother for permission.

As I was walking up the road, my buddy *Ruff,* a German Shepherd mix, spotted me. Eagerly, he tore down the lane full speed toward me while barking and carrying on. As he plowed into me practically knocking me down, Mother came out of the henhouse to see what all the ruckus was! I could hear the hens cackling. Quickly, Mother placed the bucket of eggs in a safe place and ran out to meet me. It was so great to see her and Ruff.

Mother told me that she and Dad were both sorry that he could not be home: he was down in Del Rio working at the Army Air Base. As we walked up the rock steps and entered the house thru the backdoor, she asked me if I was hungry as if she did not already know the answer. It was that time of year when *blue whistlers* paid frequent visits, and it was rare that we used the front door during the dead of winter. Instead, we chinked and covered it to keep out *Old Man Winter.*

Everything appeared the same as it did the day I had left for the Army. Actually, not too much had changed since the day I had been born in our two bedroom wood-framed house— except it did seem to get smaller as each new member entered the world and staked a claim to his/her space.

The door still had that familiar squeak, the floors creaked, and I could smell the oak wood burning in the kitchen stove and hear the sheep bleating out in the pasture. However, I did notice a new linoleum floor, with a peach floral pattern and green leaves, had been installed in the living room.

About the most significant change in the house since it had been built was when the fireplace in the living room was torn down. The chimney had begun to lean slightly, and Dad was afraid it might fall and injure someone. Oh, but what wonderful memories I had of the times when my brothers, sisters and I would roast our pieces of ham or marshmallows on clothes hangers over the live coals in the fireplace, or whenever we would huddle to get warm and just watch the flames dance around.

When the wind would be blowing up a gale, sometimes a *naughty* puff of smoke would sneak back down the chimney and spring out into the room as if to scare us! That is when we would let our imaginations run wild and think up spooky stories to tell or to claim *something* was trying to come down the chimney after us!

With twinkling blue eyes and a shiny baldhead, Dad was a great storyteller. He could hold us spellbound for hours. I really missed not getting to see my jolly ol' Dad. At sixty-four years old, he was still very active. He had farmed and raised horses, mules, sheep, hogs and cattle all his life, and I might add *children* to that list, since he and Mom had seven sons and three daughters.

Dad taught seven of us how to play musical instruments, and I surely would have liked to have backed him with my new guitar while he played some of his hot fiddle tunes. If it had strings on it, Dad could play it! However, the fiddle was his favorite.

I especially liked to hear him play "Soldier's Joy" and "Zenda Waltz". He was quite the harmonica player, too! We knew we could always count on him to play on January 8 of each year. Quite a character, he would grab his harmonica and play "Eighth Day of January" as if it were a national holiday.

During the summertime, when we were working long, sweltering hours in the field, we would come inside the house around noon for dinner. After we had finished eating, Dad would toss a pillow on the floor, lie down and read the Bible. Next, he would take a nap. We would be quiet as a mouse with hopes that he would sleep the rest of the day. It never happened.

He and Mom were pretty much opposites. A tall, thin, hardworking woman who barely weighed more than a hundred pounds, I do not remember Mom ever taking a nap. She was as fair-minded as the day is long, but she was also very firm and strict. She didn't mince words, and she didn't like to repeat instructions.

From an early age on, I learned it was not advisable to argue with her. However, she worked her fingers to the bone for her children. When we came in from school, she usually had a snack for us after we had changed into our work clothes. Each one of us had chores that we were expected do without being reminded.

The youngest children would feed the dogs and cats. The next level of responsibility would be taking care of the chickens. As we got older, we graduated into slopping and feeding the hogs. The older children milked the cows twice a day, fed the livestock and watered and fed the horses three times a day. After our chores, we had to do our homework. The rest of the evening was free time to do anything that we wanted within reason.

We were taught right from wrong as babies and were expected to live up to what we had been taught. Mom, who was one of the leading alto singers in church, also played hymns at home on the piano. There was no doubt that her faith in God was her number one priority. As a matter of fact, Mom and Dad had actually met at a summer singing school at the church.

That morning, Mom did the unusual and set aside her morning chores. Instead, she sat in her chair at the end of the long, wooden table, and I sat on one of the side benches while we visited for a spell. Her scrumptious home cooked breakfast of oatmeal, hot buttery biscuits, and homemade sausage patties sure hit the spot. It was my favorite, and I thought I had died and gone to hog heaven. As I savored every bite, I could see and hear thru the backdoor Ruff whimpering and licking his chops with hopes that I would save a little *something* for him.

Naturally, Mother wanted to know all about the things that I had been doing during the past four and a half months, and I wanted her to fill me in with what was happening with the family. She told me that Dad had been able to take a week off from his job to come home for the holidays. Lester, who was in the Army Air Corps, came home on a three-day-pass. He had been able to enjoy Christmas dinner with the family.

Of course, my younger siblings who were home, chopped down a cedar tree and draped it with the red rope and lots of shiny icicles. They did their part in eating their share of turkey and the delicious sage dressing Mother always prepared at Christmas time, not to mention the ham, fruit salad, cranberry sauce, fresh baked bread, cakes, pies and homemade candy.

Neither Cecil, who was in the Army Air Corps, nor Alfred who was in the Army Medical Corps, had been able to come home. Since it had been raining cats and dogs, the muddy roads were practically impassable. Therefore, my two older sisters, Vivian and Grace and their families, and brother Raymond and his family, did not attempt to come for the holidays.

Although I had barely missed all the holiday parties, musicals and firecrackers, it was so neat to be home. I wanted the moment to last forever, but I knew I would be leaving soon. The fact that I might not *ever* see my family again was never far from my mind. Since my three older brothers, Alfred, Cecil and Lester were all stationed in the United States, it was apparent that my heading overseas had a *chilling* effect on Mother.

The need for foot soldiers was tremendous in the *Pacific Theater.* I was not certain, but knew the reason I was being shipped to the West Coast, was probably because I was being sent into the war. I had so many important questions swirling in my head. But, for some reason, I could not talk to anyone about them. It was like all future plans were on hold until after the war.

Mother allowed me to take the green two-door 1936 Plymouth to visit friends and relatives while I was home. Some offered advice, some offered encouragement, and some just stood by me. It was a very tense time—a time when I wanted to stand-up like a man, but deep down inside I felt more like a little boy. I was so grateful to have had the opportunity to make this unexpected trip home.

When the time came for me to leave, I decided to part with my guitar. I gave it to Lowell and told him to think of me every time he played it. He was shocked speechless, which was rare for Lowell. He was so tickled to finally have a guitar of his very own.

Leaving everyone was not easy; since I had no idea how long it would be before I would see them or *if* I would see them again. For the most part, I was in denial. Perhaps, I did not know how to express my feelings or possibly, I just did not want to talk about the *what ifs*.

For certain, I did not want my folks to worry about me, as if I could stop them. I did not want any tears shed when the time came for me to leave. I did not want to feel like I was heading to my funeral. I always believed that my Mother could read my mind and that she was thinking only of my safety. I believe she sensed how much harder it would be for me to leave if she became emotional.

If Dad had been there, he probably would have said something like, "Well, Son . . . Remember that you are one of the Ray Boys. Stay out of trouble, and don't do anything to bring reproach to the family name. Things have a way of working out. You'll be fine and back home before you know it." Then, he would have given me a firm handshake.

During World War II, millions of families had to say good-bye to their sons, daughters, husbands and wives when Uncle Sam needed them for overseas duty. There was surely a common thread that ran through and bound all these families together. The concerns were the same—fear, anxiety, anger, long periods of separation, and the list continues. It was a very frightening time, and different families and individuals reacted in various ways.

Mother, in her quiet and stoic way, reminded me, "Be careful, take care of yourself and go with God." Sometimes, just coming together and supporting each other as a family, speaks louder than any words. As I stood at the door while waiting for my ride, I was *strengthened* by her encouragement.

I took one last glance at the only home I had ever known, gave ol' Ruff a pat on the head as he looked up at me with his sad brown eyes, and waved to my family when Gerald and his Dad, Mr. Henson, came puttin' up in his Model A Ford.

After we picked up Milton, the weight of the four of us plus our baggage prevented the car from exceeding forty-five miles an hour. It was a special ride for us that day. Mr. Henson was a good man, and we knew we could always depend on him if needed. We took comfort in knowing we could talk to him about anything, because he seemed to understand young men. Being a hard worker, he was very firm in his discipline and expected no less than our best.

The trip down the narrow two-lane highway passed too quickly, and we were soon at the train depot in Abilene. My last memory of home was when Milton, Gerald and I hung out the train car window to exchange waves with Mr. Henson standing on the platform as he dwindled from our sight.

Soon, we were on our way to Fort Ord. The train was running late, and by the time we arrived in El Paso, Texas, we were four hours behind schedule. This caused us to miss connections with the train heading for California. We boarded the next train out and arrived in Los Angeles, California on the day we should have reported to Fort Ord. We were not too worried though.

The Los Angeles train station was jam-packed with military personnel. The next train for us would be the following day. Most servicemen did not even have enough money to stay in a hotel. Some of the local homeowners were there offering to let people stay in their homes, but most of us spent the night in the station; that was our choice.

The dining situation was bleak, and we wanted to leave the station and find a better place to have supper. Another soldier seemed to attach himself to Gerald, Milton and me, and claimed he knew all about Los Angeles and the good places to eat. He also knew which bus to take. Well, we took him at his word, and caught a city bus and stopped in a part of town that was quite different from Coleman.

Our new friend had taken us to China Town, and the place gave me the *creeps*. The streets were crowded with people shuffling along who all seemed to be in a hurry. Most were speaking in a foreign language and dressed differently from what I was used to seeing. The buildings were anything but uniformed and had strange markings on their signs. It was as if I were having a bad dream.

We went inside a bar with a restaurant in the back. As we were heading to the dining room, the first thing I noticed was a man without legs, sitting on a skateboard or a contraption with some small wheels bolted to it. He was moving around by putting his hands on the floor and pushing himself along.

We walked through the bar to the restaurant and ordered our meal without taking time to look things over, and still trusting our new buddy, that this was a good place to eat. The lighting was very dim. I soon discovered that if I moved my hand around over my head, I would be stirring-up a thick cloud of smoke. I lost my appetite, but the long wait for our food took care of that.

Although I do not remember much about the food, I do remember that when we finished eating and left the restaurant, this new buddy had some other places he wanted to show us. About this time, we saw a police officer on the corner and asked him where to catch a bus back to the train station. That is when we left our *buddy* to fend for himself!

The next day, we boarded the luxurious *Sunshine Special*, a super, streamlined train. The seats were covered in plush red velvet upholstery, and there was a speedometer mounted over the doorway of each coach. I could see that we were traveling eighty-five miles an hour!

Nothing was said to us about being a day late, and soon after arriving to Fort Ord, Milton shipped out to Oakland. The following day, Gerald shipped out to San Francisco. Later, the ship that Milton was on, arrived in San Francisco and picked up Gerald and others. Their destination was Leyte in the Philippines.

After they departed, I stuck around for a few days and did the obstacle course a couple of times—a night operation where we were trained to crawl under barbed wire entanglements. It sounded easy until I realized machine gunners would be laying down a crisscross pattern of live bullets a few inches above our prone bodies.

When I say prone, that is what I mean—horizontally on the ground. About one in every five bullets was a tracer bullet. Whenever I turned over on my back, I could see the tracers whizzing by. It looked as if I could reach up and catch one in the same way we used to catch fireflies back on the farm.

There was a story circulating about a soldier who was taking basic training at Fort Hood; he crawled upon a rattlesnake, and when he jumped up, he was hit and seriously injured by machine gun fire. I believe all infantrymen were required to complete the obstacle course during basic training.

I remember very well the first time I negotiated the course. It was a freezing, wet and miserable winter night in Arkansas. I crawled on my elbows with my rifle cradled in both arms, and was ready to engage the enemy at any time. After finishing the course, my rifle was inspected to see if it was ready to be used. After all, if this had been an actual combat situation, what good would a rifle be if it had been clogged with mud?

I trained on the rifle range each day, marched and exercised for an hour or more each morning. I also went on an overnight bivouac to learn how to survive on c-rations. Little did I know that we would soon be eating them every day for several months.

C-rations came in cans about the size of an eleven-ounce can of *Wolf Brand Chili*, and there were two cans for each meal. One can contained dry stuff: three or four round crackers, four cigarettes, hard candy, pepper and salt, toilet paper, a toothpick, a few matches, powdered lemonade, etc. The other can contained the main dish: chicken and rice, beans, ranch style beans, spaghetti and meatballs, chicken and spaghetti, etc. One good thing—we had plenty of c-rations!

When our orders came down, we were notified to report to orientation to learn about an Army regulation we had never talked about in basic training. The subject was *Loose Lips Sink Ships and Censorship*. First, we were told what we could do and could not do. Next, the punishment phase was explained if we failed to comply.

Counseling was not the word used in the Army in 1944.

All our outgoing mail would be censored. This meant that we would not be able to write a letter and mail it other than thru the Army. Someone would read all mail. The parts of our letters that did not meet the requirements would be cutout or blacked-out. On the other hand, the violator would be called in and instructed about what he was doing wrong.

Some soldiers needed to be reassured that this was not just a way to find out about their personal business. *Counseling* was not the word used in the Army in 1944; it was more like "Do this or we will make you wished you had!"

However, counseling or *something* was needed for one of my friends. A hardheaded Dutchman with a wife and family, Van Houten was a real fire-eater! This man did not adapt well to military life at all. In other words, this was a man with an attitude.

After we boarded a troop train, we were instructed to write some trial letters known as *dry runs,* a popular Army term. My stubborn friend just would not accept the fact that his mail was going to be censored. He was not going to agree to let anyone read the things he was writing to his wife and that was that! He did write his letter, but it was not to his wife. No, Van Houten wrote it to the person who would be censoring his mail.

Well, he was the first one called for some wall-to-wall counseling. When he came back from his *session,* this man had smoke billowing from his eyes, ears and nose. I mean to tell you, he was on fire! He grabbed a pencil and a piece of paper. "This time, they're really going to get a letter to remember," he growled thru gritted teeth.

He addressed his letter—*To the Reader of My Mail.* Van Houten used language so foul, that it would even make a sailor cringe. He used every dirty word he could think of to reiterate his position that his mail to his wife was to be read *only* by her. And believe me, Van Houten had an ample vocabulary of four-letter words. He read his letter aloud and asked the ones present what we thought. We were shocked and begged him to destroy the letter to avoid the trouble he would likely incur. So, he mailed it anyway.

This time, he was not called in for counseling. Instead, he was escorted to headquarters. The message was—*One more letter written 'To the Reader of Your Mail', and it will be the brig for you!* When he returned, he was still hotter than a two-dollar pistol! However, he understood that the consequences for writing another such letter would mean jail time without pay, and he did not want that. I have always wondered if his wife had to wait until the war was over for the censorship to be lifted before she received a letter from her husband.

Our troop train slowly took us from Fort Ord, California to Fort Lewis, Washington. The main things I remember on this trip were the mountains and tunnels. If the windows were down when this coal-eating-steam-engine entered a tunnel, the coaches would quickly fill with smoke and cinders. One time was enough of that. I quickly learned to keep the windows closed in the mountains and my mouth closed as well. After all, we were heading off to war.

Mom and Dad

Isaac Willis Ray and Agnes Mitchell
Married October 30, 1910

Memories of the Good Ol' Days

Takin' a Coffee Break While Bachin' it.
Front-Youngest brothers, Ed, Lowell and Dad;
Back-Ronold (14) and Lester (17)

A Visit Home to say *Good-bye*

My home in Midway about 30 years after I left and a few years before it collapsed.
On the left, Lester's and my back porch bedroom.

This letter turned out to be from a girl, named Tela . . .

Fort Lewis, Washington

Although my stay at Fort Lewis was brief, it was long enough for me to blow all my money. One day I was walking around Seattle, Washington and there in the window of the *A-1 Pawn Shop* was a beautiful blonde luring me to come in. How could I resist?

So, I went inside with hopes of finding an inexpensive used *Martin* or *Gibson* guitar, both which were top of the line and were selling new for about one hundred dollars. Well, the *A-1 Pawn Shop* did not happen to have one. However, they did have a practically new guitar, which was also a very good instrument.

This presented a little problem. I was a little short of cash. A brand-new *Kay* guitar was seventy dollars, and the used one was forty-five dollars, which was more than I could manage. It was time to do some good old Texas horse-trading.

After several minutes of haggling, I proudly walked out with that guitar plus the case and my pockets weighed thirty-five dollars less. Here I was, practically penniless, and to top it off, I had given absolutely no thought as to how long this fling would last.

Speaking of flings, during basic training I met Private Reed from Fort Smith, Arkansas. Every night he would write a letter to his girlfriend, and every day he would receive a letter from her. He kept her picture on display, and we could see she was very good-looking. Some of the guys were always kidding him about his letter writing and offering him *advice* on what he needed to write.

One night, I thought it would be funny to write her a letter myself. Reed obliged when I asked for her address. He jotted it down and handed it to me without batting an eye. The following day, I dropped it in the mail. Very soon, a letter postmarked from Fort Smith, Arkansas arrived for me.

This letter turned out to be from a girl, named *Tela,* who wanted to know how I got her address. My buddy had snookered me and had given me the address of one of his high school classmates. It only seemed decent of me to write her again and explain why she received a letter from me. We continued to correspond with each other occasionally until the war was over.

Receiving a letter during wartime was better than getting a box of Cracker Jacks as I did on special occasions when I was a kid. It was during mail call at Fort Lewis that I received a letter from Tela. She wrote to tell me the tragic news of our friend who had been killed in action. What a shock to learn of Reed's death! Deep sorrow for his family and intense anger against the Germans welled up inside of me.

I did not talk about it, but I knew that on my last day on the farm when I told Mother "good-bye" that some of the ones with whom I had trained would be left crippled and some would pay the ultimate price before the war was over. I just did not know it would happen so soon. This war was becoming very personal and *real* to me, and I had just received orders to ship overseas.

Up until then, the Brownwood Lake had been the largest body of water on which I had ever been, and a new experience was looming ahead. I was fixin' to board my first ship. And, oh, what a dinky little floater it was! It was not a large troop vessel as I had anticipated. Instead, it was more like a small prison-on-the-water.

We left at night from *somewhere* in Puget Sound and very soon, the smooth ride rocked me to sleep. Sometime later, we headed out to the open sea. When we hit the breakwaters, the bucking and pitching of the ship began. That is when I woke up needing to toss my cookies.

About the time I was feeling better, we collided with a storm at sea. The only ones that were allowed on the deck were the sailors—only when necessary. We soldiers were only allowed to stick our heads up to view the deck. Safety ropes were stretched around for sailors to grab in case they needed to go topside.

Having grown up in Central Texas, I was use to rain, hail, and severe thunder and lightening storms. However, nothing had prepared me for this violence! Thru the pitch-black sky, I could see rain beating down in sheets. The roaring wind whipped mammoth waves right over the deck, the likes of which I had never seen before!

Our little boat would be on top of a high wave and would suddenly plunge into a deep hole. All I could see was water, and each time the boat took a dive, so did my insides. My dry heaves only got worse. I was so sick that I had not been able to keep food down for two or three days.

I knew I needed to eat to keep up my strength and decided to go to breakfast. The eating areas were very compact, and had a narrow aisle down the center with tables on each side; there were five stools to each table. It was actually more like a bar with stools, which were either welded or bolted to the steel floor.

I picked up some eggs, toast and milk, and noticed an empty stool located on the aisle where I sat down and started trying to eat. All at once, the ship decided to roll to one side, and four plates of food slid down the bar and crashed to the floor! The fifth plate stopped directly in front of me as if to say, "Hey, Man ... I know just how you feel."

On the other side of the aisle, the plates piled up against the wall as if they were scared of the monster at sea and would meet their untimely death next.

What a mess! I decided that I was not hungry after all. However, I did learn a valuable lesson that day; Life can be stormy, so always hold onto your plate while sailing thru rough water. I held on, and within a week, we finally arrived in Honolulu.

We were experiencing things that only soldiers on their way to war could grasp.

Pineapple Express

Earlier in the war, the Marines had set up a jungle training camp *somewhere* near Honolulu. This training was designed to teach what actual combat would be like and to show the many ways the enemy might attack. This was some tough stuff! Although we did not talk much about it, we all knew we would not be taking this kind of training unless we were being prepared to use it. This was the most difficult training I received during my stay in the Army.

Before we started jungle training, we needed to store our c-bags that contained our clothing, shoes, personal stuff, etc. We carried our rifles, a field pack with the essentials, and the clothing we wore. Everything else was stashed in a huge ware-house. However, I did not want to leave my guitar in a place like that.

I noticed a staff sergeant standing nearby and asked him, "Are you gonna be one of our trainers?"

"No, I'll be staying behind," he said. "Why do you ask?"

"Well, I was wonderin', is there some other place I could leave my guitar?"

"Sure. You can slip it under my bed and pick it up when you finish jungle train-ing," he offered.

What a nice guy! This seemed like a better option, so I left my guitar there and hoped for the best.

One sweltering afternoon, several teams comprised of twelve soldiers each, were taking compass training. It was so stagnant, there was not enough of a breeze to move a hair, if we had hair. After finishing classroom study, it was time to put our new knowledge into practice, and of course, beat the other teams.

Our team was pumped-up, and ready for action! We went down to the sugar cane break where the cane was about ten to twelve feet high and as thick as hair on a dog's back. It was not a cultivated field planted in rows. Instead, it was wild cane that was so solid that we could hardly walk through it, and the visibility was very limited.

Each group was issued one compass and a small bag that included: paper, pen-cil, a short tape measure, one piece of heavy string and some miscellaneous items. First, we chose the tallest guy in the group as our leader to oversee the operation and a compass man who was given the assignment of figuring out the different degrees to travel for each distance. If we came out as instructed, the target, a machine gun position, would be visible. Our orders were to "knock it out!" This was a dry run, of course.

After the compass man determined the designated degree, he pointed us in the right direction to walk. This is the way we lined-up: Eight guys stood in a single file at the front of the line. Then, the compass man was next and the leader stayed at the back, so he could observe and make sure that the front eight guys were lined-up straight according to the specified degree. He made sure we stayed on course since he had a better view than anyone else in this claustrophobic sugarcane nightmare. The other two guys measured with the string and recorded the distance we covered each time as they walked beside the compass man and the leader. Since we could not see very far, we decided to cover only ten yards at a time.

After our progress was recorded, the compass man moved up to the middle of the eight guys. He then determined the next degree and correct yardage for us to advance thru the cane. Then, the four guys behind him leapfrogged ahead of the front four guys. The compass man continued this pattern and the four guys behind him jumped ahead of the front four. Although this method was slow, and we felt as if we would suffocate, we hung in there until we came out right on target. There was no way we were going to admit those Marines could outdo us!

Another time, we were crossing a river that we called the *Grand Canyon.* The bridge was about twenty-feet above the water. Two cables were stretched across the canyon. Crossbars, about four-feet long and at regular intervals were connected to and separated the cables. Mesh wire, which was tied to the cables, provided a footpath. It resembled a railroad track with wire stretched over the rails.

Crossing looked easy at first glance, but when we understood that our weight would cause the cables to drop down into an elongated "V" shape, we realized that this was not going to be a fun deal. The instructor crossed over, turned around and came back. After showing us the ropes, he taught us how to be successful. "Don't go too fast; don't go too slow; don't get off balance or you will be flipped off," he said.

The tendency was to go too fast on the front part of the "V," because going too slow would not give us enough speed to make it up the other side. Of course, one would fall off if he stopped. To make crossing more challenging, we were wearing our field packs and carrying our nine-pound rifles plus the ammunition.

The instructor told us, "If you carry your rifle in both hands, it will help you keep your balance. However, if you start down too fast, your speed will increase. This will cause you to lose control, and you will fall off into the water."

If we fell, a detail of soldiers would be waiting to fish us out. I could only hope that I was *over* the water if I should take a dive! This is one time I was glad my last name began with *R*. By watching my buddies' mistakes and successes, I was able to judge the speed that was needed. Luckily, I did not have a problem crossing and managed to keep my powder dry.

There were places on the island where vegetation and trees were so dense that it was difficult to see the light of day; part of our training was in such a place. We were instructed on how to deal with the different situations that we might encounter in jungle combat: ambushes, trip wires connected to booby traps, enemy soldiers in trees, and meeting the enemy face-to-face on narrow trails.

The Japanese soldiers had mastered the art of camouflage and jungle warfare. One time, I was walking down a dark trail when I caught a glimpse of *something* flying through the air, and it was heading right at me! I sidestepped and stabbed it with my bayonet, but it went right on down the trail almost taking my rifle with it.

I had just enough time to turn around to see it coming right at me again. This time I pulled the trigger, but of course, this was an exercise without ammunition. High above me, a rope was attached to a tree limb, and a sandbag was attached to the end of the rope, which was near the ground. Now the soldiers, who were pulling the sandbag up and releasing it at just the right time, must have been having a great day. I could hear laughter and see the rope as it was being pulled up for the next release.

One night, we ran a compass course with a four-hour time limit that began at eight o' clock. A first lieutenant was in charge of our group of twenty, and he was some kind of a leader. He was the kind that gave 110 percent, and in return, we wanted to outdo, outshine and be number one for the night.

He instructed us not to talk, smoke or make any kind of noise. He made it clear that we must stay close together, and above all, we must not become separated. It is not an easy task to stay together in a jungle at night without a light! It was almost as dark as the *Carlsbad Caverns* in New Mexico when the lights are off.

We were told it was because of a similar situation that brought about the Marines wearing leather around their necks. It was possible during the darkness for an enemy soldier to slip into the line and knife a Marine—maybe more than one. Wearing leather around the neck helped the Marine who was behind to identify the person he was following.

Whenever I attempt to relive that night of compass training, I still cannot believe to this very day that we were able to complete the course; in fact, we were the only ones who did. At midnight, we saw headlights shining and heard horns blaring. The Army trucks had arrived to transport us back to our quarters, and we all ran out to grab our ride.

The following day, we were training in the same area. What a shock it was to see the places we had been! We could not believe the dangerous situations we had been in just a few hours before: the jungle, the stream and climbing canyon walls and mountains.

I really do not know if I could have climbed that canyon wall during day-time. Maybe by not being able to see all the way down to the bottom was a blessing. Sometimes I think about the men that actually scaled walls like that under enemy fire. It reminds me of just how much freedom really cost.

One of the things I really enjoyed during jungle training was learning how to shoot weapons from the hip. I am not talking about pistols; in fact, we did not have pistols. I am talking about rifles, light machine guns and browning automatic rifles that hold twenty rounds in the clip.

Some of us became very good at firing from the hip, which was another crucial survival skill to know; since it is much faster than raising the rifle to your shoulder before firing. However, fighting a war encompasses both the physical and the mental. For instance, take the Army term, 'momentary paral-yses' and all it entails. The mind has to be trained to react *instantly* to differ-ent situations. It is a matter of survival and a problem for new soldiers.

In basic training, we were shown actual combat films and the conse-quences when soldiers hesitated to destroy the enemy. Just imagine the first time of being the point man in a line of soldiers walking down a jungle trail and suddenly coming face-to-face with the enemy. A split second would be the difference between living and dying.

The Army's method for moving on the trails was for the lead soldier to carry his rifle in both hands with the safety off and pointing forward to be ready to fire. The trees and brush had a tendency to hem in the rest of the troops, which made it difficult for them to fire without endangering their bud-dies.

Most of our weapons were the M1-Garand rifles. The clip held eight rounds of thirty-caliber ammunition, and the rifle was semi-automatic, mean-ing it will fire each time the trigger is pulled. In order to survive, we had to pull the trigger first.

Our rifle was better than what the Japanese had. Their rifle was a five-shot bolt-action repeater; meaning they would have to pull the bolt up and back and then forward and down after firing the first shot and for each additional shot. Of course, they would be carrying their rifle with the safety off, and their first shot could be fired just as quickly as our first shot.

After learning how to shoot from the hip, we spent several days on the regular firing range. It was a miserable time. Our tents were located in the mid-dle of a gigantic pineapple field. The soil was red clay, and it rained a solid week. Our shoes would sink down into that red gooey stuff and getting it off was almost impossible.

It was apparent that the tents were a recent addition. Heavy equipment had been used to push the pineapple plants aside, but nothing had been done to harvest the plants or remove them from the field. Several signs were posted around the tents: $50.00 Fine for Stealing a Pineapple. The owner of the field would be a wealthy man today if he had been successful in collecting those fines!

I loved pineapples and pineapple juice, but by the time we finished training on the firing range, it was sickening to even smell one. Our fatigues were stained red, and the Army laundry was never able to wash them clean.

The firing range was typical as we shot from 200-, 300- and 500-yard ranges. We practiced shooting the 200- and 300-yard ranges from the prone, squatting and standing positions shooting both regular and rapid fire. Shooting the 500-yard range was more like training to become a sniper. Firing from this distance, we would be in the prone position and would take plenty of time to shoot.

The pop-up range was new to me, and it turned out to be my favorite. I always liked shooting rapid fire, but this was rapid fire with a new twist. Rapid fire is always a timed event. The pop-up range worked like the following: We soldiers took turns inside the foxholes to work the targets. Telephones were installed in each foxhole and silhouette targets mounted on sticks, were stashed next to the phones.

The foxholes blended in so well with the terrain that it was difficult to recognize them. However, it would not have helped since the targets popped-up randomly. When everyone was in position, a signal was given to start. A sergeant, who would be working the phones, would ring a number—for instance, number five.

The soldier working number five target would raise the silhouette and immediately pull it down. By the time the target went down, the sergeant would ring another number. Sometimes a target with a picture of the devil would pop up, and we had only a second to fire. The targets were scattered over an area of roughly twenty-five to sixty-five yards in front of the shooter and covered about fifteen yards to each side. Shooting pop-up targets required instant action and accuracy.

We understood that in combat, missing the target was something we could not afford to do. This training was as close to a battlefield situation as they could make it. In real combat, we had to destroy the enemy before the enemy destroyed us. The better we were prepared, the better our chances were to survive.

The soldiers who took jungle training were much better prepared than the soldiers just out of basic training were. I suppose the Army brass knew all along where we were headed, so they kept us busy until we could be transported safely.

After finishing jungle training, we were sent back to Honolulu to pick up our bags and to get ready to ship out. My first order of business was to recover my guitar. The staff sergeant was in his quarters, and the guitar was under his bed just as he said it would be. He wished me "good luck" and would not accept any pay for taking care of it.

Trying to carry all my stuff and the guitar, proved to be next to impossible. However, with a lot of help, I made it to the railroad with everything intact. I had never seen a narrow gauge railroad or such small cars before. The cars were flat with sideboards, and looked much like the hay wagon we used back on the farm. They were used for hauling pineapples to the factory. When we boarded the train, we were delightfully surprised that the railroad ran right through the *Dole Pineapple Plant.*

Cars piled with pineapples surrounded us. Our train was moving at a snail's pace, and some soldiers near the front of the train jumped onto the loaded cars and began tossing pineapples to all the guys that wanted one . . . or two . . . or three. Pineapples were flying everywhere! The soldiers continued to supply pineapples to everyone, and when the end of our train was near, they reboarded.

We made it down to the dock, and boarding the ship was rather interesting. Some of us could not make it up the gangplank with all the pineapples and our extra stuff. The process of loading was slow, because each person had to be checked-off the shipping orders. However, someone had a good idea. We started handing our stuff forward, sort of like they did in the old Western movies; when a fire broke out, the people used the bucket brigade system.

After embarking, I became one unhappy camper. Roaming around the ship for two days among the thousand plus soldiers and the Navy personnel on board, I frantically searched and asked if anyone had seen my guitar. There was no trace of it.

After a couple of days, I heard someone singing and playing music. What I could not find with my eyes, I found with my ears as I followed the sound right to a soldier who was entertaining friends. Sure enough, he had my Kay! Finding my six-string friend made me happier than a redneck at his first rodeo. Since my guitar had been passed hand-to-hand up the gangplank, no one knew who owned it.

Four other soldiers on the ship had musical instruments which were in constant use. During World War II, guitars were used mainly to back singers, fiddle and mandolin players, so the melody was seldom played on a guitar. Soldiers would just join in and start singing, and no one cared about the quality of our music.

Singing off-key or out of rhythm was never a problem; bonding together for a common cause was what mattered. At times, we sounded like a pack of coyotes howling at the moon, but we could have cared less. We were experiencing things that only soldiers on their way to war could grasp.

Some of the popular songs were: "There's a Star Spangled Banner Waving Somewhere," "Elmer's Tune," "Boogie Woogie Bugle Boy from Company B," "I Saw a Rainbow at Midnight," "I'll be Home for Christmas," "G. I. Blues," and "Drinking Beer in a Cabaret."

During the moments we shared, I could have written new words to another favorite song, "You'll Never Know How Much I Miss You."

> *You'll never know how our spirits were lifted,*
> *You'll never understand how worries melted away,*
> *A moment like this can never be captured,*
> *And, it only has meaning, when you're far away.*

As we continued to sail the deep blue sea, our singing and camaraderie seemed to take on a life of its own. The musical instruments were rarely idle, because different musicians were eager to borrow them and the singing would start anew. The mood was like an *addiction* of some sort. I believe I could rightly say that the circumstances were such that we were looking for a way to escape reality, if only for a moment.

However, there were two things that remained constant—the smell of pineapples and the zigzagging of our trusty boat, I call the *Pineapple Express*. She seemed to be rocking and rolling to the rhythm of the music as she sped to her destination, and we were positive that the Japanese could smell our ship all the way from Tokyo.

As we began our twenty-five-mile-mind-conditioning-march
to reprogram our waterlogged brains. . .

Howdy, Saipan! So Long, Kay!

We were on the *Pineapple Express* for several days before docking on the island of Saipan. After disembarking, Army trucks transported us to our new quarters—*tents*! It was apparent that a war had been fought on this island, and we were warned to be extremely careful. There were still enemy soldiers hiding in the hills.

Before we landed, we had been briefed on how fierce the fighting had been, and we were now seeing the evidence. Burned and demolished tanks and various kinds of Army vehicles were scattered around, both Japanese and American. Destroyed field artillery pieces, including the big guns (*105 mm and 155 mm howitzers),* blown-up pillboxes, and damaged trees gave proof that a vicious battle had been fought and many lives had been lost.

The island had been secured for thirteen months by the time we arrived. After the fall of Saipan to the United States, five huge runways had been built within two months. There was a mad rush to get supplies, planes, military personnel and all sorts of buildings constructed.

Many of the battlesites had been cleared of debris and enemy bodies prior to our assignment. With ample rainfall, the vegetation had grown back and the landscape was lush and green. However, a vast number of trees were mangled from the barrage of shrapnel.

At the end of World War I, the League of Nations gave Japan possession of the Caroline, Palau, Marshall and the Mariana Islands. Since Saipan was a strategically located island and Japan's first line of defense in the Pacific, it was absolutely essential for them to retain control. Allowing the United States to capture the Marianas would be a crushing and perhaps, a fatal blow to their ambitions and war machine. Some Japanese admirals believed that the nation that held Saipan would eventually win the war, and this stronghold must be held at all cost.

It was Japanese Prime Minister Hideki Tojo's belief that he would be able to withstand any assault by the American military, and thus, continue to control that part of the Pacific Ocean and protect the homeland. He had an estimated army of twenty-five thousand and six thousand naval personnel on standby with a well-fortified island. Lieutenant General Yoshisugu Saito was commander of the Japanese army garrisoned on Saipan and Vice Admiral Chuichi Nagumo, who executed the December 7, 1941 attack on Pearl Harbor, was commander of naval operations at and during the Battle of Saipan.

Saipan was part of the main defense-line in the Pacific for Japan, but was also critically important to the United States. Our Army Air Corps needed a base for the *B-29* long-range bombers. Japan was only fifteen hundred miles away and within range, and a round trip of three thousand miles was manageable without having to refuel. With the B-29s in the mix, the United States would be able to rain fire on Japan like no one had ever seen!

Equally important, was establishing a Naval base and supply depot. This was the largest operation so far in the Pacific Theater. In short, the United States needed to get massive amounts of supplies and men closer to the war. Seizing Saipan would be a major step in that direction.

Perhaps the most important thing about capturing Saipan, was breaking Japan's "Inter South Sea Empire". A decisive victory would give the United States a leg up on gaining control of both the air and sea. Japan's defense line would become more vulnerable as our Navy and air power moved closer to each target. Furthermore, destroying the enemy's supply lines would handicap their effort to fight a war.

The big guns began pounding Saipan on June 13, 1944. After two days of relentless shelling, the Marines landed and were the first U.S. troops to set foot on Saipan. The next day, the 27th Infantry Division landed and the combined number of Marines and Army troops tallied at approximately seventy-one thousand.

In a way, Saipan was a learning experience for us—the bunkers, the caves, and the Japanese fierce and savage way of fighting. For instance, it was no holds barred and no quarter was given by the enemy. This kind of action set the stage and guidelines for the Americans—taking prisoners was *not* a priority for us. We did not want to waste our c-rations or deplete our number of fighting men in order to care for them.

We also learned the important role of the dreaded flamethrower and how effective it was to ferret out and incinerate the enemy hidden in caves or bunkers. Although the flamethrower was limited in range, it had a tremendous psychological impact which created much fear and anxiety on the enemy.

With our Navy surrounding the island, the Japanese were cut off from receiving any kind of outside help and had nowhere to retreat. By July 7, the Japanese army had been reduced to a mere three thousand able-bodied men. General Saito gave his final command to his remaining troops—a *banzai raid* on the Americans. In my opinion, the Battle of Saipan ranks as one of the most brutal and bloodiest of the Pacific.

The end came swiftly for Saito and Nagumo. They followed the ancient Japanese ritual by committing *hari-kari.* Civilians and remaining soldiers had been brainwashed into believing the Americans were cruel and barbaric; Instead of being captured, hundreds of the Japanese chose to jump off the cliffs. Some parents hurled their children off and then followed suit. This action was inconceivable for the new troops merely passing thru Saipan to destinations unknown.

With so many soldiers being processed and waiting for their orders and with the constant push toward Tokyo, just getting food meant standing in the chow line for as long as two hours at times. Breakfast hours started before daylight, so the chow line was an excellent place to hear the latest rumors.

Some of those rumors were rather amusing. I remember one about a Japanese soldier who would dress in an American uniform, and go through the line. He was not considered dangerous, just resourceful.

Another story floating around was how all the Japanese soldiers had big buck teeth and were so nearsighted that we did not have to worry about them; they couldn't see well enough to shoot straight. I guess someone was just *hoping* when he started that one!

For sleeping arrangements, there were enough tents, but there were not enough cots for each soldier. The cot situation worked like this: If you could find an unattended tent, you could just appropriate a cot. That sounded so much better than stealing. However, getting caught had a tendency to create some friction among the troops.

I was among the first to catch KP duty. The mess hall was the widest and longest Quonset hut that I ever remember seeing. Our instructions, when reporting for the honor of dishing out the powdered eggs, were to go down to the end of the building and enter thru the exit. Then, we were supposed to continue up the side aisle to the entrance. There would be a sergeant stationed there, and we were to tell him that we were on KP duty. He would then allow us to break into the line, so we could get our food, eat and report for work.

What a deal! I reported everyday after I discovered how easy it was to enter the mess hall through the exit and report for KP. After eating, I just somehow forgot to report to the mess sergeant. Not only that, but a few of us would get an early start and take off to the beach and spend the day swimming instead of reporting to the three-hour routine of rifle range practice and physical exercises. It was sort of like playing hooky in high school!

Well, our swimming club, *The Saipan Sea Devils,* continued to grow. One day, a soldier named Mack, wanted to turn it into a boxing club. *"When we get back to camp, let's put the gloves on for a couple of rounds,"* he said.

"Nah. Boxin' isn't my thing," I replied.

I think he got the idea that I was afraid of him and started acting cocky, like he was some tough *hombre.* Almost everyday Mack would come up and say *especially* in front of a crowd, *"Let's put the gloves on for a couple of rounds!"*

Each time he asked, I would do a *slow burn*. The steam was building-up, and the lid was ready to blow. He asked the question one time too many. Several of us had just finished swimming, and had gotten dressed and were ready to return to camp. Then, Mack asked *the* question again.

"I don't need any boxin' gloves," as I doubled up my fists and jumped on him like flies on flypaper! Mack tried to run, but a couple of guys grabbed him and held me until I calmed down.

Orville said, "Cool it, Ray! He just wanted to spar a couple of rounds."

"Then, why'd you stop it?" I challenged.

Before he could answer, I said "Look, I've had enough of his bull. I've told him over and over. . . I . . . don't . . . like . . . to box! But, I sure as heck don't have anything against a good fistfight!"

This was the only time I came close to having a fight with another American soldier during my Army career. After the war, I did put the gloves on with a buddy one time.

The adage, "All good things must come to an end," proved to be true for *The Saipan Sea Devils*. We were caught, booked and sentenced. If we had been stateside, taking off without a pass, would have been considered being AWOL, (absence without leave) and the punishment could have been severe. Being within a couple of miles of our tents, we just considered ourselves *misplaced* soldiers. We were in a situation where it did not seem like anyone knew what was going on; in fact, it was ten days before we were missed.

Our punishment was something that most soldiers hated with a passion— a twenty-five-mile-march in the blistering sun. We each were allowed only one canteen of water. I am not sure that we marched the entire distance, but we definitely marched for eight hours. About every two hours, a relief crew arrived with new leaders. After all, they were not being punished.

We had heard in the chow line that the KP list of names and the names to report to the rifle range were not correlated; *surely*, that was not just a rumor. Besides, if it were, what was the worse thing that could have happened . . . *send us to battle?*

As we began our twenty-five-mile-mind-conditioning-march to reprogram our waterlogged brains, some of *The Saipan Sea Devils* began to mouth-off. Orville barked, "Well, what an *honor* it is to be selected to do this special training! Why with all our volunteer swimming and additional conditioning, we will be the envy of the camp!"

He flexed his biceps and lowered his voice about two octaves. "Man, I could go toe-to-toe with Joe Louis any time any day."

"Sure you could, Orville . . . in your dreams," I chuckled.

"We'll be so physically and mentally fit that we will be able to run fifty miles without breaking a sweat. What a privilege to be among such distinguished reprobates," Orville said.

"It's not fair!" A sniveling voice emerged from the group. "I was with you guys for *only* one day. All I did was be at the right place at the wrong time."

"Well, now," Orville snapped. "You know the old saying—if you want to dance, you have to pay the fiddler!"

"Yeah, but we're being used. They're making examples out of us," he whimpered.

"Oh, stop whining!" Orville demanded. "You've been in the Army long enough to know better!"

Another soldier loudly exclaimed, "Just one canteen of water! That's enough to barely wet our tongues every thirty minutes."

"Well, maybe we can snitch a few coconuts here and there," Orville suggested.

"It's obvious we have more than one kind of nut on this island. Who's gonna climb the tree? " I shot back.

The following day after the march, we were back on the rifle range. In Saipan, we were in a holding pattern or a staging area. We had a lot of free time to where we could swim, play cards, box or play music *after* we finished our daily training. There was a black soldier among us who was a gifted musician and could he ever play "Boogie-Woogie" on the piano. What an entertainer! Singing, cracking jokes and tap dancing, this guy could do it all. Oh, how we loved to hear him tickle those ivories!

When I recall the period of time between basic training and being assigned to the 27th, one thing comes to my mind—the constant meeting and parting of friends. Each time we shipped, *farewells* were exchanged with old friends and *hellos* were said with the new ones. Now three or four weeks might not meet the definition of an old friend, but during wartime, bonding and shipping out can happen in a hurry. With the third cruise at hand, I had hopes of seeing a friend or two listed on the shipping roster.

After bidding farewell to some friends, I boarded the USS *Bosque* and soon the island of Saipan disappeared from sight. The USS *Bosque* was a Haskell Class Attack Transport, which spanned 455' in length, and would travel up to 19 knots. She was named after Bosque County, Texas and carried 26 boats and landing crafts. The Navy personnel consisted of 56 officers and 480 enlisted men, and there were 86 Army officers and 1475 enlisted soldiers. There were so many of us on that ship that there wasn't enough room to cuss a cat!

The bunks were something to behold! They were stacked five high with about eighteen-inches of clearance in-between each and were made out of heavy canvas, like the bottom of a cot. In fact, the bunks were about the same width of an Army cot and were laced to each side of the frame. Just picture in your mind, five legless cots stacked on top of each other at eighteen-inch intervals and imagine a soldier sleeping on each one. Our sleeping arrangements were about as *cozy* as it gets.

When living in such close quarters, personal hygiene was a must. I certainly missed bathing in my private little lake with the catfish back home! One of the benefits of being on the ship was an unlimited supply of water—good old salt water, that is. Since the water was cold and salty, a special soap was needed; the soap had a tendency to roll up on our skin like small balls of chewing gum. Scrubbing too hard would cause a stinging sensation, and I never did get used to taking a bath in that salt water. I often wondered if the sailors had fresh water for their showers.

Somewhere along the way, we were told our destination was Okinawa. This was when it became obvious to me that a separation was imminent. I was going to walk out, never to return, to my beautiful, blonde *Kay*.

Even during wartime, some individuals look for ways to take advantage of another's misfortune. Soon as the word was out that we were headed for Okinawa, some of the sailors began scouting around to find things that soldiers would not be able to take with them into battle. Of course, my guitar was a real find. I was pestered day and night with offers up to five dollars, including the case!

I told the ones who made that outlandish offer that I would toss the case in the ocean, and if they could fish it out, they could have it for free. There was one sailor, a small redheaded kid who was just learning how to play. He was always hanging around and wanting me to teach him. I would let him play my guitar and would show him a few things. It was obvious that he really wanted my guitar, but he never mentioned it.

When Okinawa came into sight, I asked him, "Why haven't you made me an offer?"

"I don't want to insult you. I only have ten dollars," he replied.

"Do you really like the guitar? Do you really want it?" I asked.

"I would be the happiest sailor on the ship if I could buy it!" he said.

He also told me that the Navy would not pay them until the soldiers disembarked. I knew this to be true. There was constant gambling going on day and night, and that was the reason the Navy held up paying the sailors.

Time was running out, and destroying my guitar was something I could *never* do. I had to make a decision fast! I could have put it with our c-bags with hopes of recovering it later; but the chance of it being crushed or getting wet was almost guaranteed. I decided to sell my guitar to the little red haired sailor for ten bucks. When I told him, he was so elated, that the freckles seemed to pop right off his nose!

And, that was the last time I saw my beautiful, blonde, *Kay* that had lured me into the *A-1 Pawn Shop*.

I shuddered each time I heard a bang
on the bottom of the ship.

Oops!

The invasion of Okinawa, the largest amphibious invasion of the Pacific Campaign, commenced on Easter Sunday, April 1, with a strong Naval force of fourteen hundred ships. I was on Saipan where fifteen hundred troops were in the process of boarding the USS *Bosque*. On April 15, we sailed to the Western Caroline Islands and anchored on April 17, while we waited for a safe trip to Okinawa. However, more than a thousand kamikaze flights were flown, which created a situation so hazardous and a risk so great, that the landing of additional troops in Okinawa would have to be delayed.

On April 22, we pulled anchors and soon headed to our destination and the zigzagging began. The USS *Bosque* was the flagship, and we were near the middle of the convoy. All we could see in any direction for miles were ships and more ships. There were so many, and they were so spread out that counting them was impossible. This convoy carried the first group of Army and Marine replacements since the landing of troops on April 1.

It is unbelievable how much cargo it takes to fight a battle the magnitude of Okinawa. A very limited list of items would include all kinds of weapons and ammunition, jeeps, trucks, equipment for building roads and airfields, building materials, tents, food, toilet articles, and the list goes on and on.

Not long after sailing, the USS *Bosque* began to shimmy and shake. It was determined that all engines would have to be silenced. We would have to float around until repairs could be made. Something had gone wrong with the propellers and divers had to go down under the ship to fix the problem.

What a perfect target for the Japanese! The tension was building, especially among the sailors. How could they defend an attack from a stationary ship? The commander of the convoy transferred to another ship, and soon all the ships disappeared out of sight. We were instructed not to throw anything overboard or make any noise; if the Japanese detected us, we were goners.

Our anxiety level intensified by the minute. In our minds, we knew what would happen if a Japanese plane or submarine spotted us. The sailors continued to warn us about making loud noises and how it could travel under the water and how submarines could detect sounds. It was impossible for the repairmen down under the ship to do their job without making some noise. I *shuddered* each time I heard a bang on the bottom of the ship.

What a disastrous set of circumstances we were facing! More than two thousand lives were at stake! We did not need to be told twice to remain quiet. Now the question of how far away a submarine could detect noise was never answered, but some thought anywhere from where we were to Japan. However, thinking rationally is hard to do when you have wet underwear.

While repairs were being made, we were just floating around for four or five hours, but to me it seemed like a month of Sundays. It is possible that some ships were lagging behind to protect us, but if that were the case, they were too far away for us to spot.

When the repairs were completed, the engines were immediately started, and we moved full steam ahead without any zigzagging. The USS *Bosque* caught up with the convoy the following day. What a relief to see the first American ship! On April 26, the large convoy of ships anchored near the island of Okinawa and had transported all the things that were needed to fight a war, including the first replacements of Marines and Army troops.

When the USS *Bosque* anchored, small boats began pulling up by our left side; the nets were lowered, and we were told to take our rifles and packs, go down the nets and board the landing crafts. The nets would swing back and forth, so dropping into the small boat at the right moment had to be perfect timing. This was really scary, because the waves caused the boats to bump and spread apart; getting caught in-between could be a crushing and deadly experience.

The landing crafts would take a load of soldiers to a floating dock, dump them off and return for another load. Land and sea crafts were waiting at the floating dock to carry us to the beach. We were instructed to dig a foxhole in which to spend the night on the beach, in case of an air raid, and to be ready for orders.

Bright and early the next morning, a soldier drove a jeep back and forth along the beach. Another soldier rode with him, and yelled into a bullhorn, "Walk up and down the beach, until you see a sign with the name of your ship and assemble next to it."

It was not long before trucks began to line up near each sign, and another soldier with a bullhorn began calling the roll; all assignments had been predetermined. When our names were called, we were to take our rifles, packs and load-up. For most, the next destination was to join their new company on the front lines. No one called my name. As it turned out, I had been designated as an alternate on the shipping orders and should have never left Saipan!

*Rubbernecking is bad business
when you are in a foxhole.*

Hey, Who Invited You!

The brass on Saipan must have thought that one of those man-eating sharks devoured me, because transportation back to the United States was unlikely. Here I was, on Okinawa without orders; no one knew I was coming, and they did not know what to do with me. However, during wartime, the Army has many quick fixes.

Riflemen were sorely needed, and within a couple of days, I was assigned to the 27th Infantry Division of the New York National Guard and was given a complimentary ride in a supply truck right up to the front line. It did not matter where my name fell in the alphabet that day, nor did it matter what my original orders were.

By midmorning, I was sitting in a first-class foxhole with no one blocking my view. Little did I know, this would be one of the luckiest days of my life. Had I stayed in Saipan, I might have missed what all combat veterans experienced—*the utter horrors of war.*

Our position was on a range of small hills. Stretching out before us was a valley, and just beyond was a range of large hills held by the Japanese army. Although we could see the enemy walking around, we were separated by approximately one thousand yards, which was out-of-range for small arms fire. The valley was called, *"No Man's Land."* Most of the terrain between the hills, was more or less, open with rice paddies and had very little cover. There was a village off to the right of our position.

Prior to my joining the company, a push to advance the front line had been stopped by fierce fighting by the Japanese army. This was a setback, and a rude awakening to our military strategists. They had underrated the enemy, and we were in a very vulnerable position. A strong counterattack could have been disastrous for us. While I was on the front, we were in a holding position waiting for additional men before making another assault.

During daylight hours, the Japanese seemed willing to rest and to wait until it was dark before attacking. Their attacks reminded me of a colony of ants at a picnic; if they were not everywhere, my imagination convinced me that they were.

By daylight, our stress levels would be pegging the meter! Our strategy was, "Dig in, hold on and wait for daylight." Our movement or assault would come during daylight hours and only when the military strategists agreed that the timing was right.

During my time on the front line, the Japanese used their artillery more during the night. Okinawa was the artillery-training base for the Japanese army. The adage, "Practice makes perfect," seemed to apply to their artillerymen. For sure, they knew the range of every important target on the island and were very effective in hitting it.

Much of the enemy's artillery was mounted on tracks and could be moved in and out of tunnels or caves at their choosing. Rolling the big guns out at night to shell our positions and hiding them in the daytime, made it very difficult for us to locate and to destroy.

Once the artillery shells were fired, we could hear them gliding through the air. It was possible to estimate where they were going to hit. Naturally, we would be very edgy when we knew the missile was coming close to our foxhole! And, we knew to crouch down as low in the hole as we could with hopes that the shell would hit a few feet away and the fragments would fly over us. Of course, we were always wishing that our foxholes were deeper.

As I was sitting in that foxhole on the front line that lucky day, all of the sudden, we could hear the sound of planes approaching. We did not know if they were enemy planes or ours. The possibility of being strafed with machine gun fire from a low flying aircraft would make even the bravest cringe. We more than hoped they were friendly. As it turned out, they were U.S. Navy Corsair fighter planes. What a relief!

The first plane appeared to be headed directly over our foxhole. Imagine our surprise when rockets were released *behind* us! What was this guy doing? Was he fixin' to blow us to smithereens? If he didn't, what about the four or five planes that were following him?

As the rockets glided past us, it became apparent that their mission was to destroy the village. The pilots positioned their planes, and began to fly in a large circle. Then, they took turns firing rockets at the target until the village was transformed into a burning inferno.

I was in the foxhole with the platoon sergeant and a couple of other guys, because it looked deeper than most, and the loose dirt from the hole was piled high around the top. I became so enthralled in what I was seeing, that for a moment, it seemed like I was watching a picture show! The roar of the engines, the sound of the rockets as they were released and struck their targets, the smell of black powder and watching the village disappear could not be captured in a movie. This was front line action at its best!

The spell was suddenly broken when the dirt from the top of our foxhole began flying all over me! Each time a plane flew over and fired a rocket, I stuck my head up a little higher to get a better look. *Rubbernecking* is bad business when you are in a foxhole.

A Japanese machine gunner must have noticed more than the burning village and the planes firing their rockets. At the cost of revealing his position, which was approximately six hundred yards or more away, he opened fire on me with a light machine gun. Luckily, for me, he missed! I cannot remember if I needed a change of underwear or not, but I did learn a valuable lesson—keep my head down! Well, the machine gunner paid the ultimate price for revealing his position.

When practical, telephone communication was available to each platoon sergeant and commissioned officer. Our sergeant made good use of his binoculars in searching for the machine gun position. It must have taken him fifteen minutes, but eventually he noticed something that looked like one side of a bipod for a light machine gun. It was just barely sticking up above the ground. Since we had not seen the gunner, it was obvious that he was in a foxhole and had left part of his gun visible to us.

Mortars were normally fired from a concealed position, and an observer was needed to communicate with the mortar crew, because the success of the mission depended on him. Our sergeant immediately called the sergeant of the mortar section, gave an estimate of the position of the target, and ordered the first round to be fired. Observing the landing of the first shell, he was able to estimate the distance over or under and right or left of the target. By observing the landing of each shell and by repeating the same steps, success was soon in coming. In this case, the target was hit and the enemy was destroyed.

New recruits to the front line had been trained and were warned that one little bobble could cost us our lives, but putting the game plan into action was something that had to be learned. Unfortunately, not everyone got the second chance.

Rifle shots rang out, and we lost one of our own.

Front Line

After the nerve-racking experience on my lucky day, things were so calm the following morning that it was *eerie*. It reminded me of the lull before a storm. Although we had a clear view in front of us and could readily detect any movement from enemy troops, tension was building. The mind is prone to work overtime when things are too quiet.

On this warm day, some of us had moved from the front to the back to rest for a spell. It was during this period of time that I met a mountain-of-a-man, Private First Class, Nick Nicola. At nineteen years old, we both had recently been assigned to the New York National Guard, 27th Infantry Division.

There were about a dozen of us taking it easy; most of us were the first replacements assigned to the 27th since the invasion of Okinawa. None of us knew each other or anyone in Company K, so we were trying to get acquainted with our new buddies.

Fun loving, outgoing, and friendly, Nick was the kind of person that people liked to be around. You could tell by looking at him that he was in control of his life. It was apparent to me from moment one that Nick was genuine, and there was nothing deceitful or false about this soldier. Towering well over six feet and weighing well over two-hundred pounds, Nick ambled over to me and stuck out his big paw. "Nick Nicola from Indiana. Where're you from?"

"Ronold Ray from Texas. Glad to meet you."

"Texas? Man alive . . . I love horses! All you Texans must have a big corral full. Well . . . we need to have ourselves a good ol' talk!" He flashed a smile.

Nick had a passion for horses and seemed to know the name of every racehorse that had ever won a competition, the owner of the horse, their lifetime earnings, and their complete history. For some reason, he just assumed that I came from a huge ranch with a pasture full of horses. Anyway, we had a lot of things in common and became foxhole pals from the get-go.

Even when things were quiet and nothing was happening, we still had to be alert and protect ourselves from snipers and uninvited guests. It just so happened that we were hunkered down in an old roadbed where rain had washed away the soil. There, we had ample protection from small arms fire. The ditch was deep enough and long enough for all of us to gather inside, so that Sergeant Cedric Maxwell could talk to us. It was also a good opportunity to get acquainted with each other and for some to take a smoke break.

Even during the battle at the most doggone times, some soldiers just had to have a cigarette. One of the c-ration cans always included a couple and a few matches. The supply truck usually carried boxes of kitchen matches—the kind with two and one-half inch stems. Each soldier was issued a waterproof matchbox, and Nick decided he was not about to run out of matches. In order to cram more inside his box, he decided to shorten the stems. So, he pulled his knife off his belt and began to whack away. Soon, he had a pile of match heads with quarter inch stems.

There was a striker in the end of the matchbox cap. After he filled his box, *things* began to happen. When Nick screwed the lid onto the box, the striker came in contact with a match head and set off an explosion! And, the fun was underway! The ignited match heads blew the cap off the box and made a noise that sounded like a hand grenade when the safety pin is pulled and tossed.

Maxwell yelled, "Grenade! Hit the ground! Hit the ground!" The mad scramble was something to see. Well, Nick and I knew what had happened, so we just continued our conversation. Needless to say, Maxwell was not a happy camper although it was an accident.

Another night, while we were still on the front line, our company was covering a section of the line that had a major road running through it. Maxwell, a veteran of two previous campaigns, had given the order, "Do not ask for a password. If you see someone moving around, let em' have it! We'll all be in our foxholes."

There were a handful of reserve soldiers, who were behind the line to hold the road just in case of a breakthrough. Our company constructed a fortress in the middle of the road with huge rocks that had been pushed aside by heavy road equipment. We were about fifty-yards behind the line. On this night, Nick and I were in the fortress, and a few more reserves and medics were behind us. We were to hold the road at *all* cost.

Flares were continually fired-out in front of the line, which made it more difficult for the Japanese to slip up and attack; at times it was dark. There were no flares back where we were, but the moon was shining some light. The problem was when the gulf clouds sailed by and covered the moon.

During the night, we saw a man who was slowly walking up the road toward us. We had only a moment to decide what to do. Our decision was to let him come closer, and call for the password; if he did not answer, then we would take the necessary action. Nick, who had a strong voice, called out; the answer came instantly, *"Apple Dumplings."* The guy who gave the correct answer was none other than Maxwell in the flesh! I will remember those words for as long as I live.

Maxwell had been out of his foxhole, because the medics were needed. Just minutes before, a Japanese officer had crawled up to the front line, jumped into the foxhole with two of our friends, and used his saber to kill one and wound the other. One of our soldiers in the next foxhole shot and killed the Japanese officer, which saved the wounded soldier. Firing in the dark, while two men are fighting each other and hitting the right target, calls for real skill or a lucky shot.

So, when Maxwell sent Nick back to get the medics, I almost panicked. I had an awful feeling that he would be killed. If it had not been for one corporal, he would have. When Nick came near the soldiers positioned behind us, this one soldier did not request the password. Instead, he shouldered his rifle and fired! It just so happened, that the corporal pushed the rifle barrel upward, and the shot was fired into the air. I could hardly believe my eyes when Nick came walking up with a couple of medics.

The next morning, the dead Japanese officer was searched and a map was found inside his helmet. The map showed the position of one of our machine guns, and he went belly-up for trying to destroy the gun. He came close to the gun—as close as the next foxhole. Suffice it to say, the order "not to call for the password" was never given again.

Our main concern was trying to survive the enemy's strategy of trying to send us home in a box. However, there were other problems; for instance, trying to maintain a healthy body under such poor conditions was difficult. The dreaded *GI trots* was really bad news! When we needed to go, we needed to go badly.

Going to the restroom was not an option. In fact, restrooms were nonexistent and most of the time, getting out of the foxhole was hazardous to our health. We were living in very unsanitary conditions. Dysentery was sapping the strength from all who had it, and there were many who did.

C-rations were the only thing on the menu, chlorinated water was all we had to drink, and the loss of sleep from pulling guard duty each night compounded our problems. A hot bowl of chicken broth might not have been what we needed, but I certainly thought about how good it would taste.

One night, one of our soldiers had a severe case of diarrhea. He decided to leave the foxhole and go back behind our positions to relieve himself, which was not according to Army procedure and orders for that night. Army procedure was to take care of our business in the foxhole. He let it be known to the soldiers near him what he was going to do and not to mistake him for a Japanese soldier and shoot him when he returned.

Since the enemy was sometimes able to infiltrate our positions, we always had to watch our backs. Shooting up flares was normal and this night was no different. If we were caught out in the open when a flare was fired, our instructions were to freeze, turn our face to the ground and cover our eyes with our arms.

A moving object is easier to spot than a still object. This soldier was well-trained, but as he was returning to his foxhole, a new flare was fired. He froze, lowered his head and covered his eyes. Another soldier, who was way down the line and too far away to know that one of our soldiers was out of his foxhole, caught a glimpse of him the instant he was covering up.

What happened next was a tragedy. Rifle shots rang out, and we lost one of our own.

My steps might have been wobbly,
but my speed was excellent!

Let the Mop-up Begin!

Divide and conquer was the name of the game during the invasion of Okinawa. On April 2, part of the mission was accomplished early on by the 7th Infantry Division when they gained control by overtaking a strip of land that stretched east and west entirely across Okinawa. Another goal was to seize the southern region and the capital city of Naha where the Japanese generals chose to position most of their warriors. To establish the rear echelon safely, it was necessary to rid the North of all enemy soldiers.

The 6th Marine Division had stormed thru the northern section; however, vast numbers of the Japanese soldiers were still hiding out in heavily fortified caves and in the dense underbrush. The battle for Naha and the southern region was proving to be much more difficult than anticipated. The 27th Infantry Division, which was designated as a floating reserve, landed on April 9 and took positions on the front line adjacent to the 96th Infantry Division.

About all the grunts know during a war is to take orders, so it came as a complete surprise when we were told that the 6th Marine Division would be relieving us from front line duty; we would be moving back to a staging area to regroup. Our new assignment was to track down, kill or capture all enemy military personnel who had been hiding out. In addition, we were ordered to move the civilians into military compounds after we burned down their homes to keep them from returning. We mopped-up the northern region while unusually fierce fighting was going on in the southern part.

As the Marines were moving in, and we were getting ready to move out, the added activity was drawing more attention than usual from the enemy. I am sure the Japanese were anticipating another assault on their positions, and they started dropping more shells to let us know that they were watching our every move. When the Marines were ready, they moved forward with determination to capture the big hill.

One of our tanks, which led the Marines down the hill, was hit by enemy fire. Although one of the tracks was blown off, the crew was unharmed. They managed to burn the tank and destroy its weapons before making their escape. This was a precaution just in case the enemy overran our position and tried to use the tank weapons against us. Company K was beginning to move away from the front when this happened.

We had to exit down a road that had been carved out on the side of a steep hill. There was nothing to prevent a person or vehicle from dropping off the ledge. As we were walking in a single file, the Marines were meeting us walking in a double file. We were also meeting some military vehicles along the way, and the enemy was firing artillery and mortar shells in our direction.

A shell *whizzed* past us and hit off to the left. Another *whooshed* by and was pretty much in line. I cannot remember the third shell or what happened. All I remember is a Marine officer holding me up by the shirt collar, kicking my rear end and yelling, "Get out of here!"

I ran down the hill *lickety-split* and was told later what had happened. A shell had hit the middle of the road, which was filled with military personnel; a Marine was killed and others were seriously wounded, including my squad leader. I had been knocked out. The two guys walking in front of me must have shielded me from receiving any fragments from the shell. This was truly another lucky day.

We did not waste any time in getting back to a secured area. My steps might have been wobbly, but my speed was excellent! We stopped for a couple of hours while our company commander was given our new assignment. During this brief period, an Army Chaplain had set up to hold services and communion for all the soldiers that wanted to attend. Those of us, who had just received a good dose of *foxhole religion*, were more than happy to participate!

Shortly after the services were over, we moved out and headed to our new assignment and to a place to spend the night. It was a cold, miserable, rainy evening and the wind was blowing furiously. We were drenched all the way down to our shorts by the time we stopped at a reasonably safe place. The sergeant sent us out to find anything that would burn, so we could build a fire, warm-up and dry-out. I joined Nick to see what we could find, and this is where it all began.

"Hmm . . . I wished I knew how to disarm this grenade," he said.

"Heck. . . I learned how to make 'em and disarm 'em during' jungle trainin'." Of course, I reminded him of our need for grenades. "Why do you wanna destroy one?"

He raised his brow. "Oh . . . I thought I would have a little fun."

Well, how could I deny a buddy from having a moment of pleasure? A little entertainment would be a welcomed change from what we had been doing. We would all get a kick out of it. Sure, we would! I disarmed the grenade. Nick looked at me with a mischievous smirk and hooked it back on his belt. Then, we headed back carrying a couple of discarded wooden boxes we had found and joined the others as they were trying to get a fire started.

After we warmed-up somewhat and were just beginning to get comfortable, Nick began to act *strange*. Tilting his head and looking upward, he started babbling incoherent words. His voice trembled as if he were talking to a spirit.

As he appeared to be in a trance, he had definitely attracted everyone's attention.

All at once, he started fiddling around with the grenade that was attached to his belt. Man, oh man! Now, I knew what he was up to! Before anyone could even utter a word, he ripped that grenade right off his belt!

Next, he stuck his finger inside the safety pin pull ring, fumbled around for a moment and yanked the pin. The situation looked very grim. We had all witnessed the devastation a grenade caused at close range. Nick then stumbled around and let the grenade drop to the ground.

The reaction from the group of about twenty soldiers was instantaneous. Some were yelling, "Grenade! Grenade!" Everyone fled for a couple of seconds and hit the ground just as we had been trained to do.

Most of the fragments from an exploding grenade will go upward and out, so getting a few feet away and falling flat on the ground will increase the chances of survival. No one was wounded, but there were plenty of four-letter words shouted when the group found out what had happened. For Nick, it was a rerun of the time the match heads blew the cap off his matchbox.

My biggest mistake was failing to run with the crowd and hit the ground as if I were scared to death when the grenade dropped. Even uttering a few choice words like the rest were doing might have been wiser than calmly standing there. Instead, I just looked at Nick and helped him enjoy the high point of his production. Sometimes enjoyment can make a one hundred and eighty degree turn in a hurry. The consequences of that little prank lasted much longer than the fun did.

Prior to my being assigned to Company K, Lieutenant White had been killed, and my new platoon had been without a leader. We had not yet been introduced to the new guy, who just happened to be among us. Since he was not wearing his silver bars, we had no idea at the time who our leader would be. Soon after the scare, our platoon sergeant introduced Lieutenant Peters as our new platoon leader.

Peters wasted no time in taking command, and if harsh words could have taken the hide off backs, I know two guys that would have been skinless. In addition, seventeen soldiers would have gladly stood in line to help him. Probably the *only* reason they did not shoot us was, because our help was needed to secure the island of Okinawa.

Squad Leader

After pulling such a crazy stunt, it is amazing to me that merely a few days later, I was appointed to be a squad leader. However, that is exactly what happened. Now mopping-up the north-end of the island was much less

Probably the only reason they did not shoot us was, because our help was needed to secure the island of Okinawa.

dangerous than front-line duty, so we used some different tactics. For instance, we would sometimes set up an ambush on a trail or a road or any place we thought the enemy might be moving. My squad was called on to do this task on several occasions.

After dark, I would take four men with me and move out in front of the company to a predetermined site, which would sometimes be as much as fifty-yards ahead; then, we would dig a hole about eighteen-inches deep and large enough for five men to lie in. Each soldier had a woolen blanket and a poncho. After we finished digging the hole, we would put a couple of waterproof ponchos in the bottom of the hole to protect and keep our blankets dry. Next, we would spread a couple of blankets over the ponchos and use the rest for cover. If it was raining, we would make a tent out of the ponchos.

My wristwatch with a florescent dial is how we kept time for guard duty. Two guys were always on guard duty and would serve two-hour stints, but we rotated only one guy each hour. We hoped that the fresh guard would be fully alert his first hour since he would be the timekeeper and have the responsibility of waking the next guard. Of course, we hoped both guards would be alert, but fatigue and sleepless nights have a way of taking its toll even in such dangerous situations.

For sure, both soldiers would be observing each other and would be trying to keep each other awake and alert. This was the way we rotated guards when on ambush detail, but it was not only on ambush detail that someone had to be watching at all times; this went on until the end of the war. The procedure varied at times, but looking out for our hides was the number one priority.

We did not setup ambush details on a regular basis, but one time we setup a detail in a rice paddy. The rice had been harvested, and although the ground had been drained, it was still wet. We had put down a couple of ponchos and had spread the blankets on top hoping we would stay dry. However, the water managed to seep through, and we slept most of the night on those soaked blankets. I did learn something about wet wool blankets though—you can wrap-up in one and still get warm. This might not be true in freezing weather, but Okinawa was not that cold from April until September.

On one occasion, we received information from the Battalion Headquarters that the enemy had been using the night as their *cover* to move their troops down a back road and out of our area. Plans were made for Company K to move in after dark and setup an ambush. Moving a company of men plus two jeeps in the dark was not an easy task, and the possibility of an enemy attack was not far from our minds.

Our site for the night was in a small valley with a seldom-used road that ran down the center. Both jeeps, facing in opposite directions, were placed in the middle of the road. Machine guns were mounted on each jeep. Our positions were up in the small hills on each side of the road overlooking the jeeps. We spread out about 200-yards on each side of the road and dug in. We also had positions guarding our backsides. We had no way of knowing where the enemy was hiding, and we could not take any chances of a surprise attack.

The Army had dropped leaflets all over the island to warn the civilian population to "stay in their houses and get off the roads and trails after dark." Things had been quiet all night, and nothing was going on. However, just before daylight, a machine gun opened up. Chills ran up my spine. It sounded like one of our guns, but I could not tell for sure. Our machine guns fired faster than the enemy's did.

Things were very intense until daybreak when we learned of what had happened. An elderly civilian man, who was wearing a pair of those forked-toed tennis shoes, (the kind with a place to put the big toe and a single section for the other toes, sort of like a *foot mitten*) came walking down the middle of the road. He moseyed right up to one of our jeeps. It was not easy to hear a person walking on a dirt road especially if they were small like the old man and were wearing lightweight shoes.

Whenever the machine gunner saw the old man, the gunner went into action by pulling the trigger and holding it for a long burst. Naturally, our imaginations ran wild! We were so sure that we were fixin' to be in a firefight. When we heard the whole story, there was a good side and a bad side.

The bad side was if it had been a Japanese soldier coming down the road, the machine gunner would have probably been killed. The good side was that the machine gunner fired over the old man's head, and he continued his journey down the road.

The second machine gunner in the other jeep was able to tell that the man was a civilian and was no threat to us. As the old man came in front of the gun, the second gunner let him pass. The interesting thing about this incident was that the old man did not speed up or anything; he just kept pluggin' along as if nothing had ever happened.

Another time, we had a few days off to regroup, dry-out and rest. Our Command Post was accessible on one side by boat, so our c-bags had been transported to the area. It had only been a month since we last cleaned-up, but we took advantage of the opportunity whether we needed it or not. How nice it was to be able to take a bath in a nearby stream! We even had the luxury of a bar of soap.

I had been worried that Japanese snipers would start locating us by scent rather than by sight. Getting a fresh shave, a change of clothes, new socks and underwear, and some new shoes were just what the doctor ordered. Shucks! It was as if I had morphed into an actual human being.

The ocean was good protection for us—the Navy saw to that. From the beach, the ground was level for about two- or three-hundred yards. Then, there was a steep mountain with a well-traveled trail that led to the top. Since we were still in enemy territory, the captain decided we needed to maintain a position on top of the mountain just in case. The area was considered safe, but we did have to guard against snipers.

The site was chosen by our captain, and I was selected to take four men with me to maintain the outpost, both day and night. Rations and water would be brought to us. During daytime, we would take turns coming down one at a time. The site was on a side trail which led to a small potato patch. Tall pine trees surrounded us, but the trees had been thinned out around the garden.

A dozen or so soldiers were chosen randomly by the first sergeant to help setup our little fort. Telephone wire was installed around the site and circled about one hundred feet in radius and was attached to bushes at a height of about eighteen inches. C-ration cans were hung on the wire and each can had gravel inside.

The wire was concealed by small trees and other vegetation. This was our alarm system. If we heard the cans rattle, we knew something or someone was out there. In addition to the alarm system, a booby trap was set each night.

The c-ration cans were also just the right size in which to slip a fragmentation hand grenade—perfect for setting booby traps. First a small hole was made near the bottom rim of the can, and another hole was made on the other side just above the rim. This was easy to do with a knife or bayonet.

Next, telephone wire was run through both holes, twisted together and the loose end was attached to a tree adjacent to the trail. Then, the tripwire was tied around the handle of the grenade and placed inside the can and was strung across the trail and tied to another tree. Rocks or sticks were used to raise the tripwire a few inches above the ground.

With the grenade stuck tightly inside the can, the safety pin could be removed without pulling the grenade from the can or allowing the lever to fly off. Therefore, as long as the grenade stayed inside the can, it was safe. If the enemy walked or crawled into the tripwire, the grenade would be pulled out of the can, and the handle would fall off. The spring-loaded striker would activate the primer and a live, mini bomb would be on the ground; the chance of survival would be nil.

After we had everything set, I would gently pull the safety pin from the grenade and get the heck out of Round Rock! Hand grenades are very effective at short range, but the timing of the fuse is crucial. The effective killing range is approximately sixteen feet and the casualty range is up to fifty feet, but is still dangerous at fifty yards. As the fragments travel further, they are dispersed at a higher elevation which prevents them from being as effective

There is one minor problem with using grenades as booby traps; someone has to muster up enough courage to put the pin back in the grenade the following morning. If the lever were to slip off the grenade, there would be only four seconds to make a choice—either grab and toss it faster than a cat can lick his eye, or it would be, "Katy, bar the door."

Although our company was way understrength, my squad was almost full with seven soldiers, all teenagers. Whenever I was on an ambush detail or in the mountain fort, I only needed four guys. I chose my Hungarian friend, Nick Nicola, from Indiana; Juan Rios, from California; Nervous Ned Bailey, from Illinois; and Jessie Cooper, better known as "the Kid" from Fort Worth, Texas.

Juan, a small Mexican guy, was good-natured, but he did not let anyone push him around. I could joke or kid with him all day long. No problem! He knew that I treated him the same as all the other guys, and we became close friends. He was a judo expert and was the most courageous guy in my squad, including myself. Sometimes, I would be asked to send one man to join a night scouting patrol. I always hated to choose, because I did not know if they would ever return. As it worked out, I never had to make that decision, because Juan would always volunteer.

Nervous Ned was a good soldier, but he had a problem with his overactive imagination. At night he could see things or hear things that the rest of us could not. To make matters worse, everyone in my squad was having anxiety problems. Ned reminded me of a high-strung racehorse, dancing and prancing just before the race was to begin. However, when time came for action, Ned was a winner, and that was why I choose him for the ambush details.

The Kid was from a rich ranching family near Fort Worth, Texas and spent a lot of time gambling and chasing women before he was drafted into the Army. None of us could stomach his arrogant attitude, but he was indeed, a good soldier. During the day, the best way to deal with him was to play poker. We had a big box of kitchen matches, and he would divide them up and win them all back—divide them up and win them back again. This would go on and on. No doubt, he was a professional card shark, but this was not the worst thing about him. He had no use for Juan and was angry, because I included both of them for all the ambush details.

Nick was strong as an ox and was in a good mood most of the time—a big teddy bear would be a good description for him. However, he was much more than that. When things got rough, he knew what to do, and he would do it.

An excellent storyteller and actor, Nick loved to talk about his mother and what a good cook she was. He could have us practically smelling her Hungarian goulash that he craved. Nick loved life and fun, but he loved God more. He was dead serious about his faith in Jesus. We were sitting in our little fort one night when Nick pointed up to the beautiful moon and rejoiced, "God is really shining his blessings on us tonight."

It *was* one of those magical nights! The full golden moon was radiant and the clouds were drifting by casting shadows all about. It was a spectacular sight to look out and see millions of stars reflected in the ocean below and the majestic mountains surrounding us. It made me think of other times and other places, and for a few moments, I could almost forget that I was more than five-thousand miles away from home in a faraway land fighting a war.

It almost seemed like I was back at home on the farm during more innocent times enjoying the company of my family and friends, and doing the things I had been doing prior to graduating from high school. However, reality is never far away when one is engaging the enemy during wartime. I had to face the fact that the plans and dreams I had made for my life, might never come to fruition.

The tranquility of the night was soon shattered around midnight. I was getting ready to wake Juan to take my place in the guard rotation. Nervous Ned was wearing the watch on his arm, which meant that he was the fresh guard, and was more or less, in charge.

According to his orders, he was supposed to wake me if he spotted the enemy. Of course, if the enemy was nearby, he knew to shoot him. Ned turned to me and frantically whispered, "I see a Japanese soldier crouching down! He's on the trail that leads up here!" I then woke the others, and we all grabbed our weapons and took our positions.

I could not see anything or anyone on the trail. However, Ned was so sure of what he was seeing. I told him, "Blast away!" Ned opened fire, and immediately, we heard the cans rattling like crazy! Although we could not see anyone, we knew we had visitors crawling around in the weeds and brush.

I immediately gave orders, "Fix your bayonets, keep your heads down and get ready!" I can honestly say that there was no more sleep for any of us that morning. Nothing happened. It seemed like daylight would never come, and what a relief it was to see the friendly, bright sun finally peeking up over the ocean.

Now was the time to put the pin back in the grenade and scout out the area. There could be a wounded or dead Japanese soldier nearby. While I was putting the safety pin back inside of the grenade, one of the guys shouted, "The wire holding up the cans has been broken!"

He had followed the wire and found that the break had occurred at a tree near the trail. He determined that the tree was the *crouching Japanese soldier* seen by Ned. The wire had been wrapped a couple of times around the tree, and one of Ned's bullets had severed it. This had caused slack in the wire and had set off our alarm system. It would be next to impossible to shoot a small wire in two during daylight, but at night? No way! However, strange things do happen in war.

After that incident, I needed to go down to the Command Post and report the reason for the rifle shots. There, I visited for awhile and upon returning to the fort, Nick had some things to tell me. He explained that everyone was uptight after losing sleep and having had such a stressful night, and the hard feelings between the Kid and Juan had finally erupted into a physical confrontation.

The Kid had invited Juan out to the potato patch and the contest was on! Juan was about thirty-pounds lighter and much shorter, but he *was* a judo expert. According to Nick, the Kid charged him as if he were one of those raging bulls on his Texas ranch. Much to his surprise, Juan flipped him over his back and onto the ground and the Kid bellowed like a wounded animal! However, the Kid jumped up, charged Juan again and was flipped once more.

Then, Nick jumped into the fray, grabbed each fighter by the collar and told them, "Stop or I'll bash your heads together!" I suppose the Kid was ready to stop. Juan had certainly had his fun, and I am sure that neither one of them wanted to cross the big teddy bear. Word spread about the brawl, and the Kid was reassigned to a different squad. Soon, we were back mopping-up the island . . . instead of each other.

*I could run with the best, and there was not
a horse living that I could not ride.*

The Stud

A lot of tumbleweeds have rolled across the highway since the war, and some of the things readily understood back then, have changed dramatically. During that time, there was no transistor, and television had not been marketed to any extent. Telephones and radios were considered a luxury, and travel for most people was very limited. Finishing high school was the goal for the majority of Americans.

Attitudes were also somewhat different then, such as a Yankee's attitude toward a Texan. Some of us Texas guys were frequently asked about Texas and what our lives were like on the trail under the stars. Western movies were popular worldwide, and many people believed that the movies portrayed the true lifestyle of a typical Texan—a cowboy, who lived on a gigantic ranch with thousands of horses and heads of cattle!

By now you might be thinking, what does this have to do with Okinawa? Well, hold your horses! Let me explain. Some of my buddies shared that cowboy mentality, and not only did I let their imagination continue to work overtime, I actually encouraged it. I was always ready to tell a Tall Texas Tale.

Of course, I was a *wild, rootin' tootin' cowboy*! I could run with the best, and there was not a horse living that I could not ride. If this was what they wanted to believe, who was I to ruin their day? Now, the part about the horse turned out to be a heck of a mistake.

The 27th was pulled off the front line and given the job of mopping-up the north-end of the island. For certain, our first orders were to destroy the enemy, and as we moved toward the north, we were to force all civilians to move into the military compounds. We gathered all their livestock and burned down their houses to prevent them from trying to return to their homes. In the compounds, they were provided with food, clothing and shelter.

Now, about those livestock! Portions of the island were suitable for farming, and some horses were used—mostly for pack animals. We took about four or five days to collect the horses and a few cows. These animals were small and weighed between seven hundred to eight hundred pounds. They were larger than donkeys, but smaller than most saddle horses.

Talk about mean horses! These animals must have been fed a steady diet of wild oats. They did not like American soldiers, and if one of us tried to mount one, we took the chance of being bitten, kicked, or pawed. Anything that a vicious animal could do, they would do it. But, that did not discourage us from wanting to have horse races.

I was not one of the lucky soldiers to find a horse of my own; however, fate dealt me a one-eyed black mare. Her behavior was so wild that no one could even get on her back. That's when some of my good buddies remembered how Pfc. Ray, the cowboy from Texas, could ride anything that had hair on its back. Whoa!

Well, sometimes things can change in an instant. I noticed a soldier leading a horse, and he came up and stopped in front of me. "Are you the Texas cowboy?" He asked. "If you are, I have a horse to give you."

I had just been given the fastest and most ill-tempered racer in our group, and I knew that I had to ride or eat crow. I was not about to eat crow, at least not at this stage. I managed to mount the one-eyed racer and miraculously, I was able to stay on.

I had been to a couple of hog killings and several goat ropings, but the thrill of racing my fiery steed and winning each time was almost more than I could stand; and my reputation, as a Texas bronco rider, quickly got around. Of course, I needed to put on a show for the Yankees, and I *might* have even put a little swagger in my walk. Well, that turned out to be another big mistake.

Unknown to me, another group had located a stallion, which was the only one I saw on the island. However, I am sure there must have been others. He was fair-sized, but the black mare was tame compared to him. No one, but *no one,* had been able to ride him. This was not a run-of-the-mill nag. He weighed about one thousand pounds, had small pointed ears, a flared nose and pig-eyes! He was prancing, snorting and showing signs of being a real outlaw!

Two guys could hold him until the rider mounted, but after that, it was high sailing! Well, the word was out, "This guy from Texas can ride anything with hair on its back!" And, this stud had plenty of hair. *"Oh, what a tangled web we weave when first we practice to deceive,"* ran thru my mind more than once.

Suddenly, being a rootin' tootin' cowboy wasn't nearly as much fun as it had been just minutes before. I desperately needed to figure a way out of this mess. I had ridden horses all my life, but this was different. I was never cut out to be a bronco rider, and I knew it. I had these Yankees fooled, and I wanted to keep it that way. Besides, I did not like the taste of crow.

I needed some way to even the odds, so that I could ride this *hoss.* All at once, I knew what I needed to do! There was a potato patch next to the road, and it was soaked from all the rain we had been having. I told the guys that we were blocking the road, and we needed to move. Then, I led the horse out into the potato patch and told them I was ready to ride. One thing for certain, the potato patch would be a softer place to fall.

I looked down to see how far the horse was sinking into the mud—maybe as much as six inches. The odds were looking up! As soon as I could mount, I rode that sucker around and around in the potato patch, and jumped off. Then, I led him out to the road and gladly gave him back to the other guys. I don't know how the potatoes felt after being trampled on, but I can truthfully say, "My ego pegged."

As it turned out, I was the only one to ride the stud. Later in the day, the guys wanted me to give a repeat performance, but I declined. After all, we had moved away from the potato patch, and were heading toward the military compound to leave our four-legged beasts. Although the party was over, and the fantasy of starring in a cowboy movie and charging to the front line on a white stallion with guns ablazin' had ended, the Tall Texas Tales continued to *grow* as we rode off into the sunset.

Rootin' Tootin' Cowboy

Steer Clear

We're already dead if the voices are comin' from Japanese soldiers, so I might as well use the element of surprise and see what happens!

Fire on the Mountain

Lurking high on a mountain trail, a Japanese heavy weapons company consisting of a sizable number of soldiers equipped with *81 mm* mortars and heavy machine guns were detected, according to the latest air surveillance report. Our company was immediately trucked to the base of the mountain where we met other ground troops when we arrived. We were to dig in, hold on and wait until morning.

I had recently been transferred from Company K to Company B, and that is when I met Staff Sergeant Tim Turner. I was never in the same platoon with him, but we did see each other almost everyday. Sometimes, the foxhole is a good place to have some serious conversations; such as what really matters in life—survival and loved ones. Tim told me how he planned to get married just as soon as he returned home. Naturally, we discussed the strong possibility of meeting an entrenched enemy holding the high ground when we started climbing up the mountain.

During the night, the Navy moved ships in near the beach. At daybreak, the shelling started. It looked and sounded like the Navy was blowing the mountain apart! The raining barrage of fire went on and on until we wondered if anything on the mountain could possibly be alive. I wondered how the mountain could possibly be standing. Finally the shelling ceased, but soon we heard planes roaring in the near distance.

As the Navy planes arrived, the thundering bombardment resumed, and continued for quite some time. In the meantime, the Navy ships left the shore and retreated farther out into the ocean. Then, all went silent. Now it was time for us to do our thing— climb the mountain and destroy the enemy.

The battle plans were ready for execution; our company was to assault and take the top of the mountain. Since our commanding officer had been either wounded or killed, and I never did know which, Captain Leonard Rogers was appointed to be our commanding officer. And, this was his first day.

A narrow river flowed down the mountain, and our approach was to follow it as far as possible. The map indicated a fork in this stream, which was more than half way up. Considering all the shelling we had just heard, I was thinking, "What are we gonna find at the top?"

Our orders were to move out at 10:00 a.m. My position was near the front as we strung out and began following the stream. It was treacherous climbing up the steep, slippery rain-soaked mountain. Finally, we made it up to where the river divided without any mishaps. While Rogers decided which direction to take, we stopped for a breather.

Then, we continued up the main stream where the climbing became extremely difficult as the narrow pathway became steeper and more constricted. As we moved farther beyond the fork, we became more and more boxed in; the dense vegetation prevented us from seeing much of anything. At last, we came to a waterfall and a dead end. There was no place to go.

What a predicament! A machine gun positioned behind us could have easily pinned us down. The enemy that hid in heavily fortified caves during the day could have been watching our every move. Since the Army never retreats, Rogers told us to do an about-face and double-time it back to where the stream split.

At the fork, there was a fairly good trail along the side of the smaller stream. For Harry and me, this is where the rubber met the road. Rogers pointed at us and said, "You two! Come with me!" Then, he scampered up the trail as if he had a bee in his pants. He continued to climb higher and higher. I don't know what he was thinking, but we both knew that we were sitting ducks for a sniper.

We mentioned this to Rogers, and he called us "yellow-bellies." A few minutes later, we noticed an old man ahead of us walking down the trail. He was carrying one of those long poles across his shoulders. Tied to each end of the pole was a rope, and a bundle of firewood was tied to the end of each rope.

We tried to stop Rogers once more to tell him about the old man, but he called us "yellow" again. When he spotted the poor guy, he raised his carbine and fired!

Several things happened simultaneously; the old man tumbled down the creek bank and out of sight, Roger's gun jammed and would not fire again, and we soon learned that he had missed! As it turned out, the old man was scared *only* half to death.

The situation only got worse. Rogers ordered Harry, "You stay and guard this old man." Then, he looked at me and said,

"You'll come with me." By this time, we were a good three-hundred yards away from the company, and he was acting as if he was out for a Sunday afternoon stroll.

I couldn't help but notice that Rogers's uniform was *overkill* for combat duty as he donned his bright, silver captain bars—a *no-no* rarely seen in the field. Most field grade officers were brighter than the bars they had earned and knew they were prime targets. They could see that it was to their advantage not to give the enemy a glimmer of hope on the battlefield as the sunlight could easily reflect light from their insignia. Therefore, most officers merely penciled their rank on their collar. Perhaps, Rogers wearing his glistening bars was merely a reflection of his experience or intelligence.

The malfunction of his weapon indicated that he had never led soldiers into battle, and his rank indicated that he had been in the Army for a few years. It was later when I found out that his expertise was commanding a cannon company.

We continued to follow the stream, and as we rounded a bend, we could see several houses ahead. Rogers picked up his pace, and we were soon at the first house. He told me to watch while he searched the house. I mentioned to him that some of the houses our platoon had previously searched had been booby-trapped. Again, I received the yellow-belly treatment.

The houses in the mountain villages were very primitive. Most were wooden with a thatched roof and had only one large room with a dirt floor and one door. The natives lived a hard life. As we moved from house to house, I could hear we were getting closer to a waterfall.

During the monsoon season, the water would rush down from the mountains and create many streams and waterfalls. I heard muffled voices mixed with the sound of falling water. When I told Rogers, I was starting to get used to being called "Old Yeller Belly."

On the backside of the waterfall, surrounding the base was a semicircle of huge boulders where I was positioned. I kept listening and decided the voices were coming from the other side of the boulders. I was thinking, "We're already dead if the voices are comin' from Japanese soldiers, so I might as well use the element of surprise and see what happens!"

Since Roger's gun was jammed, I thought, "Why tell him what I had in mind?" Besides, I was tired of his mouth. I decided shooting from the hip would be the best approach. I eased around the last boulder with my gun ready, and I could not believe all of the screaming, crying, and carrying on when they saw me! It was a moment I will never forget.

Huddled around the waterfall and protective boulders, were twenty-five or thirty elderly men and women and children. After all the shelling, strafing and bombing they had just endured, they were *now* being threatened by an American soldier staring and pointing a rifle at them. This was almost more than they could bear. And, what a relief it was for me.

When Rogers heard all the screaming, he ran to see what was going on. "Ray, go back down the trail and bring the old man up here to these houses. Then, tell Harry to go back to the company and have them join us up here," he snapped.

On that mountain, I had expected to see dead and wounded soldiers and natives all over the place, but I did not see even one. The soldiers must have slipped down the backside of the mountain and escaped. If even one had stayed behind, three more American soldiers would have probably been added to the nearly 13,000 Americans killed on Okinawa.

When the company caught up with us, the first sergeant and Rogers moved out of hearing distance. By the tone of the voices, I could tell it was a heated discussion. After that, the sergeant questioned Harry and me about what had happened.

Okinawa was the third battle for the sergeant, and he knew how to fight a war. He assured us, "I will be talking to the battalion commander, and come morning, Rogers will not be around." The sergeant must have had a good relationship with the major, because the next morning, Rogers was no longer shining. He had been fired from the mountain.

*Just how do you think you can defend yourself
with that tin-plated cap gun!*

Cool Hand Lester

The big hunt was on. We were in the process of ridding the north-end of the island of all Japanese soldiers. At the beginning of the mop-up, we were on the peninsula and the majority of the area was farmland, mostly rice paddies. Our line of soldiers stretched from one side of the peninsula to the other. There were so many of us that we could easily see and talk to troops on either side of us. Moving forward by day, we dug in at night hoping that none of the Japanese soldiers crawled thru our lines. Our objective was to flush-out and destroy the enemy, but above all, to prevent them from moving in and attacking our positions from behind the front-line. Cutting them off from rejoining their units and keeping them separated was imperative.

As we moved farther north, the terrain was mountainous and heavily covered with vegetation. Our tactics changed, and we began to use aerial maps to locate the trails and villages. Our orders were to burn down the villages and move the civilians into military compounds. The civilians were given a few minutes to pack what they could carry before we set the fires. Then, we blocked the trails, and continued to advance.

When we came to a narrow part of the island, half of us pushed forward for three days and half of us rested. When our time came to relieve our buddies, we traveled in small amphibious boats to catch up with the troops that were moving forward. During one of those rest periods, some of us were playing cards and some were just taking it easy. Others were cleaning their rifles and checking their gear. Don, a small soldier from Iowa, was a company runner and was prone to playing practical jokes. That day, he came to where I was playing pinochle. "Ray, you have a phone call!" He announced all excited.

"Sure, Don. Are you outta your mind? Get lost."

How ridiculous! Who would ever get a phone call out in the field with a war going on!

Within a few minutes, he came running back. Out of breath and in a panic, he said, "Ray, you've got a phone call. You need to come up to the Command Post!"

This time, I was more forceful, "Man, what kinda idiot do you think I am? You'd better get outta here while you still have two legs to run on!"

He looked nervous and stood there a second with a furrowed brow. Scratching his temple, he opened his mouth as if he were about to say something. Instead, he turned around and ran back once more to the Command Post.

Next, the first sergeant came storming down the hill. He was definitely on a mission. He was blowing smoke out of both of his ears! Man, he was so angry that I thought he might explode! He informed me in language clearly understood by every soldier. "Pvt. Ray! Get your stinkin' hide up here immediately! I'm *not* goin' to hold this phone-line open all day for you! I'm about to cancel your call. Understood?" Then, he stomped off.

It was at this point, I realized that I really did have a call. When I answered the phone, what a delightful surprise! It was my older brother, Lester. Three years my senior, he had enlisted in the Army Air Corps shortly after Pearl Harbor. He was stationed in Louisiana when I shipped overseas. I did know from his APO number (Army post office) that he had been shipped overseas, but I did not know where he was stationed. He was calling me from the 27th Infantry Division Headquarters and wanted directions to get up to where I was.

"Don't even think about it, Lester! You don't have the foggiest notion of what you're askin' me to do. Don't do anything foolish. It's not worth the risk," I almost panicked.

I quickly explained, "It's too dangerous! I've seen at least five different ambush sites recently. I'm positive there are others. These Air Force and Navy officers are nuts! They had the same ideas— thinkin' they were safe and could take care of themselves if they ran into trouble. But, I've seen first hand what happened."

"Oh . . . I know how to take care of myself," Lester reassured me. How do I find ya?"

"It's not worth it. You'd be belly-up before sundown, Lester," I reiterated.

I painted him a true picture of the gruesome and dangerous circumstances he would be facing to shock him out of his stupid thinking. The burned jeeps, the decaying worm-infested bodies and the stench of rotting flesh were all the results of that kind of logic.

"You know I wanna see you, Lester . . . but why put yourself in a dangerous situation? Maybe we can get together later on . . . or maybe there's a way I can come see you," I suggested.

"Well, since nobody's gonna help me, just give me a G-chord on that guitar, and I'll find ya," he laughed.

"What song do you wanna sing—'Back in the Saddle Again'?"

"I was athinkin' about 'Drinkin' Beer in a Cabaret'."

"Better make it, 'Pass the Biscuits and the Ammunition'."

"Well, I can say one thing about your outfit, he added. They gave me the *De-luxe* royal treatment at division headquarters."

"Hmm. Wished they'd pass it around."

"Yeah, a sergeant major took the time to find and contact ya by phone, but he advised me not to try to find ya. He told me that he wouldn't have any part in helpin' me get shot."

"Glad someone's usin' their brain."

But, he told me that he'd do all he could—he 'd try to get ya outta there and over to headquarters so we could visit."

"Great. I hope he can."

Captain Richard Henry had gone *somewhere* in one of our jeeps, and we only had one left at the command post. It was not prudent to take the other jeep, because unforeseen emergencies might arise. I was told that if Henry got back by midday that they would try to get me out; otherwise, it would be the following day. As it turned out, they got me out the next morning.

When the driver stopped the jeep in front of Division Headquarters, I immediately spotted my tall, black-haired brother. I shouted, "Hey! Over here, fly-boy!" He turned around and was almost to the jeep before I could even get out.

Man! We just stood there for a moment looking at each other and smiling like a couple of mules eating briars. The Ray boys were not into the *touchy-feely* kind of greeting; Dad had taught us that a good firm handshake was the way real men greeted each other. True to form, we carried on the tradition.

It had been more than a year since we had visited, and Lester could not get over how much I had changed. I had gone from one hundred and forty pounds to one hundred and seventy-five pounds. We got to talking about the different things we had done before the war, and I just had to remind him of all the times he tried to *outfox* our Mother.

Growing up in the Depression and being part of a large family, we had to share beds. Lester and I slept out on the back screened-in porch year round. There were curtains to let down when it rained and during the cold months. Electricity had not yet arrived to the farming communities, and most people heated the kitchen and living room with wood stoves or fireplaces; usually other rooms were not heated.

During the winter before Lester volunteered for the Army Air Corps, it seemed as if he always wanted a smoke before going to bed. However, there was a catch. Mom was very much against his smoking.

Well, there was usually a good supply of *Bull Durham* and *Dukes Mixture* tobacco and plenty of paper to roll a cigarette stashed inside the kitchen cabinet. The problem was—if Mom had ever found a sack of tobacco with the seal broken, Lester's hide would have been in the hands of an irate Scottish Mother. In addition, there might have been another part of his body smoking! However, if Lester had gotten caught, he could have always used the excuse that he was merely trying to help her empty them, so she would have enough to make a tobacco-sack lining for another one of her patchwork quilts.

The top of the tobacco sack had two yellow pull strings and one of the strings was looped and glued underneath the paper seal. Now getting enough tobacco out without breaking the seal or loosening the string was just the kind of challenge most people would have avoided, but not Lester. If anything, it actually encouraged him.

After Dad put a few extra logs inside the old cast-iron heater before going to bed each evening, he would instruct the last person who was up to turn the damper down and bank the coals with ashes. That way, he would have live coals to start a new fire at five o'clock the following morning.

Usually Lester and I would stay up playing our guitars, but if we played too long, Mom wasn't bashful about telling us to put our instruments away and do more studying. Even after we stopped jammin', Lester had a routine that he went through most nights, and it was so entertaining that I would stay up and watch. Besides, I did not want to warm-up that ice-cold bed by myself.

After Lester was sure that Mom had fallen asleep, he would then tiptoe into the kitchen, open the cabinet door and sneak a sack of *Dukes Mixture*. With the patience of Job and grinnin' like a possum, he would very slowly start to work his magic on his little project.

He would carefully ease the looped yellow string out from underneath the seal. After pulling the string free, he would work open the top—just enough to pour a small stream of tobacco without breaking the seal. Closing the sack and looping the string back under the seal was even more difficult. By golly, he could do that, too! He would then ask me to inspect his work, and it would look as good as new.

The funniest part for me was when he would return the tobacco to the cabinet and come back into the living room. This is when his big old grin spread from ear-to-ear. With nary a word spoken, he would roll his cigarette, open the damper and door of the cast-iron stove and light his *masterpiece* on a live coal. Then, he would take a big puff, lean down and blow the smoke inside the stove. With the damper opened, the smoke and his little secret would go right up the chimney and vanish into thin air. That way, Mom would never be the wiser.

Well, we had a good laugh as we remembered how he got away with his smoking, but the biggest laugh I had was when I saw the rig he was wearing! Lester had on a fancy, hand-tooled leather belt and holster, supporting a beautiful pearl-handled .45-caliber revolver, equal in looks to any pistol John Wayne might have worn in a movie.

If Lester had been wearing boots and western wear, he could have easily passed for a cowboy star with his blazing blue eyes and flashy smile. I snickered, "Just how do you think you can defend yourself with *that* tin-plated cap gun!" Smirking, he raised his eyebrows as if he had something up his sleeve. I didn't know *why*, but I did know that I had just stepped in it.

Without batting an eye, he nonchalantly said, "Well, come on. I'll show ya." We walked along the beach where he stopped to stick a match in the sand. We backed-up a short distance, and he challenged me, "Go ahead. Shoot the head of that match."

"Sure, Lester," thinking he was nuts. "You're kiddin', right?"

He shook his head, "There's nothin' to it." And dang, if he didn't whip out that ol' pistol and *boom*—off goes the match head! To finalize his demonstration, he held the barrel of the pistol up to his mouth and blew the smoke away.

I did not know until later that Lester was the best pistol shot and pool player in his squadron. However, I was not surprised about his marksmanship, because swimming, shooting and riding wild horses were things in which he excelled, not to mention sneaking smokes.

I reiterated, "Lester, surely you don't think you can defend yourself with that fancy pistol! Why the enemy would cut you down before you could even get close enough to use it. And, if you did, you'd never live to reload it."

"Man! You Air Force guys don't have the slightest idea of what the infantry is doin' out there in the bushes. We're not exactly havin' a picnic and eatin' fried chicken, that's for sure!" I added.

Each branch had their specialty and the Army and the Marines were trained in jungle warfare, hand-to-hand combat and things with which the other branches were not familiar. We were witnesses to what might happen when Navy and Air Corps officers took to the hills for a little sightseeing in a jeep while carrying their pistols and thinking they could actually take care of themselves! Some would take a joy ride in the middle of a battlefield, and for many, it was their last ride. It would only take one sniper to wipe out several guys.

I was curious and asked Lester how he knew what division I was in and how he found me. All our mail was censored and about the most I could write was, "Hey, I'm doin' great!" Well, Lester went to his grave without ever telling me how he really knew. However, this is what he told me:

Ie Shima was a few miles from Okinawa, and he just happened to know the pilot who delivered the mail to both islands. Lester told the pilot that he wanted to hook a ride with him to Okinawa, but the pilot told him that he could not take him. However, Lester insisted that he could, and it would not be any problem since he had a pass. "So, what time are we leavin'?" Lester asked the pilot.

Eventually, the pilot agreed and told him that he was going to deliver mail to the north end of Ie Shima and then to Okinawa. He instructed Lester *when* and *where* to be out on the runway. The pilot told him the approximate time that he would be flying back from the north end of the island and if he didn't see any brass, he would set the plane down near Lester. He made it clear to Lester that he had better be ready to jump in!

This is the way it worked. After they were airborne, the pilot asked Lester, "Where to?" He told him, "Take me to the 27th Infantry Division Headquarters." The pilot replied, "I don't know where that is!" Within a few minutes, they were flying over Okinawa and the pilot said to Lester, "See that little clearing strip down there? That's where I'm dumping you!"

When Lester got out of the plane, an enlisted man eagerly came running up to him and saluted. "Sir! Can I call you a car?"

"You could, but I suspect you'd better not. I'm just a GI like you. Do you have any idea where the 27th Infantry is?" Lester inquired.

The soldier said, "You're on the 27th Infantry's landing strip. He pointed, "Headquarters is not far from here. It's just a short way down the road and around the corner. If you stand out there on that road, any military vehicle that comes along will be glad to give you a lift."

Within a few minutes, Lester was at headquarters and was inquiring about my whereabouts. He was sent to a sergeant major, who told him that I was out mopping-up the island.

I have been able to figure out how the pilot knew where the 27th Infantry Division Headquarters was located, but the question I have never been able to answer is —'How did Lester know I was in the 27th *and* on Okinawa?'

By the time I arrived at Division Headquarters, Lester was scheduled to leave for Ie Shima within three hours. We had to get our visiting done in a hurry! "Hey, what's this I hear about some girl from Louisiana visitin' Mom and Dad? Are you thinkin' about gettin' hitched?" I asked.

"Heck, no! That's just a rumor. You and me are gonna be back home before ya know it playin' all those parties," he quickly set me straight.

When the clock ticked down to the final minute of our visit, and it was time for Lester to catch his ride, we both were well aware that this had been quite an unusual experience for two brothers to meet as we had in the middle of a war. It was a time when we realized just how much we really did mean to each other. We parted that day not knowing if we would ever see each other again.

Lester caught a ride on a plane headed for Ie Shima, and the next day, I caught a ride on the supply truck to join my company as they were getting ready to board those amphibious boats and move up to the forward positions.

Cool Hand Lester

Jammin' on the Farm

Brothers-Lester, Ed and Ronold Ray

A Sunday Afternoon

Good Times at Gotcher Get Togethers

Plannin' Our Next Escapade
Front-Ronold, Lavan Gotcher,
Milton Terrell
Back-Lavan's Dad

Hangin' Out
Lavan and Ronold

Peter Sanreno reminded me of a little puppy dog whenever it gets scared and wets on the floor.

First Lieutenant Pogue

My encounter with First Lieutenant Hugo Pogue began on Okinawa when the mop-up was winding down. Company B was taking a much-needed rest for a couple of days. Captain Richard Henry called us together and told us that our company had received two new members. After introductions, he informed us that both soldiers would be assigned to our platoon. Pogue would become our platoon leader. And, what a jerk!

When Henry went back to the Command Post, Pogue called our platoon together and marched us down to the beach out of hearing range from the rest of the company. There he ordered us to sit down and began ranting and raving, the likes of which we had never heard—not even in basic training. We thought he would never shut-up!

He barked, "You are a disgrace to the Army by the way you are dressed! From now on, you will wear a clean uniform every day, and you will shave every morning! You are going to look like soldiers even though you're not, and if I tell you to go jump into the ocean and start swimming to Japan, you will do just that!" These are merely the highlights of what he said.

What was the reaction to his long spiel? Well, some of the guys in the platoon were veterans who had earned up to three battle stars; one might say they were survivors. What a slap in the face to a group of combat soldiers! His arrogant manner was so uncalled for. Now, we had *two* wars to fight! A couple of the old vets went so far as to say, "The next time we come under fire, Pogue will definitely go home in a black bag."

A large, tall man, with a milky white complexion, Pogue's hands were way too soft for *any* man, and his physical build was a bit on the *cheesy* side. His appearance indicated to us that he had probably been working inside an air-conditioned office. In civilian life, he was an attorney who had spent three years at Fort Benning, Georgia training cadets. Ironically, he had never been overseas or in combat, had no idea what combat was like, and had no common sense whatsoever.

How could he actually expect us to shave or change our uniforms everyday when our c-bags were miles away? Plus, sitting in a foxhole was not exactly conducive to shaving or changing uniforms. Call me crazy, but the last time I checked the foxhole bathrooms, there was a month long waiting list of huge, blue-green blowflies.

What a shame the way our platoon was being treated! To make matters worse, the second soldier, whom Henry introduced that day, must have invented backstabbing. He was an ex-Marine named Peter Sanreno. We never did find out much about him, except that he was a jerk, second only to Pogue. While we were discussing Pogue, Sanreno would make mental notes and then report everything to him. For this bit of information, Pogue made him our platoon sergeant.

We called Sanreno, "The Squealer" and found out he had been a Marine sergeant at one time and came to us as a private first class. We never knew how he happened to be in the Army. He might have served in the Marines before the war and was discharged and drafted, or he might have joined the Army after the war started. Since he had been in the Marines, he wanted us to think he was tough. He saw to it that a boxing ring was built when the war on Okinawa ended, and that he was the boxing instructor.

By this time, we were living in "tent city." Our mess hall was operating for the first time since the invasion. Breaking into the chow line was no big deal since we all knew each other. Most of us preferred to eat with our close friends, so we usually granted this courtesy.

One morning, Tex, who was not in our platoon, walked up the line and joined some of his buddies. The Squealer, who happened to be standing near the front of the line, abruptly left his place and ran back to jump on Tex for breaking in front of others. Tex walked back to the end of the line without saying a word.

As a career soldier in the regular Army, Tex was among the first replacements that had been added to the 27th. Not everyone in the Army was buddies, but all of us were united by one common goal—to win the war. However, the mix was not good, because the regular Army career soldiers, who were mostly from the South, felt like they were being treated like stepchildren. The National Guard had a tendency to favor their own whenever it came time for promotions or preferred duties.

In addition to the tense situation, in the barracks at night, discussion of the Civil War was a hot button! There was still plenty of fire in the bellies of some of the southerners, and the yanks could set off things very easily. Things continued to simmer until one night, the pot boiled over! A fight erupted between some of the regulars and the National Guard soldiers. Tex was the main player on his side.

He had been drinking and took the opportunity to get rid of his pent-up anger. Well, Tex did some mighty stupid things, but the worst was when he set up a machine gun in the company street and riddled the outdoor privy! Of course, there was no one inside at the time. When the battalion commander ordered him to stop his rampage, Tex got in his face and sprayed him with choice words.

He was court-martialed, stripped of his sergeant stripes and sentenced to a few years in the brig. Since he could not leave the island, he was allowed to drive a tractor to cultivate vegetables that the Army was raising in the meantime. When the 27th was preparing to leave for Okinawa, Tex was offered a *deal*.

Either he could choose to be sent back to the United States to serve his time, lose his Army benefits and receive a dishonorable discharge or he could volunteer to go with the division into battle. If he decided to go with the division, his record would be expunged, but his rank would be private first class. Since he was a career soldier, staying with the division was his choice.

The Squealer had learned about Tex's past and was constantly prodding him. After we finished eating breakfast that morning, the Squealer came down to Tex's tent and started mouthing-off again. He boasted to Tex that he could whip him with one arm tied behind his back! Tex informed him that he would be in serious trouble if he hit a sergeant, and he could not afford to get into trouble again.

With utter contempt, the Squealer said, "If that's all you're waiting on, I can fix that!" He jerked off his shirt and stripes and egged him on. "Well, what are you waiting for!" he yelled. The fight happened so suddenly that most of us didn't have time to get out into the company street to see it.

Tex knocked the Squealer down twice before he could say "Jack Sprat." The Squealer did not make any effort to get up after the second knockdown. Tex was just getting warmed-up. He was a volcano waiting to erupt, and he wanted more! He challenged the Squealer to 'put the gloves on,' but it never happened.

The news of the fight spread like wildfire throughout our company and battalion. There was much speculation and many wondered why Tex had not been escorted to company headquarters. It was such a hot topic that Capt. Henry called the company out and explained why nothing had or would be done. What he said was news to most of us.

"It has been an unwritten code in the military for years that when a non-commissioned officer removes his shirt, bearing his stripes, and challenges another soldier, he is fair game and Sgt. Sanreno and Tex both fully understood the code. Therefore, no action will be taken," he said.

What a debt our platoon owed Tex. It was so interesting to observe the change that was taking place in the Squealer. He was so seldom seen at the mess hall, we were beginning to wonder if he was back on the c-ration diet. And, it was obvious that he didn't want to be near Tex. The only time he came around our platoon was strictly in the line of business.

I guess the adage "the bigger they are, the harder they fall" applied in this situation. Peter Sanreno reminded me of a little puppy dog whenever it gets scared and wets on the floor.

When Dago had pulled the jumper up between his knees,
little did he know that this would save his life.

This and That

Japanese soldiers were spotted inside a house way out in the boondocks in a range of mountains a reconnaissance plane pilot reported. About a dozen of us were sent out on patrol. The only way to the house was by walking, and it would take us between two and three hours to get there as we *teeter-tottered* all over the mountains.

We were not able to march at the usual pace of three miles per hour, because climbing the mountains slowed our progress. To make it even more challenging, some of us, including myself, were battling severe dysentery. We also had to be cautious to avoid walking into an ambush.

As we reached the top of still another mountain and gazed down the other side, we finally located the house. It was down in the valley and was surrounded by mountains on three sides. In fact, the mountain was shaped like a horseshoe.

We came in on the frontside which left the backside open for an easy escape. A couple of dogs that were tied to a tree began to bark. While the officer in charge decided what to do next, we rested for a moment. He did not ask for our advice, but we were facing quite a dilemma.

First of all, we did not know if Japanese soldiers were in the house or not, and if they were, we did not know how many. Second, without knowing what we would encounter and without backup troops available, would it be wise to try and circle the house with such a small force?

If we decided to circle, we would be too spread out. With only one radio, how would we be able to stay in contact with one another? How could we get the wounded out in case we took casualties? We were also cut off from our home base.

It was pretty well a given the dogs had announced our coming. If there were Japanese soldiers in the house, they would have plenty of time to prepare for an attack if they chose to stay and fight. However, they were the hunted, and we were the hunters.

Two of our soldiers eased down the mountain and into the valley to scout around. The dense trees and brush provided them ample cover, and the rest of us followed from a short distance. Before we could get into rifle range, three Japanese soldiers came out of the house, untied the dogs and escaped into the thicket. Ironically, the dogs did not go with the Japanese soldiers; instead they headed for our soldiers!

We watched to see how our buddies were going to handle the menacing mongrels as they growled and charged toward them baring their fangs. One came within a hundred yards of our soldiers, and the other, within fifty yards. We got our answer within a minute when both were sent on a one-way ticket to doggie heaven. *"A dog rushing at you is not as easy to hit as it looks,"* one of the soldiers told us later.

I do not know what the officer wrote on his report for that day. However, he could have easily written: three enemy soldiers ran for the hills and escaped; burned down one house; two charged head on and were killed; two sets of collars and dog tags attached as evidence.

Here we were, three hours away from camp, so we began to retrace our steps. On the last climb, I struggled to stay up and was not sure I could make it to the top. I felt weaker with each step that I took and became more and more lightheaded. At times, I thought I might pass out. I knew I had to make it back to camp, but my energy was drained.

The sun was starting to set when the platoon reached the top. There was no time to rest, but they waited for me to catch up. I crawled part of the way and finally managed to reach the top. Although my strength had escaped, I was able to stagger down the mountainside. Never have I been that tuckered-out.

The Runny Gunnies

The mop-up operation was not always a one-way street. A story I heard gives a good example of how things worked—the tale is about two guys who went up into the mountains to hunt for grizzly bears. They spent most of the day looking for bear tracks. First they looked along the riverbanks and next out in the brush. Then, they looked on the mountaintop, but never found a bear track. What a surprise when they discovered that a grizzly was tracking them! Sometimes the hunter becomes the hunted. It reminds me of what happened to Private Dago.

A short, stocky guy, Dago was a cook, but only when he had a stove and *something* to cook! Our menu consisted primarily of c-rations, so Dago was issued a rifle and became a hunter and rifleman. He was also a real live wire and quite the storyteller. His home was New Orleans, and he loved to spin tales about his experiences down on Bourbon Street. It was hard to top his Bourbon Street stories with my Tall Texas Tales. However, the time that old Dago was battling dysentery, takes the prize!

We were still hunting down the enemy when this happened, but the number of enemy soldiers was becoming few and far between. We were nearing the end of the war. Leaflets had been printed in the Japanese language and were distributed by dropping them from planes. The message to both the civilians and soldiers was "Come out of hiding, and you will be taken to military compounds and cared for."

The soldiers were instructed to leave their weapons, dress in civilian clothing and give themselves up. Surrendering for Japanese soldiers was not an easy thing to do, and the ones that did, were considered cowards. They were brainwashed to fight until death! A few chose life, but most did not. Therefore, we still had snipers with whom to contend, and we still had civilians that would not leave until they were forced.

It was easy to understand the anxiety that the civilians suffered knowing that we were going to burn down their homes and what few belongings they had. Nevertheless, soldiers had to deal with many anxieties too. One smaller anxiety we dealt with was the use of our steel helmets, not to be confused with the helmet *liner*.

The helmet was not only used for protection, but it was also used as a cooking pan, a sink in which to wash, bath and shave, and in the absence of a shovel, it was used for digging. Wearing a steel helmet could sometimes be like having the stomach flu . . . not knowing on which end to wear it!

Standard procedure on the front line was to use it as our personal toilet. It was very important to remove the liner first. Then, we would put dirt in the bottom of the helmet, do our jobs, and hurl the stuff at those nasty Japanese! It was, united we flung and always with great pleasure. Nothing, but *nothing* was wasted!

Well, Dago's bowels were really causing him some pains, and it would be an understatement to say that he needed to go in the worst way. Since it was late afternoon and the sun was still bright, he disappeared into the brush. There he found a place, leaned his rifle up against a tree and proceeded to relieve himself. Being a short guy, Dago's fatigue jumper that he wore over his pants hung too low. When he squatted, it hit the ground. He said that he had to pull the backside up on his hips and secure the front between his knees and hands.

With the sun at his back, Dago said that he noticed a shadow moving up behind him as he was taking care of his business. He could tell from the shadow that a Japanese soldier was creeping up behind him and had a rifle with a fixed bayonet pointing directly at him. It was obvious that he intended to use the bayonet, or else there would have been no reason to come so close. A shot would have alerted those of us that were nearby, and that may have been the reason he chose the bayonet. However, it was also a known fact that the Japanese preferred to use cold steel instead of bullets.

Dago was one of the very few that carried a pistol. He always had a .45-caliber Army pistol in the pocket of his fatigue jumper. I do not know how he came about having it, because pistols were not issued to riflemen. We were in a rifle company. It is possible that the cooks were issued pistols.

Dago said that he could not move until he had his pistol in his hand. With the Japanese soldier seeing his rifle leaning against a tree and believing he was unarmed, this might have been the break that Dago needed. The Japanese soldier's view was from Dago's backside, and he could not see Dago's hands.

When Dago had pulled the jumper up between his knees, little did he know that this would save his life. With the pocket and pistol in front of him, he had a chance to defend himself. Slowly, Dago pulled out the pistol. When he had it in his hands, he quickly jumped sideways! The element of surprise allowed Dago to get off the first shot, and he kept pulling the trigger until he emptied his pistol. Everything came out fine in the end, and one more Japanese soldier died for the Emperor.

Feetments

One of the other health problems was keeping our feet functional. During basic training, foot soldiers are taught the importance of caring for their feet. It was raining constantly on Okinawa, and keeping our feet dry was impossible. Wet feet caused big problems for some of us: problems like crud or jungle rot, especially between the toes. If we even got a blister on a foot during basic training, a trip to the infirmary was pretty well mandatory.

On Okinawa, this was impossible, but some kind of treatment had to be administered. The medics carried a bottle of *stuff* with them, and I am sure it was straight from *Hades*. I never figured out how the bottle kept from melting. The bottle contained a ten-percent solution of salicylic acid that we referred to as liquid fire. When applied, it was excruciating! One time, it seared my skin and stopped my toes from bleeding, at least for a while.

It took two to three people to administer the treatment: two to hold the patient down and the medic to apply that fire! The truth is, it was hard to be *macho* after a few treatments. We just wanted to skip one now and then. In a case like that, the medic would threaten to have some guys hold us down. However, I don't remember it ever happening.

Hairrors!

Keeping healthy, feeling good and keeping a positive attitude was something we all needed to do, but someone decided we needed to do something about our looks. This just dumbfounded most of us!

The closer we came to the north end of the island, the fewer men were needed. Part of us would get an opportunity to rest while the others pushed on and vice versa. At one point we were given a brand-new set of barber tools which consisted of shiny, sharp clippers and scissors plus an actual barber's comb; we were then instructed to cut each other's hair. I would estimate that ninety-five percent of us had never played barber before.

The conditions for opening shop were not that great either, because it was pouring rain. Our shelters were made by joining two ponchos together, which allowed just enough head room for us to sit up. My barber partner, Slim, wanted to clip my hair first, and I was pleased with his request. I was thinking that after I cut his hair, he might want to shoot me; if he does, then I will at least die with a fresh haircut.

Slim was about the tallest soldier in our company. His hair reminded me of an angora goat: baby fine hair with small ringlets, especially when it was wet. A couple of other guys were present watching and waiting for the tools. When it was my turn, I started right off with the clippers. Slim let me know immediately that he did not want his head clipped, so I changed to the scissors.

I did not have the slightest idea of how to cut hair and his wet hair curls only complicated the matter. I combed and snipped, until he had about one half inch of hair left. The next thing I did was clip around his neck and around his ears. With his hair still drenched and slicked down, he looked great. Even the two guys watching wanted me to do their hair.

When the rain stopped and his hair dried, Slim was one funny-looking soldier. I must have cut right in the middle of every ringlet, because his hair was too short to curl, and it just stood out in every direction. He actually reminded me of a six-foot-six-inch porcupine.

However, there was one happy ending. We did not have a mirror and my buddy never did get to see what a mess I had made. As a matter of fact, I never did know what kind of a haircut he gave me either.

Cleaning-up

Before the end of the war on Okinawa, dual runways were constructed for the new long-range heavy bomber, the Boeing B-29 Superfortress. The bomber had an advanced radar system and could travel over 5800 miles without refueling. Security had to be set up around the airfield before the Army Air Corps would land the B-29s.

Previously, the Japanese had slipped inside the airfield on another island. During the skirmish, the airmen actually caused more damage to the planes than the Japanese had. An infantry outfit now surrounded the airfield with troops to stop any attempt to sabotage the planes. Serving on guard duty was a real break for me.

The runways were side-by-side with a separation of approximately fifty yards in-between. Hundreds of B-29s flew to Japan on the bombing raids. In the morning, the roar of the engines would start and soon the pilots would begin to taxi the planes out onto the runways. Two planes, one on each runway, would simultaneously take off and as soon as they cleared the runway, two more would follow.

It was interesting to watch the planes after they became airborne. The lead planes would get into a holding pattern, while waiting for all the planes in their group to become airborne. After they were in formation, the P-51D Mustang, the best fighter in the world, would escort them all the way to and from their mission. I do believe that this was the first time during the war that land-based fighters had enough range to fly to Tokyo and back without refueling.

As that group took off, another one would already be forming and this pattern would continue. Hearing those engines roar, smelling that burning oil, and watching those B-29s lift off the runway and knowing they were devastating Japan with incendiary bombs was something to behold! The seventy-pound canisters that were usually dropped were capable of exploding one hundred feet above the ground and scattering dozens of cylinders of napalm, a jellied gas. They could destroy up to sixteen acres at a time.

When the last planes were out of sight, we would have peace and quiet for a few hours. It would be about mid-afternoon, when the planes would return and began to circle the field again. The landings were even more exciting than watching the take-offs!

Excluding the shot-up or damaged planes, this was the landing procedure; two planes would drop down side-by-side and one would land on runway number one while the other would land on runway number two. About the time the first planes reached the far end of the runways, two more planes would touch down. This pattern continued until all the planes were on the ground.

It was just amazing how so many planes could become airborne or land in such a short amount of time. Our outfit did not receive any information on how many planes were lost each day, but we did not lose many. Later, I did get to see the devastation of the bombings.

During this time frame, Iwo Jima had been taken, and American fighter planes were based there—some were based on Okinawa. I remember P-38s zipping around. They looked so neat compared to the B-29s. However, the Army's P-51 and the Navy's Corsair were our two best fighter planes.

One of the reasons the Japanese defended Okinawa (approximately 340 miles away) with such great force and to the last man, was because the loss of Okinawa would have given the United States complete superiority in the air and on the sea. Another reason for their last ditch stand, was their belief that if they could inflict enough casualties on our military personnel, a *negotiated* settlement might be possible. This, of course, would save the mainland from being occupied by a foreign country.

Now guarding the airfield had some benefits that we had not had for a while—one was safety. If the Japanese were going to try to infiltrate our positions, it would be during the night. Therefore, daytime was pretty much free time for us.

We even had tents and cots. There was an outdoor amphitheater nearby, and about half of us could go to the movie every other night. A well had been drilled which provided fresh water. We found a barrel and punched a few holes in the bottom. Then, we built a platform to elevate the barrel and cut a hole in the bottom of the platform to accommodate the showerhead, which were actually nail holes in bottom of a barrel. What a fantastic shower we had! The Army Air Corps was very appreciative for our services, so they furnished the water tank truck, pump, soap, the tents, cots and a few other things. The one thing they would not do for us was dig our foxholes.

During our free time, some of us would go to the beach and skinny-dip during the day. I loved swimming in the salt water. Sometimes we would comb the beach for shells, although there was no way to keep them. For a country boy raised up in Central Texas, it was something interesting to do. One beautiful day, some of us were taking it easy on the beach when a group of soldiers came walking by.

One of the guys looked very familiar. What a shock! It was none other than Ed Maurice Whittington from Coleman, Texas! I had no idea that he was even on the island, let alone in the 27th Infantry Division. But, there he was . . . in the flesh. And, here we were, standing face-to-face . . . naked as jaybirds halfway around the world.

The fig leaf shops had just closed for the day. So, we quickly plopped down in our makeshift sand suits and chewed the fat for a while. Our visit was brief, but what a morale boost. It was so nice to see and visit with someone from home and my spirits soared.

Before Maurice had shipped overseas, he married one of my best friends, Ruth, a dark-haired beauty with a feisty personality. She lived on the next farm just down the hill where our properties joined. We had started to school together, and we were like family. After retirement, they moved back home and lived ten miles from Coleman, Texas. We continued to stay in touch over the years and continued to laugh about that day. So, Dago was not the only one who got caught with his pants down!

There was another time I was at the beach that I had another surprise encounter. I loved to swim way out into the ocean and float back to the beach. My buddies did not like getting so far away from the shoreline, and most of the time, I would be out by myself—living on the edge. Like so many lessons, some of us have to learn them the hard way.

Everything was going great . . . until I met a *Portuguese-woman-of-war.* These babies are bad news—one of the worst when it comes to jellyfish. She was one of those clinging types and her body just kind of stuck on my arm and her tentacles covered my upper torso. Talk about being set on fire! I am firmly convinced that my body was so hot, that the water in the ocean actually began to boil.

I managed to break away, but she reminded me of an octopus in love. She seemed to delight in embracing me with all her appendages and was not about to let me escape so easily . . . at least, not until she thoroughly branded me. Each time I managed to get away, the waves washed her back over me for one more hug. Huge red whelps begin to pop-up on me every place she grasped. When I finally managed to escape, I was still a long way from the beach.

And, here we were, standing face-to-face . . .
naked as jaybirds halfway around the world.

I knew I had to keep my cool in order to keep from drowning. The first thing I had to do was conserve my energy. After breaking away from that stinging creature, I relaxed for a moment—long enough to get rid of the negative thoughts swirling in my mind.

I had managed to escape injury in the war up to this point, but now I was hurting so badly that I found myself thinking, "What if I can't make it back to the beach? Have I really traveled halfway around the world and survived a war only to lose my life to a jealous, red hot, she-devil of the deep?"

It was only when the tide was coming in that I ventured out into the ocean, and I knew my only option was letting the waves carry me back to the beach. I was worried that I might pass out. It seemed like forever before my feet touched the sand. When I finally floated to the beach, I collapsed. One of the medics who was with us said, *"I really don't know what to do."* He rubbed a bunch of junk on me and told me to rest for a while.

When I stumbled back to the tent, no cot ever looked better. I flopped down and had a little talk with myself about the stupid thing that I had done. For the next few days, I wore those red whelps like a uniform. There was a large blue spot on my arm that stuck around a couple of weeks, where the jellyfish had taken up residence. I don't know whether or not the junk helped, but it was not long until I begin to feel better. I continued to swim as long as I was overseas, but I never ventured out so far again.

Shortly after that incident when I was off duty, some of my buddies and I were hanging around and waiting for it to get dark enough for the show, *Diamond Horseshoe* starring Betty Grable. The outdoor theater was jam-packed, and getting a good seat was always a problem when *Grable* headlined. No one was going to miss seeing the glamorous blonde swimsuit poster girl with the famous gams!

How peaceful it was to sit out under the starlit night, and to smell and feel the seabreeze blow gently across my face. I do not know about the other soldiers who were there, but it was a perfect night to just relax and enjoy a lighthearted comedy.

For a moment in time I felt, "There is nothin' to worry about and everything is gonna work out. I'll soon be home with my family and friends." I told myself, "Hang on! Things are gonna be just like they were, and the war will be over soon."

Well, the Grable show was going great. We were waiting to see if she would choose the mink coat or the guy. The projectionist was doing a swell job, without the usual starting and stopping or breaking the film, and everything was running smooth. Then, it happened.

The screen went black. The booing began. Nothing happened for four or five minutes. Then, the angry outbursts and yelling crescendoed. Suddenly, a very excited voice announced over the speaker system, "**OKINAWA HAS BEEN TAKEN!**"

Within seconds, tracer bullets lit-up the sky and anti-aircraft guns teamed-up and made inverted V's all over the island! Navy ships were doing the same. Of course, we all had our rifles with us, but we didn't have tracer ammunition. However, we managed to make plenty of noise without any help.

Celebrating was the order of the night! This was no movie. This was no fantasy. This was the real McCoy—a reality with which we had no problem.

But the truth is, Ronold, your age group never really got to be normal teenagers.

Surprise Visit

The Japanese military surrendered the island of Okinawa to the American forces on June 22, and organized resistance ceased. My division was moved to permanent quarters where we had the luxury of sleeping six to a tent. For sure, the cots were much better than what we had been sleeping on—the ground. In addition, our rations were better, and we were able to receive five-hour daytime passes.

In some cases, three-day passes were granted, and we were allowed to leave the island. However, they were rarely given. In order to get a three-day pass, Captain Richard Henry would have to get permission from the battalion commander before he could grant it. I requested a pass to Ie Shima to go visit Lester. The invasion of Japan was imminent and word was out—there would be no more three-day passes. I gave up on the idea of getting to leave the island.

One Sunday morning while I was standing in the chow line waiting for my powdered eggs, the company runner, Don came to tell me that Henry wanted to see me. This time I didn't question him. Instead, without hesitation, I went to the Command Post and reported to him.

When I arrived, Henry announced, "Pvt. Ray, I have some good news. I have passes for you and Lt. Austin Casey to go over to Ie Shima. You'll need to pack immediately. Stick close to Casey. He'll know how to get you a ride."

Casey was the favorite lieutenant of our company. During one of the skirmishes, a grenade had been thrown into a foxhole with him and a wounded soldier. The wounded soldier rolled over on top of the grenade and saved Casey's life while sacrificing his own.

When we arrived at the base, one that we had guarded previously, a C-47 was warming-up on the runway. Casey asked the Air Force officer on duty, "Is that plane headed to Ie Shima?"

"Yes, it is."

"We want to hook a ride then."

"Let me see your orders."

"We don't have any."

"Then, you cannot board," the officer firmly stated.

My hopes of boarding vanished, but Casey remained confident. "Don't worry. We'll get on that plane. Just be ready," he assured me. About that time, three Air

Force officers walked in and asked if the plane was going to Ie Shima. The officer on duty said, "Yes, but you must have orders."

One of the three officers snorted, "You have got to be kidding!" Then, they walked out and boarded the plane.

That is when Casey went into action! A big, rough and tough guy, Casey was ready to yank the Air Force officer out from behind the desk and tear him a new one. He roared, "We are going to board *that* plane, and I don't want to hear anymore comments!"

"Well, if the plane goes down, there won't be any record of what happened to you, and when you fail to report back for duty, the Army will list you as a deserter," replied the officer. We could have cared less!

Soon, we landed on Ie Shima. After our arrival, Casey called his girlfriend, who was a nurse there and whom he had come to visit, so we could set a time to meet back at the base for our return flight to Okinawa. Ironically, she had just left Ie Shima for Okinawa to see him. This looked like it might be a problem for me, but Casey reassured me that getting back to Okinawa would not be difficult. After he explained to me what I would need to do, he hooked the next plane back.

The next thing I needed to know was where to find Lester. An airman sitting behind the desk had been observing me, so I asked him, "Do you happen to know Lester Ray?"

"Sure! I know Lester!" he replied with enthusiasm. He told me exactly how and where to find him, which was about a mile and a half down the road.

I got my gear together and started heading toward the door. The airman shook his head, "Where're you going?"

"Well . . . to see my brother."

"Hang on. I'll get someone to drive you," he chuckled. After he made a phone call, a jeep pulled up almost immediately, and I was on my way.

The driver insisted on delivering me in person to Lester instead of dropping me off at company headquarters. "Oh, I don't want to miss this. I have to see the look on Lester's face when you just walk in," he said.

Just as I couldn't believe I had gotten a phone call a couple of months earlier, Lester had a real surprise when I showed up without warning. He was sprawled out on a cot dressed in his government-issued olive drab drawers. He stood up and spoke slowly in his typical deadpan mannerism, "Well, ya could've told me ya was acomin'. I would've dressed-up."

"Hey, why're you bein' so formal?" I exclaimed, "Surely, you haven't forgotten all the times we skinny-dipped in all those creeks in Coleman County!"

His buddies just *hee-hawed* and I was off to a good start with them. I even met the soldier that owned the fancy, pearl-handled, .45 caliber pistol that Lester had been wearing when he came to visit me. He was from a wealthy ranching family near Wimberley, Texas.

"Ronold, tell us some tales about Lester. We want to hear about his fancy four-cylinder hotrod," one of the guys piped-up.

"Oh yeah!" I laughed. "Every guy needs a 1928 Model A Ford! That was Lester's dream car. Yep! He sure was the envy of everyone in town!"

The guys howled! Lester shook his head.

"Well, you see. . . Lester didn't have any money to buy a car. Heck, he didn't have enough money to buy a second-hand three-cent postage stamp! But, he *sure* wanted a car. He heard our neighbor, Mr. England was gettin' rid of his old Model A, because he blew the engine and was sellin' it for salvage. So, Lester made a beeline thru the pasture to his house."

*"*What's on your mind, son?" Mr. England asked as he opened the screen door to invite Lester inside. Lester was so excited and out of breath that he could hardly talk. Huffin' and puffin', he managed to gasp, "I . . . wanna . . . buy . . . your . . . Ford!"

"Son, I've known you all your life and sellin' you a pig-in-a-poke is somethin' I could never do; that engine's no good. And, what about your Dad? Why I've known Isaac for years, and I'd never do anything to jeopardize our friendship," Mr. England said as he spat tobacco juice on a black beetle that was crawling up the porch steps.

Mr. England of average height, with a stocky build and a ruddy complexion, peered over his wire-rimmed glasses. "Got 'em!" He smiled as if he were proud of hitting his target. Then, he shook his head, "No, Lester. I'm sorry. I can't do it. This would be a bad deal for you. I can't take advantage of good friends like y'all."

"But, Mr. England . . . I've *already* talked to Dad, and he said it was okay with him! Besides, I know ya need help on the farm," Lester persisted. "I was hopin' ya would let me work to pay for the car. I can pull that engine apart and fix all the problems. I just know I can make it run again!"

"Hmm," Mr. England pondered a moment as he rubbed his chin.

"Aw, come on, Mr. England. I can make her good as new!" Lester tried to persuade him.

"Well, okay, Lester. You certainly seem convinced that you can recondition the engine, and I know that it can be repaired. Let me saddle my horse. You can jump on behind me, and we'll go talk to your Dad. If he's agreeable, we'll settle on how many days you'll work for me, and you'll be the proud owner of your first car."

I continued the story with the guys, "So, early the next morning, Lester harnessed a team of horses, hooked them to a wagon and was on his way to claim his prize. He had plenty of volunteers to help guide the car as it was being pulled. Lester was on top of the world! He was going to be flyin' high in his 1928 Model A hotrod.

"Since Dad had a blacksmith shop on the farm, Lester had all the necessary tools available to overhaul the Ford's engine. And, let me tell you a little secret. Lester could take a pair of pliers, some bailin' wire and make *anything* run. I don't care if it had four wheels or four legs!"

The guys chuckled as if they *knew* Lester was capable of doing all sorts of things. Lester was enjoying every minute as he ate up the details. With an amused look and a little smirk, he rolled his eyes, "Well . . . what'd ya expect?"

"By the end of the week, that old Ford was purrin' like a kitten. The body was in good shape, so Lester came out with a pretty dependable car . . . well . . . uh . . . except for the brakes,"   I added. The guys broke up and one snorted loudly, "Yeah, I can just see ol' Lester in that car thinkin' he was *really* somethin' . . . struttin' around like a big ol' Thanksgiving Turkey!"

Things were quite different in the early 1940's from the present age. One thing for sure, people took good care of the things they possessed and being wasteful was frowned upon. The Model A hotrods were not gauged on how fast they would run. Instead, they were actually judged on how slow they could run in third gear/high gear while still running smoothly.

The ones that were tuned-up the best would *cadillac* along slowly and smoothly on a little uphill grade. We could almost count the strokes of the four pistons as they pumped up and down. Lester was a gifted mechanic and his hot rod always won for precision.

Now speed was another matter. Whenever someone got their first set of wheels, it was natural to want to show it off and haul around their friends. With so many private parties going on out in the country, there were plenty of opportunities, and Lester was no different. We got invited to most parties, since musicians usually had a special invitation.

One Saturday night, my brothers Lester and Lowell, and I were down in the Glen Cove area entertaining at a party. Lester played the mandolin, Lowell was on guitar, and I was playing the tenor banjo. Lester and Lowell did the singing. We always played "Home Sweet Home" at midnight to end the evening. Getting your date home soon after was a *must* for most if they wanted to live long enough to see daylight.

We spent the night with the Gotcher family, which was not unusual. It didn't matter if we crammed three to a bed or slept on a pallet. Pitching a blanket on the floor was more than adequate for us. However, sleeping outdoors on a cot with a summertime breeze to blow away the mosquitoes was especially nice.

The Gotchers had recently moved from Midway, which is located in the northwestern part of the county where we lived, and where they had lived for years before moving to the Glen Cove area. After sleeping-in late, we dressed and soon after Sunday dinner, we started jammin'.

People began arriving to play Forty-two and soon the walls of the house were bulging at the seams with singers, players and partygoers. The young folks were congregated in the living room and on the front porch, while the

Forty-two players were hanging out in the kitchen near the coffee pot. Time flew! Unnoticed by most of us, the sun was starting to set. However, some party pooper blurted out from the kitchen, "It's getting late. Time to get home and do the chores." Several let out a groan, and the party ended.

Lester's best friend, Eddy Gotcher said, "Hey, I know! Let's go over to the Howell Theater in Coleman and catch that new show, *Western Union* with Randolph Scott." Going to the picture show on Sunday was not popular with parents, but sometimes we went anyway. Eddy, his younger brother Lavan, and we three Ray's piled into Lester's limo and headed off to Coleman. There was one minor flaw in Lester's car—the ability to stop fast.

The brakes on most cars were mechanical, and mechanical brakes were for the birds. Those kinds of brakes could not be trusted; one minute they worked and the next minute they were gone. Even at their best, they were difficult to push down and slow to stop. It was sometimes necessary to use the gears to help stop the car. For instance, dropping down to the lowest gear would help slow the car.

Eddy and Lavan lived only eighteen-miles from Coleman. We flew down the ol' cow trail and were soon inside the city limits. Shortly, we approached a steep hill right before hitting downtown. As we started descending, the fun began.

Lester stomped on the brakes to slow down and to comply with the speed limit. However, the trusty Model A seemed to have a mind of its own and decided to give us a joy ride instead with no sign of slowing down. The harder Lester pushed on the brakes, the faster we flew! He tried to gear down with hopes of the clutch remaining intact. Everything held in second gear, but we were still going way too fast!

Lester double-clutched and dropped to the lowest gear. Man, alive! Eddy, who was sitting in the front seat, was doing his best to help slow us down by bracing his hands on the dashboard. I nervously looked over the front seat at Lester. I could tell from that familiar profile that he was grinnin' like there was nothin' to sweat. In fact, he actually seemed to be enjoying himself!

However, when he let out on the clutch, the engine revved-up. It was so loud, we sounded like a B-29 blasting off! Lavan looked as scared as rat caught in a trap, and Lowell looked like he might hurl a fur ball. People came storming out of their houses to see what all the commotion was.

We learned how quickly exhilaration can turn into despair as we saw the red traffic light speeding right toward us. But, ol' Lester went charging right thru the intersection at forty-five miles an hour and continued to pick-up speed. We were petrified. Were we going to crash? How many cars or people were we going to hit before it was over? What if we kept going until the car ran out of gas?

We barreled thru a couple of other lights. Luckily, one was green! By the time we reached the next light, the Model A had slowed to a safer speed. Then,

Lester took us careening on two wheels around the corner onto a bumpy dirt road. Several blocks later, the hotrod coasted until it jerked us forward a few yards, took a final lunge, and shimmied until it conked-out.

For a moment everyone was quiet as if to catch his breath. The dogs were barking and singing *howllelujah* throughout the neighborhood. Clearly shaken, we slowly looked around at each other thru our spiraling eyeballs without uttering a sound. Then, all of the sudden, we burst-out laughing! *What* picture show? Heck, we were ready to go again!

Choking and coughing with laughter, I picked myself up off Lavan as he groaned. We both had taken a dive to the floorboard about the same time and collided to save ourselves from the unknown. I yelled, "Dang, Lester! You must have been floorin' it with that size twelve of yours! How fast were you doin'?"

Chuckling under his breath, cool and collected Lester dryly said, "Yeah. Well, apparently not fast enough. This doesn't cut it. We need to find us some bigger hills. Let's go over to Santa Anna next time and check out those mountains for some real excitement."

On the next steep hill, Lester tried a new approach. He decided it might be better to start downward in *low* gear from now on. Lester's buddies were amused, but not surprised. After all, they had gotten to know Lester pretty well over the past years.

Pop, the senior sergeant in Lester's company spoke up, "Ronold, seeing you over here visiting with Lester reminds me of my youngest brother, Charles. He's in the infantry serving in the Philippines. I sure miss him. I pray he's okay."

I nodded.

"We were born into a military family, and I must admit, we're certainly proud of our heritage. Like you, Charles was only sixteen when the Japanese made their sneak attack on Pearl Harbor. After he finished high school, he went into the Army when he was eighteen. Lester has told us stories about all those parties."

"Yeah . . . some would scorch your whiskers," I interjected.

"But the truth is, Ronold, your age group never really got to be normal teenagers. Even in your senior year of high school, your thoughts and actions were tempered by the war. You were ushered into manhood at a very early age."

"True," I agreed.

Pop continued, "I've had a hand in training most of the young men in this guard squadron. Unlike you and Charles, we've all been together from early in the war. We laugh together, cry together and when one hurts, we all hurt. I was just wondering, how do you cope with being overseas and going into battle so soon? Have you been able to establish such a relationship in the short time you've been in your division?"

"Well, although I've only been in the Army for less than a year, the trainin' and the process of gettin' to Okinawa took about eight months. I've been in Okinawa for about three months, and when I joined Company K on the front line, I didn't know a soul. Then, I joined Company B after a couple of months. Didn't know anyone there either. But, havin' to move around so much tends to make us bond faster. We don't really get the chance to learn much about each other though. Of course, many have sacrificed their lives," I responded.

Pop shook his head and sadness filled the tent. No one spoke for a couple of moments. Each one of us were remembering our friends whom we had lost to the war and wishing it was over. Lester's friends had many questions and concerns about the war and wanted to know more about Okinawa.

Riding with Lester in that out-of-control car thru the mountains sounded pretty good to me right now. One thing I had to rub in to Lester before leaving was the huge box of Mother's delicious homemade sugar cookies/teacakes that I had received by mistake. The box had been double-wrapped and on the inside wrapping was *Lester's* name. This was such a surprise; I was not sure what to do. It was so rare to receive goodies from home and when someone did, they were shared with friends. My friends just happened to be standing there when I opened the package.

Lester asked me, "Well, what'd ya do?"

"Didn't take long to finish those cookies!" I boasted. "*M'm . . . m'm*! They *sure* were good! Yep! My buddies sure appreciated your generous contribution, Lester. They went down faster than a hog can slurp its slop!"

This time Lester smirked. The guys chuckled as if they knew *something* I didn't know.

"Well," Lester said, "Do y'all have anything to say to Ronold before he leaves?"

"Thanks, Ronold!" they chimed-in and quickly glanced around at each other. Pop said, "They *sure* were good."

Lester said, "Yep! But, I reckon the ones we got were bigger and better." Apparently, our boxes had gotten mixed-up.

We enjoyed a couple of days and nights of visiting. Lester's buddies were friendly, interesting and full of stories among *other* things. Time passed too quickly, and I had to get back to Okinawa. Lester made sure that I was given a ride back to the landing strip. Once again, I was thankful for this unusual, yet very special gift of time that I was able to spend with my brother. I was now on my own with no orders to board a plane, but I did have Casey's instructions.

Standing tall with confidence, I walked right up to the information desk and told the corporal that I needed to board the next plane to Okinawa.

"You got orders to board?" He asked.

"No, but here's my pass." I replied.

"Too bad. I can't let you board a plane without orders," he added.

I then walked over to where some other guys were sitting and joined them. They all wanted a ride to Okinawa. Pretty soon a plane pulled up, and the corporal came over and pointed, "You . . . you . . . you and you can board." When the next plane arrived, I was soon on my way back to Okinawa. I don't know why waiting for the second plane was important, but it worked out just as Casey had said.

Things were really popping when I got back to Okinawa. Our division was getting ready for the *big one*. The invasion of Japan was just around the corner. We did not know when, but for sure, it would come within the next few weeks. The rumor was—we would be making a beachhead landing over the flat terrain, covered only with rice paddies and not many places to hide. We were getting new shoes, fatigues, and the things foot soldiers needed to fight another battle. I can tell you that in our minds, we were planning to sink Japan to the bottom of the deep blue sea!

However, at the same time, we knew it would be one heck of a battle! Okinawa would seem like a cakewalk compared to what we would be facing in Japan. The U.S. military had lost approximately thirteen thousand troops in the Battle of Okinawa. The Japanese lost ten of their military people for every one of ours; and thirty thousand to one-hundred thousand civilians were killed on Okinawa.

Our military strategists projected the loss of lives for the United States at one-half to one million if we took Japan by conventional means. Using the ratio of one-to-ten, based on Okinawa's figure, the loss to the Japanese military could be as high as five to ten million, not to mention the civilian population which would be *astronomical*.

The Japanese civilian population would now be fighting beside the Japanese armies, and we would now be forced to kill women, children and elderly men—the same as we would the soldiers. Just as in Okinawa, the dazzling white beaches and emerald-green seas would soon be transformed into red from the blood that would be sacrificed. We certainly did not look forward to it, but it had to be done. There was no stopping us now.

War is hell and contrary to what some people might think, there is no nice way to fight a war.

Out on the Town

War is hell and contrary to what some people might think, there is no nice way to fight a war. The American flag was raised, signifying that Okinawa was now under the control of the United States of America. Our military strategists were in the process of planning the invasion of Japan and millions of lives would be lost.

President Truman would not accept anything less than *total and unconditional surrender* from Japan. The fierce fighting and loss of life on Okinawa and Iwo Jima must have been a deciding factor on his decision to drop the atomic bomb. On August 6, 1945, the first bomb was dropped on Hiroshima, Japan. The expected result was unconditional surrender. The Japanese military was not ready to admit defeat.

On August 9, the second bomb was dropped on Nagasaki, Japan. On August 15, Emperor Hirohito announced via radio that Japan was surrendering to the United States and was accepting and submitting to the terms as laid down by President Truman.

The formal surrender of Japan, which lasted only thirty minutes, was executed on September 2 in Tokyo Bay, aboard Commander in Chief of the U. S. Pacific Fleet, Admiral Chester Nimitz's flagship, the USS *Missouri*. Japanese Foreign Minster Mamoru Shigemitsu led the Japanese delegation and signed the Instruments of Surrender on behalf of the Japanese government and General Yoshijiro Umezu signed on behalf of the Japanese Imperial General Headquarters.

General Douglas MacArthur accepted the formal surrender on behalf of the allies: China, the United Kingdom, the Soviet Union, Australia, Canada, France, the Netherlands and New Zealand. Admiral Nimitz signed for the United States. There has been much criticism about dropping the atomic bombs on Nagasaki and Hiroshima, Japan. However, more lives were lost by conventional means in the War of Okinawa, than the lives that were lost in the dropping of both atomic bombs.

Is it easier and any more humane to be killed by a rifle shot, a grenade, a mortar shell, artillery or any other means, than it is to be killed by an atomic bomb? In the real world, it is understood that dropping the atomic bombs saved many lives. I for one believe it saved mine.

The surrender set the stage for my departure from Okinawa, and the rush was on to occupy Japan. The quicker we could get boots on the ground in Japan, the better! To the best of my knowledge, the 27th was the only infantry division flown into Japan. We first assembled at one of the landing strips to do some dry runs on exiting the plane without puncturing holes in the roof with our bayonets.

The 11th Airborne Division flew in first. As the planes flew around the clock, we stood by ready to board. Then, we were flown in a C-54 and landed in Japan the night of September 7. I felt uneasy; why were we ordered to fix our bayonets just before landing? And, if we were to encounter enemy fire, how were we supposed to dig a foxhole on a runway?

However, things went off without a hitch. A guide met us and escorted us to an open field just off the runway to spend the remainder of the night. The next morning, Japanese flatbed trucks arrived and transported our company to a small town, Odawara. We stayed there a few days while arrangements were being worked out for one battalion of the 27th to take over a naval aviation and machine base at Koriyama.

Charcoal burners were used for transportation, and I have no idea how they made the engine run. Each vehicle had a charcoal burning stove on the bed of the truck and somehow this was their gasoline. (I am not making this up!) I suppose the fire put off gas fumes or something like that. The trucks would not run very fast, but it sure beat walking. I think the vehicle had to be started on gasoline, so after a day or two we just used gasoline.

The first morning after we arrived in Odawara, we were ordered to get our *suntans* out of our bags and to make them look as presentable as we possibly could, get dressed, fix our bayonets and to be ready to fall out for a parade. Then, we marched about a half-mile into town. We were instructed not to talk or even look around and to look the sharpest we could under the circumstances.

As we marched into town, I was in the fourth platoon near the back and a first lieutenant was bringing up the rear. An infantry platoon usually consisted of about thirty-six to fifty soldiers, but we were way understrength at this time. There was not a single Japanese in sight. But, when I glanced around, I saw people starting to pour into the street.

The town was laid out pretty much like our small towns back in the United States with a central building similar to our courthouses on the squares. I thought we would march around the block, but when we got to the end of the block, the captain yelled out, "Halt! About face! March!" Now, the lieutenant was leading the company, and I was near the front. Then an amazing thing happened when we turned around.

The Japanese people began running and scrambling! They were literally falling and crawling all over each other trying to avoid being seen. Within a few seconds, we could not see a single soul anywhere. The town appeared deserted, and our goal was accomplished.

All at once, we realized the fear in which the Japanese civilians were feeling. And, to tell you the truth, we *liked* it. Why shouldn't we? After all, we were the conquerors! We still did not know how they would react to just a couple of soldiers walking around town, but we did want to explore their little town.

Sometimes you think you know someone fairly well; however, under different circumstances, things can sure change. My friend Red, who was from Georgia, was like that. After a short time at Odawara, we were allowed a five-hour daylight pass into town.

Nonetheless, there were stipulations. We could not go alone and were required to carry a weapon. Well, Red and I got our passes and took our M-1 rifles with us. As soon as we got to town, my friend found a place where he could get some spirits. Since we could not communicate in Japanese, and at this point in time, the Japanese were more afraid of us than we were of them, things were more or less, *free*.

I don't know what my friend was drinking, but he was getting red-eyed and rubbery-legged fast! "Let's head back to camp. I think you've had enough," I said.

Red didn't seem to hear me and was lost in his own little world. He continued to weave down the sidewalk. Then, he spotted a barbershop and swayed in front of the window for a minute. As he ran his hand thru his thick, red curly hair, he lost his balance and stumbled.

"Boyz. I haznutz haz . . . (hic) . . . noz hairz cutz and . . . . shavez . . . shavez...inza barberz shopza inza . . . aaaa...gez," Red slurred. "Letz getz ourz selvez spruzed upz. Wez. . . mightz...seez somez... (hic)... gri. . .grilz."

There was no way to talk to this guy! "Come on, Red. Let's get back." I insisted. "It's time to go."

However, he was in a stage where everything was funny. Red staggered into the barbershop, and fell into the wall as he leaned his rifle in the corner. While trying to keep his balance, he crawled up in the middle barber's chair. Then, he rolled his eyes around, belched loudly and looked at one of the barbers as his head wobbled. Red wiggled his fingers to imitate scissors. He then used his index finger to make a scraping motion on his face to indicate that he wanted a shave.

I was more than pissed! "Get outta that chair! We need to get back to camp now!" I barked. "That barber might let that razor slip and slice your dang throat!"

Red slurred, "Raaayz... Raaayz. Juz holdz yourz riflez on himz. If hez cuz my throatz. . Awwww. . . juz shooz himz." Then, he howled like a maniac as he slapped his knee and missed. It was amazing that he didn't tumble out of the chair and fall flat on his face.

We had been fighting a war just a few days before, and this was our first contact with the Japanese civilians. My mind-set was, "We don't know how these people will react to us. Stay alert. Stay cool and keep our powder dry. They aren't our friends, and we're way outnumbered."

I certainly did not like the way Red was acting, and I did not see anything amusing about it at the time. As it turned out, one of the barbers gave him a shave and a nice haircut. And, the only payment that he wanted was for us to leave immediately!

Shortly after we left the barbershop and started walking back to camp, we heard someone behind us yelling and dragging *something* over the boardwalk. By this time, I was nervous as a cat in a room full of rocking chairs. I turned around ready to defend myself if necessary. What I saw blew my mind!

The barber was trying to catch up with us, and was pulling Red's rifle by the sling which made a *bumpity-bumping* sound over that boardwalk. The barber was desperately trying to get rid of my buddy's rifle. He was probably worried that another GI would come along and see him with one of our rifles, and that would not be good for him.

Our walk back to camp was beautiful along the ocean, yet uneventful compared to what had happened earlier. I do not recall ever seeing Red's clear blue eyes again. From that day forward, his eyes were usually patriotic—red, white and blue. I will never forget that day—my first day out on the town in Japan.

Being in a new environment came with some new rules. One rule was not to eat any Japanese food, but I did pick up a couple of onions while we were in town. What could be wrong with an onion? We had been living on bland old c-rations for so long, an onion would certainly spice-up things!

The following morning, we marched down to the beach to do calisthenics. Off to the left of the road were a few acres of cultivated land. Being an old farm boy, I was surprised to see such pretty vegetables growing so near the ocean. The land could not have been more than a few feet above sea level.

Out in the field, I noticed two black cows hooked up to a cart. The cart was loaded with two barrels. Three or four people were using long-handled dippers to scoop *something* out of the barrels. I mean these handles were six or seven feet long. And, the people were pouring the stuff all over the plants. I just figured the plants were thirsty and were being watered.

Later, we were marching into a gentle seabreeze, and all at once, I got a whiff of *something*. I knew it was bad, but at the moment I could not tell what it was. Getting a little closer to the workers, the stench was horrendous. We began to yell out, "What's that odor!" It was so bad that even the buzzards needed gas masks.

One of the soldiers shouted, "See those two black cows hooked to the wagon? That's what you call a *honey wagon*." Someone hollered back, "Don't smell like honey to me!"

Well, the two barrels were loaded with human waste. Much of Japan did not have a sewer system. Instead of a sewer system, they had a honey wagon service. The honey wagons would service the homes, and my guess is that the waste was sold to farmers for fertilizer. They were double-dipping. The honey wagon people had to keep emptying the barrels by selling it to farmers for fertilizer. Therefore, they actually got paid twice for the same job.

That morning, the light bulb flashed on in my head! Now, I fully understood why we were told not to eat any of the Japanese food. Boy was I glad that I had never gotten around to eating my onions.

I was awakened that night to a noise that sounded like baseballs hitting the ground. The next morning, there were onions all over the street. I did not try to identify mine, but they had plenty of company. I was wondering how my buddies, who had eaten their onions the night before, were feeling. However, we never discussed it; some might have considered it very distasteful.

HEADQUARTERS FIRST BATTALION
105TH INFANTRY
APO # 27

22 October 1945

MEMORANDUM:

SURRENDER OF KORIYAMA NAVAL AIR BASE

1. On 26 September, while this battalion was still at Odawara, the commanding Officer of Japanese forces at the Koriyama Naval Air base surrendered that installation to Major ROBERT H McKAY, Commanding Officer of this battalion. The ceremony took place in a conference room in the building now housing the battalion command post. Captain CURJIKO NAKANO, Imperial Japanese Navy, with staff, took his place along one side of the long conference table, while Major McKAY and the officers of the battalion advance party were on the other.

2. After signing the surrender document, Captain NAKANO spoke as follows:

We lost and by command ceased fighting. Here we meet each other

The Japanese spirt of war is characterized by the samuria, therefore we are glad to present to you, as a memorial to our soldiers, these our sabers.

We fought bravely at Saipan, Iwo Jima and Okinawa, as you know. We fought to the end but now we abandon warlike ways and initiate steps to build a new Japan as civilians. I am determined to do my best to fulfill that mission.

In Japan there is a proverb: "Yesterdays enemies, todays friends." Under present circumstances, of course, we cannot be considered equal friends, but I am hoping that day comes soon.

There may be some points about us which you cannot understand fully, but I pray that you endeavor to understand us, and receive these sabers to keep them forever.

3. Major McKAY acknowledged the receipt of the surrender of the installation with the following remarks:

My Officers and I acknowledge the presentation of your swords, and accept them in the name of our Government.

In America there is a proverb "Beat your swords into plowshares." We know that Japan, by following peaceful pursuits, can take its place among other nations. To accomplish this Japan needs the skill and intergrity of its former soldiers.

We, in America, do not desire to carry enmity in our hearts tword anyone. We, too, hope that the day will soon come when we can all resume our former state.

So long as it is necessary for us to remain we shall endeavor to understand your people, at the same time showing them, by example, the American way of life.

We accept your sabers in the spirt in which they were given, and shall always keep them.

The time frame was short,
but the effect has lasted a lifetime.

Not My Cup of Tea

As soon as the formal surrender of the military bases at Sendai and Koriyama were signed, we left Odawara. Although the weather was pleasant, the train moved at a slow pace and stopped in many small towns. The tracks reminded me of our roads back home; some were similar to our two-lane highways with trains traveling in different directions at the same time. In the small towns, the depots had a long wooden platform on each end and were built between the two tracks.

Passengers used the platforms to board or exit the train while the freight was being loaded or unloaded. On this occasion, a train which was headed south, was waiting on the opposite side of the tracks. Our troop train was heading north when it pulled into the station. As we stopped in the different towns, some of us would exit the train to stretch and get some fresh air while others would light up a cigarette.

The delays were usually for fifteen minutes. When the train started moving again, we would make a mad dash for our seats. However, this occasion was different; Army guards were standing on our side of the platform and ordered us to stay inside the train.

At first, the guards were pretty tight-lipped and would not tell us anything. We could see a few people standing on the platform on the far side which was not unusual. Passengers would become exhausted from a long tiring ride and taking a short break from sitting would help. But, it was unusual for guards to order us to *stay put*.

The old saying, "curiosity killed the cat" seemed to describe those of us riding on the train that day. We wanted to know *why* we could not get off and *what* on earth was going on! Why couldn't we visit with the people on the platform?

Our eyes told us we were seeing Americans who were frail and weak. And, our minds wondered if there were soldiers inside the other train who were unable to get out. Our minds also told us that we were seeing American prisoners-of-war.

How shocking! What a pitiful sight to see our emaciated American soldiers! It was obvious they had been starved. They were soldiers our age who had probably been enjoying their high school years not so long ago—soldiers, who had probably weighed at least one hundred and eighty pounds, were now skeletal weighing sixty and seventy pounds, if that much.

Their uniforms hung on their fragile frames. It was reminiscent of children playing dress-up in their parents' oversized clothing. Although we could not see underneath their uniforms, we were certain they had been tortured in other ways.

It was heart-wrenching to see how stooped and feeble they had become. We wondered how many had been brutally beaten to cause their bent and contorted bodies. Some were so weak that it took every ounce of their physical strength to get out of the train and to walk around. It looked as if their frail bodies would snap like twigs.

Others had trouble lighting a cigarette, because their hands trembled so badly. We could see sores around their lips and on their gaunt faces. Their eyes were hollow and cavernous. These soldiers were our living dead.

There was no telling how many more soldiers, who were in even *worse* shape inside that train, than the ones we were seeing! We were devastated, yet relieved for them; at least they had been rescued, and we were hopeful they would get the medical treatment they desperately needed and deserved before it was too late.

Our hearts hardened and anger welled up in our throats when we saw how cruel and inhumane the Japanese had treated our American prisoners of war! It has been said, "War is hell. There is no honor or glory in war." We were now seeing another side of war that we had not encountered on Okinawa, and we were more than outraged!

After the disturbing experience that we had just witnessed, both trains departed from the depot, each to their destination. The time frame was short, but the effect has lasted a lifetime. What a horrific thing to have been captured by the cruel, barbaric Japanese military!

As we continued our journey, we came to a fairly large town, Koriyama. One battalion was scheduled to disembark and Company B was included. The bulk of the troops, including my good buddy Nick, continued northward until they reached the city of Sendai, where Division Headquarters had been established. Sendai was quite a distance from Koriyama. Although, I never had any reason to go to Division Headquarters and was sent to Koriyama instead, some interesting things happened during my tour of duty there.

Our first priority was to destroy the Japanese army's ability to resume the war by demolishing all their weapons and planes. A scouting party was also appointed to search the smaller towns nearby to locate and take inventory of stashed weapons while our troops mutilated the planes at Koriyama. There was a hodgepodge of small crafts that would have been used as kamikaze planes had we invaded Japan by conventional methods.

Our company grouped the planes three at a time and stood them up vertically with the props to the ground and the tails to the sky. Then, we smashed the engines with sledgehammers, sprayed the planes with gasoline and burned them beyond any chance of use except for salvage.

We took great delight each time a hole was knocked in one of the planes' engines as we shouted in rage using colorful language, "This lick's for . . . take

that you sorry . . .!" What a great way to release our anger that had been building for months. We named the planes after high-ranking Japanese military men
before slinging the sledgehammer. The most common target was, "Take this,
Tojo!" *Wham*, went the hammer! The metal was later given to Japan to rebuild
their industry.

Captain Richard Henry handpicked and ordered a detail to scout out a
section of Japan where American soldiers had never been. The detail included
First Lieutenant Hugo Pogue, who was in charge; Sergeant William Riddle,
two jeep drivers, a Japanese interpreter, and four other soldiers, including
myself. I was the only one chosen from the Okinawa gang for this trip. Our
orders were to take inventory and map out the locations of stacked weapons.
We were to scout out three different towns in one day.

The next day Pogue trained and gave us instructions on how to conduct
ourselves during this scouting expedition. We mostly studied Japanese eti-
quette. For instance, if we were offered tea, we were required to drink it; refus-
ing their hospitality would be considered an insult. I did not want to insult
them when we were just eight soldiers carrying only pistols and rifles.

We left the company before sunrise and returned late that evening. Our
first contact was with the mayor and the fire chief of the first town. We were
graciously received, but I thought they would *never* stop bowing and showing
their respect.

We understood that tea would probably be offered, which was part of their
custom. I can honestly say that we did not have too many tea parties back
home on the farm, and this was my very first one. And, this is how the Japanese did it that day.

The water was boiled and the tea, the green kind, was made. A couple of
tables were set up and covered with white tablecloths. Six small cups were
placed on one table and five cups were placed on the other. The tea was poured
into two different pots, one for each table. Pogue and his driver, Riddle, the
interpreter, and the mayor sat at the head table.

The rest of us sat with the fire chief. The mayor filled four cups and
placed the pot in the center of the table. Pogue picked up the pot and filled the
mayor's cup. The fire chief filled five cups and placed the pot near the center
of our table. As previously instructed, one of us filled the fire chief's cup.

So far, everything went according to protocol. When I took my first swallow of Japanese tea, I almost spewed it across the table! It tasted to me like
ragweed smells. For a moment, I had a mental lapse. I had to remind myself,
"Hold your breath, finish off the cup and this will be your good deed for the
day." Then, I gulped the rest hoping no one noticed my nostrils flaring.

After I set down my cup, the fire chief reached over and poured me a
fresh cup of tea. That's when I remembered that the host will continue to fill
our cups, and we were supposed to keep his cup full. During the tea party, the

mayor insisted that we stop by for another visit on our way back to the base after we had inventoried the two smaller towns. Pogue agreed to do just that.

As we went about doing the things we were sent out to do, we encountered many Japanese men who were still wearing their military uniforms. I have often wondered what was going on in their minds—eight American soldiers had just rolled into town and were in the process of having their war machine seized and destroyed. What a shock it must have been to the mind-set of these proud samurai warriors!

Their weapons and ammunition were about every place we looked. Rifles were neatly stored in square stacks. On the bottom layer, every other rifle was laid in the opposite direction: one rifle was pointing north and the next rifle was pointing south until the width of the pile equaled the length. On the second layer, the rifles were pointing east and west at a ninety-degree angle in alternating directions. This pattern was continued until each unit reached about four feet high. This method of storing, kept the rifles secured firmly together and made counting easy. There were more than two thousand rifles stored in the largest city.

Light and heavy machine guns, different sized mortars, artillery pieces, pistols, sabers, grenades, bayonets, various vehicles and about anything used in fighting a war were stashed in a large barricaded section, which consisted of several streets in each town. At times, we encountered several men in a group, which was troubling to us. They never made any moves to indicate that we were fixin' to be under attack, but since we had just been fighting a war a few weeks prior, it was natural for us to be apprehensive in this situation.

Pogue pointed to a Buddhist Temple. "Go in there and search for weapons," he ordered me. Outside the building was a statue of the Three Monkeys, "See no evil. Hear no evil. Speak no evil." As I walked inside, I observed a man wearing a robe. The temple reeked of burning incense and a heavy layer of smoke filled the dimly lit rooms; it gave me the *heebie-jeebies*.

Although there was nothing inside of which to be afraid, my imagination started working overtime. I did not feel at ease searching this place. Maybe I was just spooked, but *something* told me that I should not be inside their temple. I wondered, with all the weapons that were stacked outside in plain sight, why would anything be hidden inside the temple? After making a thorough search, I did not find any and was very relieved to walk back outside into the sunlight.

We spent most of the day counting and mapping-out the locations of their weapons. I never did ask, but I am sure there must have been some contact between the Japanese and our division commander before we scouted out the three towns. I know that Japan's surrender was unconditional, but still many things would need to be worked out. Soon, U.S. Army trucks would pick up the weapons, take them to be smashed and the metal would be returned to the Japanese for recycling.

We finished our mission, boarded the jeeps and headed back to the base. Just as Pogue had promised, we stopped for a second time in the first town that we visited where the mayor and fire chief were waiting for us. Only this time, they served us peeled sliced pears, peeled tangerines, and instead of tea, *sake* was poured.

Sake, an alcoholic drink made from fermented rice, was popular with the Japanese as they tanked-up on it before pulling one of their banzai raids during the war. Consuming too much sake can sometimes make a person stark raving mad! It was very different from American alcoholic drinks.

While we were getting situated, my mind flashed back to the time I had seen vegetables being fertilized with human waste. I cautiously asked Pogue, "Are we gonna eat the pears and tangerines?" He shook his head and assured me, "The things grown on trees are safe to eat."

This was about the time our hosts filled the small glasses with sake, and the show was on the road. Pogue started to object to the sake, but Riddle beat him to the draw. "You know our orders. We're forbidden to insult our hosts," he said. And, down the hatch the sake went!

At the end of this little party as we were preparing to leave, the mayor presented Pogue with a large jug of sake. Not to be outdone, the fire chief gave Riddle the same. Alcohol was never a thing with me, so I ate more than my share of the fruit. As we made our escape, luckily we had at least two sober guys who were still able to drive us back to the base. Although, it was a long tiresome day, it was a day that only a few soldiers ever experienced.

For once, I had to give credit to Pogue. Apparently, he had been briefed on what to expect, because he knew exactly what he was doing. And, for once, he treated us like soldiers—with respect. However, when we got back to the base, the party was over.

He pointed the cocked pistol at middle of my chest.

Flying Fists in Koriyama

After the planes had been destroyed, the wrecking crew had disbanded, and we had finished scouting the towns, it was time to turn to other duties. The Army certainly knew how to keep us busy. However, time to relax, play, enjoy fellowship and make friends was also an important part of Army life. I had been missing my buddies Nick, Ned, Juan, and the Kid when I was transferred from Company K to Company B.

During my stay at Koriyama, physical education was a requirement. I had done calisthenics in basic training and just hearing the word made me shudder. Playing touch football was my choice and what a bad choice it was. I thought the word *playing* meant having fun, but the college players had a different definition; playing meant bleeding. I had already seen enough blood, so I switched to volleyball.

Staff Sergeant Tim Turner, a fellow Texan, was one of the first soldiers I met when I was transferred from Company K to Company B. We just hit it off from the start, and it seemed like we had been friends for years. Although he was a staff sergeant, we played as partners in card games and were always picking on each other. I was never in his platoon, but we hung out together most of the time during off duty, and I considered Tim one of my best Army buddies.

Tim was a Champion Golden Glove boxer in his classification. He had survived a nasty wound to the groin when a knee mortar shell was dropped into his foxhole and hit the butt of his rifle. The rifle did not survive, but Tim's life was saved by a miracle. When he was released from the hospital, he was good as new and rejoined the company.

One of the first things we did, after getting settled in at Koriyama, was to build a boxing ring. The first match was between the two Japanese workers who built the ring. Some *moron* offered them chocolate candy to fight each other—two boxes for the winner and one box for thc loser.

Since the Japanese were starving for chocolate, they really got after each other! When they finished the match, the moron paid them with three boxes of Ex-Lax. Talk about a dirty deal! They were scarfing down that stuff and smiling as they went on their merry way.

The second match just happened to be between my buddy, Tim and me. I never did know how this actually came about. I must have had an enemy in the company.

Maybe there was someone who did not like my pranks. Before I knew what was happening, the guys were shouting, "Watch Ray whip up on the sergeant!" I had never liked to box, did not know how, and sure did not want to get in the ring with a Golden Glove Champ!

Well, Tim came over to talk to me. "Aw come on, Ray. We'll spar around a little. I'll let you hit me occasionally, so you won't look so bad."

When we put the gloves on and were ready to start, the guys stood up and hollered, "Ray, whip Sergeant Turner!" Well, I must have had an adrenalin rush, and it must have increased each time I heard, "Whip the sergeant!" Man, I got so excited, and the first time Tim gave me an opening, I socked him in the jaw just as hard as I could!

It was hardly a knockdown. I did not even draw blood. Tim recovered within a jiffy, and I had never seen so many fists flying around in my life! He then demonstrated *why* he was a Golden Glove Champ. Blood was spurting from my nose, and I was really getting knocked around! He was fixin' to finish me off in a hurry when the referee stepped in.

Was I ever glad when he stopped the match! I noticed that none of my supporters came down to the latrine to see if I was *okay*. My nose had always bled easily, but this time it was taking longer than usual to stop. While I was washing my face and trying to stop the bleeding, Tim's large frame darkened the doorway. He was still madder than a wet hornet. "Ray! What were ya thinking! You knew I could've knocked you cross-eyed!"

Grinning as my nose gushed, I said. "With all that excitement, I thought I was the champ!"

Stone-faced Tim retorted, "That'll be the day."

"Look Tim. . . if a guy doesn't know how to box, then he doesn't know how to spar. You should've known better. With all the yellin' and support I was gettin', what'd ya expect?"

He stood there with no expression.

"When a guy gets really excited, he might be inclined to do things that he wouldn't do otherwise. Most sparrin' between boxers and non-boxers end the same way."

He raised a brow.

"Hey, I'm the one with the bloody nose! What are ya so pissed off about?"

Now Tim had a temper, but as we talked he began to cool off. He shook his head not believing what I had done. Under his breath he dryly added, "Just *five* more seconds and you would've been a goner, Ray." After a couple of moments, he stuck out his hand. I offered mine covered with blood. We shook and never discussed it again.

During that period of time, our company began to receive a few recruits who had just completed basic training. There was one young soldier named

Grady, who was from Georgia. He did not know anyone when he joined our company and began to hang out with Tim and me. When we asked for our passes into town, Grady would follow suit and tag along with us. The recruits, who had arrived fresh from the states, seemed to want to *prove* to the combat veterans how tough they were. This was certainly true for Grady.

He wanted to ignore off-limit signs or to go to places that we did not want to go. We never used our beer ration chits that were issued with the pass; Instead, I usually traded mine for candy. There were regular Army approved places for using beer chits. Any other place that sold alcohol was strictly off-limits. Some soldiers had actually died and others had been blinded from drinking the bad stuff that was being sold.

The Japanese soon learned how to do business with the soldiers. The ones, who could speak English, would approach us soldiers on the street and try to trade or sell us various things. On this particular pass, we were approached by a Japanese guy who had alcohol, music, dancing, and girls . . . just name it. Tim told him to "bug off*,"* but our Georgia soldier, Grady said he was going to "check it out." We told him that he was on his own, and if he went inside, he would have to take care of himself.

We watched Grady go into a nearby building with this Japanese guy. The front was all plate glass with a lot of Japanese writing on the windows. Of course, we did not understand the Japanese language, but the place appeared to be a nice restaurant with an entrance that led directly into the huge dining room.

It was not surprising that the chairs were stacked on tables. The restaurant was apparently closed, because of the scarcity of food in Japan. We could see light shining underneath a backdoor. This was a large building with extra banquet rooms and of course, a huge kitchen.

Tim and I started thinking about what might happen and how we would feel if something bad happened to Grady. If we walked away, would we regret it tomorrow? So, Tim and I decided to go inside to try and talk some sense into him and persuade him to come with us.

The frontdoor was unlocked, and we walked in. As we were heading to the backroom, the English-speaking dude came out and invited us in. We could hear some strange music. This was my first time to hear such weird sounds, and it kind of set my teeth on edge. We could also hear laughter—the kind that comes from soldiers when they have had too much to drink.

The first thing I noticed were a couple of soldiers passed out on the floor. The second thing I noticed was our friend. He was trying to exit the building, but two guys were preventing him from leaving. Tim ordered the English-speaking guy, "Tell your boys to move out of the way and let our friend leave."

They moved—right between the door leading into the dining room and us. Tim firmly and slowly repeated, *"*Move . . . out . . . of the way . . . *now*!" They stood solid.

That's when Tim said to me, "I'll take the big one. If you need help with the little one, I'll be finished with him in a minute." In a flash, Tim laid a hay-maker on the big guy! I bet it took him longer to come around than it took those two soldiers combined to sleep off a drunk. I hope they sobered up.

When the little guy looked around to see what was happening to his buddy, I slammed him against the wall and out the door, the three of us fled! Grady was a different guy after that incident. I think he realized that he was not in his friendly, small hometown of Georgia anymore, and for the first time, he understood that *acting* tough and *being* tough are two different things. Tim proved that to him.

Things can get out-of-hand not only with the enemy, but sometimes even among soldiers who are fighting for the same cause. Dale, who was from Wyoming, was the youngest soldier in our outfit. He had lied about his age when he enlisted. Although, he was a good soldier and tough as a boot, he was also very immature. He was only sixteen when he signed-up.

Dale killed a Japanese officer while fighting on Okinawa. It is an unwrit-ten code in combat, if you kill one of the enemy, all his personal belongings are yours if you want them. Dale kept a .25-caliber pistol for his souvenir. He also seemed to think it was an unwritten code to be a pain in the rear, and he was one big pain at times.

Tim, an avid pinochle player, taught me how to play, so he would always have the same partner in pinochle tournaments. Several games were usually going on during free time. Since we did not have tables or chairs, we just did the best we could with what we had. Pulling a blanket tightly over the top of a canvas cot became our table. For chairs, one set of partners would straddle each end of the cot. The opposing players would sit on the sides of adjacent cots and face each other across the table.

This arrangement worked well most of the time—that is, until Dale began to sneak up, jerk the blanket, and scatter the cards. No one said much to begin with, because we thought he would stop after a bit and find something else to do. There's one thing about pulling pranks; a person can get himself into a lot of trouble.

Pranks work something like a transistor; the hotter the transistor becomes, the better it conducts, and the more it conducts, the hotter it becomes until it finally burns out. However, with transistors, control circuits are used to prevent overheating. I think Dale lost control, and the more times he yanked the blanket and sent the cards flying, the funnier it became to him; the funnier it became to him, the more he did it!

Eventually, Tim and I did something worse than what Dale was doing. We were billeted in the top floor of a Japanese barrack. Open beams were used to support the roof. I don't know where it came from, but there just happened to be a grass rope handy. So, we grabbed Dale and tied him up to the nearest beam. Dale begged, cussed, and cried to untie him and pled that he would be a *good boy*. Well, we decided to let him stay tied up for a while. Eventually, Dale became quiet, and we became involved in our game and forgot about him. That's when it happened.

Dale had worked himself out of the ropes and had run to his c-bag, which was next to my cot. We all knew what he was after! Tim was sitting in front of the stairway, and being the athlete that he was, he flipped backwards and down the stairs! Dale grabbed the pistol from his c-bag, immediately inserted a clip of ammunition into the pistol and slipped a bullet into the firing chamber.

My legs and feet were straddling the cot, and by the time I was able to get my legs untangled and stand up, there was no place to go. He pointed the cocked pistol at the middle of my chest. We stood facing each other at no more than six feet apart.

I have heard people say what they would do if something like that ever happened to them, but I can only tell my experience. Instantly, I had this thought; "If I say anything, if I make any kind of movement, Dale will shoot me." I just knew that I had to be as still as a statue. Seconds seemed like hours as we stood there facing each other.

About twenty-five soldiers were a captivated audience. No one moved. No one said a word. No one made a sound. I don't know how long the pistol was pointed at me, but it was too long.

All at once, Dale lowered the pistol. He slowly removed the clip and the round from the firing chamber. Then, he became hysterical! Some of the guys took him outside for some fresh air. I cannot remember if I had to change my shorts or not, but I can say one thing; it was a *scary* few moments. Nothing was ever said, and life returned to normal.

A funny thing happened several years later after my wife, son and I moved to Monahans, Texas during January 1951. Many young couples were transferring in and out of Ward County. Seismograph crews were all over the place, and some of the crews stayed for a few months, while others stayed for even less time. I was doing visitations for the church at the time, and two young families from one of the crews attended Sunday school and church regularly.

Wanda, my wife, invited both families over for supper one night. After the meal, we were sitting around the kitchen table enjoying our fresh out-of-the-oven peach cobbler and visiting. Of course, we were asking each other questions to become better acquainted with one another. I said to one of the women, "Jan, I bet you're not from around here, are you? You just don't look or talk like a West Texan."

She smiled. "You're right about that."

"Where're you from?" I asked.

"Oh, it's just a little podunk place. I'm sure you've never heard of. It's probably not even on a map," she chuckled.

"Well, I know a bunch of podunk towns. I'm from one myself. What's the name?"

She finally named a town in Wyoming. After awhile, I went to one of our closets and pulled out my box of Army photos. Wanda apologized to our new friends, "Oh, Ronold, no one is interested in seeing those old pictures." However, I was not discouraged and insisted on showing them. About the third picture I showed was a five-by-seven inch photo of Dale.

Well, Jan went bananas! She jumped up from the table and screamed, "Oh, my gosh! Where on earth did you get *that* picture! You *know* him? I can't believe it! You actually know Dale? Why he's the meanest guy, I've ever known!"

I don't know who was the most surprised. After she picked up her jaw from the floor, Jan said, "Unfortunately, I must admit that I went to school with him. He was bad news. Oh, but his Dad . . . his Dad was even worse! Let me tell you . . . he was horrible! Just horrible! She cringed. "Why he was so mean to Dale and his family . . . that Dale ran away from home and lied about his age to join the Army!"

I nodded. "Yeah, he was definitely the youngest in our outfit."

"Well, you won't believe this! Dale's younger brother, Bobby, did something one time and got grounded for it. I don't know what it was, but his Dad was really sore. Of course, it didn't take much to set him off.

"Anyway, Bobby slipped out of the house one night to go to the basketball game. When his Dad came home and discovered that Bobby was gone, he went out to the barn and grabbed his black snake whip. Then, he hunted Bobby down like a wild animal at the high school. I remember we'd had a lot of snow, and it was so cold that night.... way below freezing. But, things really heated up when he found Bobby at that game!

"I am here to tell you . . . that hateful old geezer disrupted the game after he ran Bobby out of the bleachers. He was swearing up a storm and started chasing him around and around that basketball court. Why he was even cracking that whip! Well, the game suddenly ended, and so did his Dad's life. He collapsed right there . . . *right there* on the gym floor and died of a heart attack. Can you believe that?"

I shook my head. "That's really sad. It explains why Dale might've been the way he was." Then, I told them about my experience with Dale while we were in the Army.

Dale and I continued to sleep on cots next to each other until I was transferred. We both knew that this little incident was behind us. If it had happened in today's world, where we have so many ways of sending and receiving information thru cell phones, e-mail, radios, TV, magazines, newspapers, and with reporters working so hard to find a story, I shudder to think of what might have been written or televised.

There is quite a contrast of how things actually were back in the year 1945 and how they are nowadays. News from the states was nonexistent for most of us. We did receive a copy of the *Stars & Stripes*, a small military paper, occasionally. Most of our information came from the lowly company bulletin board. Mail call was something we seldom missed and reading the bulletin board was a high priority.

On one occasion, Tim was asking around, "Where can I find Ray?" It was obvious by his persistence that he wanted to see me immediately. When he finally found me, I could tell he was really excited. In fact, I had never seen him so elated.

"Ray, have you read the bulletin board?" I had not, and I asked him, "What's up? Did you make first sergeant?" This was about the only thing I could think of that would get him fired-up to this extent.

"No. It's much better than that. I'm going home!"

"Oh, don't give me that bull, Tim. You know you don't even come close to havin' enough points to go home."

He grabbed me by the arm. "Come on. I want to show you something."

"It's sure gonna be a long swim. But, those ol' sharks will keep you company," I piped-up.

He huffed. Then, he shook his head. His face was very serious as he pulled me along. I could tell he didn't want any small talk. As he marched me up to the bulletin board, he pointed and firmly tapped his finger at a piece of paper. "Ray, if you can read, read that to me!" He demanded.

The ad said something like this—If you are willing to enlist in the regular Army for eighteen months, you will receive a thirty-day furlough and leave for home immediately. Each soldier who enlists in the regular Army will receive extra compensation, and some will get an extra stripe. Wow!

"Well now, this is, indeed, very interesting." I said.

"So, what do you say, Ray? Let's get the heck out of here. I am ready to get home. Then, you and I can be one of the firsts to enlist in the regular Army." Tim said.

At the time, we were in the Army for the duration— whatever that meant. If you had earned stripes, they were temporary since we were not in the *regular* Army. I answered, "Well now, Tim, eighteen months is a long time. I'll be home much sooner than that."

We had a lengthy discussion about the pros and cons of signing up, but we had different ideas about our futures. "Ray, you're stubborn as a mule! I am telling you that you're making a huge mistake. *Huge* mistake! You need to leave while you can," he insisted while clearly frustrated at me.

And, before I could blink my eyes, my good buddy Tim shipped out immediately to start his new life. As soon as he got home, he married his high school sweetheart and started working on earning that stripe.

At *Ease* in Koriyama

Mission Accomplished

No more foxholes, no more ambush details, no more
steel helmets, no more c-rations, no more cold, wet blankets,
no more. . .

Toasting Tojo!

The raising or lowering of the flag and changing of the guard always gave me goose bumps. It reminded me of how fortunate I was to be a citizen of the United States of America, and it made me proud to be a Soldier serving our country.

Good Riddance

Since our division was way understrength, we were receiving replacements a few at a time. Our platoon was getting a fair share. It soon became very evident, that the new men in our platoon were receiving preferential treatment over the ones that were present the day First Lieutenant Hugo Pogue became our platoon leader.

For instance, when our company was on guard, the officer of the day was generally from another company; when our platoon was on duty, Pogue insisted on being the officer of the day. The raising or lowering of the flag and changing of the guard always gave me goose bumps. It reminded me of how fortunate I was to be a citizen of the United States of America, and it made me proud to be a soldier serving our country.

I suppose it could be said that changing of the guard was a 'spit and polish ceremony', and a ceremony always meant preparation. The guards reporting for duty would be dressed in their best; their rifles would be cleaned, polished and unloaded. Preparation was not on the honor system, so an inspection was always made by the officer of the day.

The inspection occurred a few minutes before the ceremony, and passing an inspection under Pogue was not possible for the members of the platoon that were present on Okinawa. We were always dressed down in front of the other guards and sent back to the barracks to clean our rifles or *something*. However, instead of cleaning our rifles, we spent most of the time trying to figure out how to make it rough on Pogue. We knew that our rifles would pass the second time around.

One of the things we tried to do during the inspection was to drop our rifle when Pogue reached for it. If we were successful, he would have to clean the rifle to our satisfaction, and it would have been impossible for him to pass.

This is how the inspection worked. We all stood in line at attention with our rifles at our sides. As the officer of the day walked down the line and stopped and faced a soldier, the soldier was required to look straight ahead, immediately snap his rifle up to a horizontal position at chest height, and open the firing chamber.

It was not as easy as it sounds. Bringing the rifle up with the right hand and transferring it to the left hand was easy enough. The problem was getting the right hand back to open the firing chamber and then back underneath the rifle within four seconds.

Our rifles had to be oil-free for inspection. Sliding metal on metal and pushing a spring back while holding a nine-pound rifle with the left hand took practice. We discovered that stretching the spring made it easier, so we would try to do that inside the barracks without getting caught before the inspection.

Whenever the officer walked up and faced me, I would look straight ahead. Thru peripheral vision, I would watch the twitch of his shoulder. Any movement meant his hand was coming hard and fast for the rifle. If I was still holding the rifle when his hand grabbed it, I would immediately be jerked out of rank. That would be bad news.

So, we released the rifle at the slightest movement of his shoulder. It was up to him to catch it. If it hit the ground, he would have to clean it. It never happened.

I do not remember how many guard posts there were, but we were guarding the entire base. Some posts were within walking distance to the guardhouse and others were scattered all over the place. Most of the time, the officer of the day would drive by a couple of times to check things out. Usually, the officer would come by once in the morning and once again before ten o' clock in the evening.

Generally, the officer would just slow down; we would give our best rifle salute, and he would drive on. We changed guards every two hours, and the sergeant of the guard was always present. If there was a problem, it was his responsibility to report it.

However, this routine was not good enough for Pogue. It appeared that he was unable to adjust to commanding combat veterans and could not even begin to understand that the war was over for us. It seemed like he thought he was still training cadets at Fort Benning. Now I can tell you that the combat veterans did not respect an officer with that kind of attitude! Another thing—we were just waiting to catch a boat home. We had finished our job.

During wartime, going to sleep on the post is one serious offense and is punishable by death in some instances. Although the war had ended, sleeping at the post was still a serious offense. The posts that were within walking distance, especially the stationary ones, were targets for Pogue. He would slip around at night and try to catch someone sleeping or doing something that he did not like. He just barely missed being shot on a couple of occasions.

Things were entirely different at an outpost. It just so happened that I pulled an outpost on the right night at the right time under the right circumstances and with the right soldier who was driving the jeep. My post was a long way from the guardhouse. I could hear and see the lights of a jeep from a mile away. My post was to guard some warehouses. Since it was a walking post, I did not have to be at any specified place.

It had been pouring rain and there was no shortage of mudholes. What a perfect set up! I took a position near a turn in the road, and concealed myself until the right moment. I was hidden from view, as I stood on the far side of a building on the opposite side of the road from the traffic that entered the gate.

I had visualized my plans very carefully and might have even had a little smirk on my face. I couldn't help but laugh out loud a couple of times just thinking about it. I was *revved-up* for the big moment! How could I help it if there just happened to be a made-to-order mudhole right in the middle of the road? I was ready for Pogue!

When the jeep approached, I took a deep breath and regained my composure as I stepped out into the headlights and yelled, "Halt!*"* as loudly as I could. The driver slammed on the brakes right smack dab in the middle of that mudhole. Then, he began to ease forward. I shouted, "Halt!" the second time, and the driver continued to creep forward. I hollered, "Halt!" for the third time. This time, my rifle was up and pointed right at Pogue! I heard Pogue say to the driver in his special blend of foul language, "Stop this jeep!"

When the jeep stopped, I yelled out, "Dismount to be recognized!" There was some hesitation; but on the second command, he grumbled and begrudgingly got out of the jeep. "Advance to be recognized!" I commanded. Standing about fifteen feet away from the edge of the *preselected* spot, I was far enough away to prevent him from grabbing my rifle.

Pogue sloshed thru the mud and reached dry ground, and I ordered, "Halt!" When he stopped, I recognized him and gave him my best rifle salute. It was interesting to see the water rising above the top of his combat boots, his mud spattered uniform and his face change from pasty white to a deep red.

All my commands were standard Army procedure and were taught by Pogue himself. The select group from Okinawa knew what we could and could not do. We did not want to get into any trouble, but if the opportunity presented itself, we would let Pogue know that it was payback time.

Judo Exhibition

There were more soldiers than were needed for the job that we were doing at Koriyama; the off-duty soldiers from the four companies were grouped together and required to do physical education in the mornings and attend class or do some kind of activity in the afternoon. Various officers from different companies would teach. Scheduling the classes in this way allowed us to meet the soldiers from other companies.

Pogue was very active in teaching, and he also took his turn serving as captain of the guard for the other platoons. His reputation was well-known in all the companies stationed at Koriyama. One of the classes, which was the *least* favorite for most of us, was studying the Japanese culture; I guess it could have been called, *"*How to be Nice to the Japanese and Try Not to Offend Them*"* class. Pogue was the instructor.

As part of this class, we marched down to a large hangar to watch some Japanese guys put on a judo exhibition. A stage covered with mats was inside the hangar where the judo matches were conducted. Those guys were very good, and they put on a super show. Of course, the last match was the best—the heavy weights.

Each one weighed at least three-hundred pounds and the stage would shake and rumble like thunder when one of those guys hit that mat. When the match was over, the winner used an interpreter to invite any American soldier to come up to the stage and take him on.

The winner's rule was—the American soldier would be allowed to fight by any method that he chose while the winner would use only judo. "Hey, you tough guys! Step right up and try this guy on! He's a judo instructor from the Japanese army," cried the interpreter.

There was a long silence. You could have heard a pin drop. Then it happened. A whisper came from the back of the hangar, "Lt. Pogue." Then, there were a couple of whispers. Then there were more. Then several. Then a group, all in unison whispering, "Lt. Pogue." And, then the whispers became clearly heard. More joined in, "Lt. Pogue! Lt. Pogue!" Soon, it became a chant. The clapping began. Then, it grew into a crowd shouting, "Lt. Pogue! Lt. Pogue!" and more joined in. The yelling grew louder and continued to accelerate. Some whistled. Some stomped their feet.

Pogue's face was priceless! He was furious, and he was not about to take the challenge. However, this little episode was very short-lived.

Capt. Henry jumped up and barked, "Attention! Company B, assemble outside immediately!" What he said to us was quite sharp, but it was quite true. We had it coming to us. I agreed with everything he said to us except for one little statement.

"You should all be ashamed and feel guilty for your actions!" He hissed. Well, I never heard anyone say that he had a guilt problem over what had happened. Instead, it was more like, "Hooray! We won this round!"

Eyes Spy

One day we were ordered to go to our barracks and lay out everything for a full field inspection. This happened occasionally, and we did not think much about it. When the inspectors came by my cot, they snatched a Japanese flag from my stuff. We were told to put our things away and to remain inside the building.

A few minutes later, a group of guards came inside and one carried a list of names. "Fall in and form a line at the front of the room if I call your name," one of the guards sternly said. More than half of our names were called, including mine. "Those whose names that I just called, are now being placed under guard. You will be taken to the guardhouse immediately, and there will be no talking," he ordered.

As the guards marched us down to the house, I was surprised to see so many soldiers standing in front on the sidewalk. There was not enough room inside the building for all of them. We joined some of our buddies and quietly waited. The line moved at a slow pace. Each time a soldier came out of the door, we would move up one slot.

Each one that came out had a strange look on his face—white as a sheet and scared to death. Now most of these guys were seasoned combat veterans, and I believe most of us were wondering, "What in the world is going on?" We could not imagine anything that could cause such fear.

A lieutenant walked up and down the line to keep us from talking. After a couple of hours, another lieutenant came out and took over. He was from our company and was a much more relaxed kind of officer. We asked him, "What's going on?"

"Apparently, a Japanese woman was raped by two soldiers. She says that one was fairly tall, with a light complexion and had light brown hair. The other soldier was short with a dark complexion and had black hair," he explained. "She said that they took her flag, and her young daughter witnessed the whole thing. We're having a line-up, so that she or her daughter can identify the men who did it," he added.

Man alive! I knew I was innocent, but *what if* she picked me? I did fit the description of one of them. And, I had that flag! The punishment for this crime could be years in prison or even the death penalty!

I imagined that she would just randomly pick any two guys and stick to her story. I was convinced that she would probably try to nail a couple of us whether she picked the right ones or not. There is nothing as scary as an over-active imagination, and mine had just pegged the needle.

We entered from a hall into a large room which had an exit door and an office at the other end. The office had a large plate glass window and a door that opened into the room. The window was completely covered with heavy paper and some letters had been stenciled onto the paper. Small slits had been cut into the paper: slits just big enough to show a pair of eyes. Several circles with numbers had been drawn on the floor and some were very close to the office glass.

When my turn came to traverse the large room, a voice from inside the office instructed me to stand on a specific number and look at a certain letter. I could hear both English and Japanese talking, and I could see *eyeballs* moving around through the slits! It was obvious that several people were inside the office and possibly more than one interpreter.

I was able to identify the mother and her daughter immediately, because the slits were closer to the floor. However, I could not actually see them. When the mother or daughter wanted to view me from another angle, wanted a close up view, or a distant view or whatever, I was told to comply. I was ordered to move from circle to circle, look at different letters, move back, move forward, hold my chin up, put my chin down, show the right side of my face, show the left side of my face, etc.

The last thing was the most difficult. This was when I was directed to the circle right in front of the glass. I was told to move up to the glass and look into the two slits one at a time and to be ready to repeat if requested. My nose was touching the glass and our eyes could not have been more than four inches apart! I'm sure this is when my blood turned to milk. Just like the guys before, I also came out of the building white as a sheet and scared as a rabbit.

Things did not turn out as my imagination told me it would. The poor woman might have, indeed, picked out the guilty parties, but she identified *more* than twenty different soldiers. Maybe the guilty ones were found, but I never heard anymore about the case.

Greener Pastures

A couple of days later, Capt. Henry called me in. "Pvt. Ray, get your gear together and be ready for departure early in the morning." What fantastic news! He did not tell me where I was going, but escaping the pompous, self-serving hypocrite First Lieutenant Hugo Pogue was the best news I had heard since the surrender of Japan!

Henry continued, "Now, you will be joining a few other soldiers in a designated coach since you are prohibited to ride with the Japanese. There will be a sergeant from headquarters who will be traveling with you. He will give each one of you your next instructions. Good luck!"

Well, I was ready to saddle-up old Paint, hit the trail again, explore new territory, and see what was on the other side of the mountain. What a surprise when the train stopped and the sergeant said, "Pvt. Ray! This is where you get off."

Tokyo?

*I think it was very unusual that a captain would intercede
where a major had already given an order,
but Captain Joyce Phillips was no ordinary officer.*

General Headquarters

Luck was smiling on me when I checked into General Headquarters (GHQ) in Tokyo. Shortly after arriving, I was taken to the mess hall for my first meal where I noticed a friend seated next to my table. Orville was one of my *Saipan Sea Devil* buddies who had been with me on that unforgettable twenty-five-mile march.

He strolled over. "Ray! What're you doing in Tokyo?" When I showed him my orders, he rolled his eyes and shook his head. "Oh, man! You don't want that," he informed me.

I asked, "What's *that*?"

Orville replied, "You don't know? Why you've been handpicked for MacArthur's Honor Guards."

I inquired, "How'd ya know?"

"Because I *am* one of the honor guards," he sighed.

Orville told me what a tough job it was wearing white gloves, white helmet and white leggings—strictly a spit and polish job. He explained, "You'll be standing guard two hours at a time at the same post with a soldier from a different country. They'll definitely expect you to outshine your counterpart."

"Lord, deliver me from this job," I muttered.

"Ray, I'm sure you were picked, because you met the three requirements"

"What are ya talkin' about?"

"Didn't they tell you *anything* before they sent you down here?"

"Orville, I was so happy to get away, I didn't ask any questions. Heck, I thought they were sendin' me to boxin' camp!" I popped-off.

"*Sure* you did! I didn't think you *needed* gloves. But, you *will* now," he chuckled. "You'll be wearing those nice, white, dust-free gloves in the honor guard."

"Now, how'd I get in this mess?" I asked.

"They selected you, because you are a combat veteran and because of your height. And, because they must think you're smart."

Well, I had pulled enough guard duty to last me a lifetime, and I didn't like anything about the idea of becoming an honor guard. I asked Orville "Is there any way to get outta this?"

To my surprise, he said, "Oh, sure! Let me tell you what you need to do. You'll probably be interviewed by three or four officers. If you *really* want to get out of this, then you're going to have to convince these guys that you're rowing with one oar out of the water."

I chuckled. "Well, I don't exactly want to end up on the funny farm either."

"If you really want to get out of this, you can't act *too* sharp. Scc, if they think you're not a good fit for the honor guard, Ray, they will probably put you in the motor pool—driving a jeep or something like that." Then he made a face.

"Really? Why wouldn't that be okay?"

"Because that's also a *bad* job. You'll have to haul officers around and wait out in the jeep until they finish their business. It doesn't matter what the weather is like either. And, you know those jeeps don't have heaters! The canvas tops and doors are certainly not going to keep icicles from hanging off the end of your nose."

"Aw, come on!" I laughed. "You're kiddin' me!"

"Seriously, you might have to sit out in a typhoon like a drowned rat. And, that summer sun will fry your brains."

"What's the good news?"

"Just keep up the act, and you will probably be assigned to the Service Battalion. That really is the best you can hope for."

"Thanks ol' buddy!"

"Yeah, anytime. I am so sick of this job! I only wished someone had warned me. Believe me; you don't want to do this, Ray. It's definitely a bad assignment. Very stressful." Orville added. "Your uniform and appearance must be flawless and your stance must be exemplary. Perfection doesn't even begin to cut it. If a fly lands on your nose, then it gets to stay for two hours. If you need to go to the bathroom, there's a two hour wait."

"Yeah, I understand. I've certainly done my share of guard duty," I agreed.

"Do yourself a favor and act a little nutty, and they will probably assign you to the Service Battalion," he advised.

I had always given my best in whatever my assignment was, but I did not want to spend the rest of my Army career pulling guard duty; or I really might go nuts! During the interview, a major questioned me, "Tell me about your grades in high school, Pvt. Ray."

"Yes, sir. I had no problems with my grades. My Dad was a trustee, so I had it made," I replied.

Another officer asked me, "Do you know how to drive a vehicle?"

"No, sir. I ride my donkey back home."

"Tell me *more* about your education, Pvt. Ray. How did you rank in your graduating class?" The major asked.

Eagerly, I stood proud and said, "Number thirteen, sir!"

"Well, that must have taken a lot of hard studying, Pvt. Ray. How many were in your class?" He inquired.

I shifted my eyes. Then, I looked down as if I were trying to count in my mind without using my fingers. Hesitating, I shifted my weight from one foot to the other before saying, "Uh . . . twelve, sir."

For some reason, I ended up in the Service Battalion and was given what I consider one of the most interesting and challenging jobs in Tokyo. I was put on detached service and became a clerk at the YWCA Hotel—an Army billet which was located within thirty minutes of downtown Tokyo and was used for housing female civil service workers. The YWCA was later named the *Surugadai,* which was located on top of the Surugadai Hill—the highest in Tokyo.

Now *why* I was put on detached service, only the major knew. I always wondered if he shipped me out in order to get rid of me, or if he truly thought I was a good candidate for the job. He came to dine at the hotel almost every evening, and I had many chances to ask. However, I did not want to rock the boat.

My first job was working as a clerk at the information center where someone had to be on duty around the clock. When I arrived, the office staff consisted of only five people: the manager and his assistant, who also served as supply sergeant and chief clerk; three clerks, who worked eight hours a day and seven days a week; the kitchen staff, which consisted of a mess sergeant, one cook and one baker. However, the mess sergeant, baker, manager, assistant manager and one of the clerks were nearing the end of their military service and had earned enough points to return home as soon as transportation was available.

Our commanding officer was First Lieutenant Benjamin Johnson, who had the responsibility of three hotels: the first three hotels to open in Tokyo for women civil service workers. Johnson also had accumulated enough points to go home and was just waiting for transportation.

The rest of us had not been in the Army for long and did not have many points of which to speak. So, we were honored by serving another year. Private First Class Aubrey Weiss was a cook and Corporal Dave Rosenberg was one of the clerks. They had helped open the hotel and were in line for the first promotions, but I had a few more points toward returning to the United States. I had received extra points for being a combat veteran and for earning a Combat Infantryman's Badge.

When I first started working at the hotel, I was instructed not to allow any unauthorized person upstairs. I was also told that sometimes the electricity would go out, and whenever it did, it would be my responsibility to light candles in the office and the lobby. If the electricity was off for more than fifteen minutes, I was supposed to go outside and start a diesel engine to generate the electricity. In addition, I was supposed to check to see if anyone was stuck between floors on the elevator. Doing all of these things would have been next to impossible.

Well, one night when I was on duty, we had a blackout. A couple of guests, and some Army officers, were hidden by the darkness. Before I could get the candles burning, two officers made a mad dash upstairs. It sounded as if they were running from room to room, and I could hear women screaming *bloody murder.* What a disaster! And, I was the only one on duty.

I had to decide what to do next. I did not think that going upstairs in the dark and trying to chase a couple of guys downstairs was going to help. I figured starting the diesel engine was what was needed the most. I tried to crank it up for about twenty-five minutes until the lights finally came back on. However, I was never able to start that engine.

Two or three days later, I was called to the office. The Battalion Commander, Major Lance Hudson was present; sitting on one side of him was Johnson, the officer in charge at the hotel; and sitting on the other side was a captain whom I had never seen before. Hudson chose not to introduce us.

Then, he pounced on me with all fours for allowing unauthorized people upstairs on the night of the blackout. I thought he was never going to shut up. It looked to me as if he were trying to impress the captain. Johnson looked uncomfortable as he kept his eyes cast to the floor.

After Hudson wound down, he ordered me to pack my bags; I was being transferred. When Hudson had finished ranting, the captain had some things to say. That is when I learned that Johnson would be catching a boat home, and this captain would be taking his place at the hotel.

The captain came to my rescue, and requested that Hudson give me another chance and let me continue to work at the hotel. I think it was very unusual that a captain would intercede where a major had already given an order, but Captain Joyce Phillips was *no ordinary officer.*

Management Changes

Johnson's departure was just the first of several. In addition to Phillips, we soon had three new noncommissioned officers in charge. When the mess sergeant caught a boat home, the occupants of the hotel formed a committee and requested that a woman be appointed to supervise the kitchen and plan the meals. Although the food was prepared well, they wanted to be involved in planning menus, and how the meals were served; in short, a woman's touch was sorely needed, according to them.

Their wishes were granted and Betty Brown, a civilian and a staff member of the Red Cross, was chosen to replace the mess sergeant. This proved to be one big disaster! The problems that she created were so many that the staff at the hotel got together and asked our new manager, Rosenberg, to request a meeting with Phillips to see if she would intervene and set things back on the right track. Our request was to have Betty replaced with an Army mess sergeant.

Our big problem with Betty was when the inspection teams came; Betty did not understand what her role was. She would point out to the team all the flaws that she could find and was always complaining about the Japanese help and how they would not follow her orders. She just did not comprehend the nature of Army protocol and was constantly getting the kitchen and mess hall gigged for things that had never happened before.

Getting the Japanese workers to understand and do things the Army's way was a problem with which we all had to deal. The kitchen staff had never had any problems passing inspections before Betty came, but now things had changed, and we needed to get back to doing things the usual way. Betty was not a bad person, but she just did not have the slightest idea of what she was doing. She really did not have a chance since she had never been in the military.

There was one thing I took a lot of heat over. I had worked a little deal to get Betty a private room. It just so happened, that the same day Betty was to move into the hotel, one of our occupants was vacating one of the few private rooms.

Well, I had this idea! If Betty was going to be one of the staff members, then getting her a private room only made sense. Looking out for each other was the way it was. However, my orders said that when someone moved out, the room had to be listed as vacant. Headquarters would then post a notice at all the appropriate places to notify all interested parties, so they would have a chance to bid on the room. The person with the highest civil service classification would get the room.

It was common knowledge, among the women living in the Surugadai (YWCA), that this room was up for grabs. In addition, they were eager to bid for it! This is the only time I ever asked to bend the rules, and this is what happened.

One of our occupants worked as a secretary for the officer who made the room assignments. I had a good working relationship with both the secretary and her boss. I asked the secretary to ask her boss if I could sort of forget to list the room as vacant and allow Betty to move in.

Well, the answer came back that he could not authorize it, but everybody makes mistakes now and then. That was good enough for me, and Betty got the private room. However, the women that were planning to bid on the room were madder than a nest of hornets, because the room was never listed as vacant. And, they certainly kept their stingers out for a good while.

After Betty's meeting with Phillips and Rosenberg, they discovered that she wanted to go back to work for the Red Cross. Betty was more than happy to get her old job back, I was happy to get the hornets off my back by listing Betty's room as vacant, and Weiss was happy to be appointed as the new mess sergeant.

When the war was over, tremendous pressure was put on our leaders to bring the men and women home immediately! Of course, this could not be done within a few days. However, in hindsight, the situation was handled very efficiently. Some just had to stay for awhile, and every civil service worker who took an overseas job, allowed one more serviceman to return home.

With the military personnel being sent home soon after the war, nineteen-year-old soldiers were quickly placed into responsible positions. With all the older men going home, we had no choice, but to step up to the plate. Whenever I reminisce about the three young noncommissioned officers—Rosenberg, Weiss, and yours truly, and how we became a very effective team in managing the YWCA, it still boggles my mind.

I'd certainly like to be a fly inside that staff car
and see how Sippora wiggles her way out of this one!

The Missed Opportunity

The first week after I had been assigned to the staff of the Surugadai, Jack Carr, the manager, called me into his office for an orientation session. He was an older guy, with almost enough points to board a ship home. After the session was over, he told me to go upstairs and talk to the woman living in *Room 308*; she thought she recognized me from back home.

Having never been upstairs before, I found the room without any problem. The woman opened the door immediately when I knocked. She came out into the hall, extended her hand and said, "Well, hello! I'm *Sippora Finkler*, and I already know who you are! You are that nice young man who has just started working at the front desk!"

She continued, "Of course, I never knew you back home. That was just my way of getting you up here, so I could talk to you."

Sippora was correct about my being young, but I had enough *moxie* to know that she had something up her sleeve. And, I needed to be very careful. Slightly past middle age and dressed to the nth degree, she had a stocky figure and was considerably overweight around the hips. Sippora did not waste any time in telling me her problem.

"Honey, this old room is so drab and the furniture is so tacky and uncomfortable. I'm just so unhappy living in such miserable conditions! Now, I can tell that you are such a fine young man and will be willing to help me. Oh, I will appreciate it so much. There are a couple of rooms with some furniture that would make my room much more bearable, and all I'm asking you to do is just exchange the furniture for me. Now you *will* do that for me, won't you, honey?" she said.

"Yes Ma'am*,"* I answered, "Just as soon as I can check with the manager to see if it is okay."

Well, I had never heard a *honey mouth* turn into a *dirty mouth* so fast! In a split second, Sippora was spewing four-letter words at me with the rapidity of a machine gun. If the ladies back home used such language, I had never heard it; for sure, she did not earn any brownie points with me. I had never ever imagined being cussed out by a woman. She ended her little tirade by screeching, "Oh, *you* are just like all the others working at this hotel!" Then, she slammed the door in my face.

Steaming, I went back to the information center, and Jack motioned for me to come into his office. "How did it go?" He asked. "Did you *really* know Sippora?"

"Never seen her before," I answered. "And, I hope I never see her again!"

"Oh, you will see *plenty* of Sippora before you ship out," Jack assured me.

I was quick to tell him everything that had happened. All at once, Jack leaned back in his chair and roared with laughter! I could not imagine what was so funny!

After he finished howling, he admitted that he knew that Sippora was lying about knowing me and that he knew *exactly* what she would ask me to do. As he put it, "It was a good opportunity for me to see how an infantryman would handle the situation. So, just consider it part of your training for your new job." Then, he gave me some background information about Sippora.

"She's a high flouting lawyer, straight out of Washington, D.C., and she is a pain in the neck! If possible, avoid her. If she comes to the information center, treat her as the other guests, but don't ever make her a promise to change her room," Jack told me.

"Sippora has the best room in the hotel, but she thinks the room stinks, and it is not good enough for her. She fully expects to be able to go around to each room and scavenge any piece of furniture that catches her fancy right out from under the other women," he continued.

I soon learned that Sippora had two colonels courting her. She alternated dates every other night. The other clerks and I had a scorecard and kept record to see how long this arrangement would last before both colonels came in on the same night.

The communication system at the hotel consisted of one telephone per floor. The phone was located on a small table in the entrance hall. It was necessary for the residents to call the information center in order to place a call. Most of the time when we called upstairs, no one would answer, but the phone was used frequently for calling out. When we received an outside call, we would check the line for the designated floor and connect it if the line was not in use. A runner would notify the lucky person to answer the phone.

When someone came in person to the hotel and wanted to contact a friend, this was how the system worked: First, the guest would come to the information center and give their name and whom they wanted to contact. We filled out a small form with a place for the visitor's name, the person he or she wanted to contact and the room number. Then, a Japanese girl would take the message to the respective room. At times the lobby would be crowded with people waiting for their friends to come down. This was especially true during the evening meal.

When Sippora's colonels came to the information center, both were exceptionally nice to the staff. Since Sippora was always late and kept them waiting for twenty or thirty minutes, they would sometimes come over and talk to us; most of the time they would stand near the elevator and wait. Sometimes when Sippora was later than usual, we would be asked to send a second message.

When the elevator came down and Sippora stepped out, the colonel for the night would bow, extend his arm, and they would do a grand march out to a staff car. Sippora, who was always dressed to the nines and usually wore black, was quite dramatic! She would stick her nose in the air and priss around as if she owned the joint while swinging her humongous hips that jiggled like a tub of Jell-O!

One night, Sippora was later than usual in coming down to the lobby. This was the big night for which we had been waiting! One of the colonels came in, and I sent his message to Room 308: "The colonel is waiting." After a few minutes, the other colonel came in, and I sent another message: "The colonel is waiting."

As previously agreed, I sent for the other clerks. And of course, we were all in the information center waiting with great anticipation! One of the colonels was standing to the left of the elevator and the other to the right. We could tell that the colonels were not acquainted with each other, and they both were becoming very impatient; Sippora was certainly taking her time!

Finally, she made her grand entrance. She bounced out of the elevator and immediately, both colonels bowed and offered their arms. Wow! Miss Finkler had really stepped into a mess this time. The colonels just stood there with confused expressions on their faces. After a few seconds, Sippora introduced the colonels to each other, then grabbed each by the arm and was out the door in a hurry. Well, the next thing we clerks wanted to know was *which* colonel would be bringing her home?

One of the clerks blurted out, "I'd certainly like to be a fly inside that staff car and see how Sippora wiggles her way out of this one!"

Jack overheard our jovial conversation and came into the office and asked, "Why are all three of you clerks standing here, and *what*'s so funny?" Jack had a good laugh when we explained how Sippora had painted herself into a corner and that we were dying to know how she was going to get out of this one.

Now Jack never missed an opportunity to talk about our problems at the Surugadai and this was no exception. He said, "You know, we have so many messes around here that need remedies; I suggest that you concentrate on finding solutions."

The all out war that Japan had been fighting had curtailed the maintenance at the Surugadai. The Army Corps of Engineers was working on the major problems: for instance, painting the exterior of the seven-story building, the plumbing and heating, and cutting a shoot into the basement where dump trucks could unload coal. Before the shoot had been cut, the coal had been piled on the ground and carried in one bucket at a time.

There were Japanese contractors, who had offices in the basement, and they had men working full time at the hotel. I do not know how the chain of command was organized, but Capt. Phillips usually gave the orders on the small stuff like interior painting.

Wet paint was just a way of life at the hotel. Although signs were displayed, there was usually someone getting paint on their clothing: most of the time, a coat sleeve. So, we kept a can of turpentine and some soft rags in the information center. When someone brushed-up against wet paint, they would usually come by and we would clean the paint from their clothing before the paint had time to set. It was just one of our many services.

Well, the telephone table on the third floor needed a paint job. The painters moved the phone over, placed it on the floor, painted the table white and displayed a big sign: *Wet Paint*. I could not believe what happened next.

Miss Priss Sippora Finkler came in from work, picked up the phone, and sat down right smack dab on that table to make a call. It's a wonder it didn't break! By the time she finished her conversation, the top of the table had been wiped clean and one of her expensive black dresses was saturated with paint. And, yours truly, the *Lucky R* was on duty.

Sippora did not even wait until she reached the office before screaming. She was already cussing up a storm when she stepped off the elevator. She screeched, *"Of all the stupid imbeciles, you must be the worst!"* She was also sprinkling in plenty of four-letter words as she continued to have a *hissy fit*! Her voice was so shrill, I thought my eardrums were going to burst. Thank goodness, we were fresh out of chandeliers.

I asked her *why* she was so upset. She turned around and flounced her big buttocks right at me and said, "This is what I'm talking about! You must be crazy to leave a freshly painted table in the entrance hall! *"*

"Ma'am, I didn't have the table painted. In fact, I didn't know it had been," I replied,

"*You* are on duty and *you* are supposed to know what goes on around here!" she snapped. "Get busy and clean this paint off my new dress!" The backside of her dress had solid paint where she had been sitting on the table, and it covered a large area.

"Ma'am, if you will go back to your room and change clothes, I will go down into the basement and get a gallon of turpentine, and then I will try to get the paint out of your dress," I offered.

"Not on you life! Just wet a rag and get started now!" she demanded.

"Ma'am, I'm not about to clean your dress with you inside it," I said.

Things only got worse; the vibrations from her shrill voice must have ruptured a blood vessel inside my nose. I don't recall her hitting me, but she might as well have. I must have blown my top though. For some reason, the right side of my nose started gushing blood. I headed to a downstairs bathroom and never did know what happened to Sippora's dress.

Since my nose had always bled easily, I was not worried. However, for some reason, the bleeding did not want to stop this time. After an hour, one of the clerks called the medics and a doctor came out. He removed a clot, and the red river finally stopped running. He asked me if I had plugged up the right side of my nose, and I told him that I had.

The Doc advised me, "Let it flow freely if it happens again, but I also think I can help you with your chronic nosebleed problem." Then, he got a cotton swab out of his bag and soaked it in a white solution. When he ran it up my nose and swabbed around, it hurt so badly that I actually thought I was going to pass out. I heard the Doc tell my buddy that the pain would not last long. Sometimes, good things happen in strange ways, because that day the Doc cured my career of nosebleeds.

As for Sippora Finkler, unless she had been wearing a rubberized girdle, I missed an opportunity of a lifetime. I could have had Sippora climbing the walls like a crazed turpentined cat from all the heat that would have been generated from a full gallon that would have been needed to clean all that paint!

The shock came when she introduced me as "Captain Ray."

Baby San

Baby San, who was one of my interpreters, was a very small woman and was probably in her fifties. Her face looked like it had been burned or scarred; in fact, her face looked like a bar of homemade soap after a day of hard scrubbing.

However, Baby San was a jewel in many ways. She was reliable, punctual, trustworthy and very focused and intense on whatever project we might be doing. I was fortunate to have her.

Although we worked closely together, Baby San remained a mystery to me. She did not talk about her personal life. I often wondered how the war affected her, but never asked. It was never expressed to me in words, but sometime I got the feeling she was trying to make amends for the bombing of Pearl Harbor. At least she did not blame any of Japan's problems on the United States.

In a way, it was as if she had a crow to pick with her own people. And, her willingness to go against tradition by wearing western attire and speaking up to the Japanese men was kindly rare. One such time was when we were having problems with the laundry service.

The Surugadai was merely one of several entities that was served by the GI Laundry. We were having a problem with this set-up—our people were running out of clothing before their clean laundry was being returned. In the meantime, we had located a Japanese laundry and thought we had our problem solved. Soon other units discovered the same laundry service, and we were back to square one.

One day, Baby San suggested we take the hotel jeep and pay a visit to that Japanese laundry. She insisted, "Wear shirt. No stripe." I argued with her about it, "If I'm caught out of uniform by the MPs, I can get into serious trouble." She shook her head. "Where we go, no MP."

Baby San won the argument, and off we headed to the laundry! I did not have any idea of what she had in mind. I just knew that she was a real *pro* at getting results with anything she attempted. As I drove, we saw miles of destruction and dilapidated buildings throughout this vast urban wasteland.

Nothing was standing except tall smokestacks and steel towers that supported their electrical system. Thousands of incendiary bombs had been dropped and burned most of the buildings. The steel towers had become so hot and molten that the weight from the top caused the tower to bend like a horseshoe. Both the tops and bottoms of the towers were touching the ground and most of the industrial section had met the same fate—reduced to mountains of rubble and ashes in the scorched city of Tokyo.

When we arrived to the laundry, Baby San had a conversation with the first person we encountered. Soon, we were on our way to meet the owner. Baby San was very animated at times, and that day she was at her best as she started her discussion with the proprietor. She reminded me of a choir director as she quickly moved her hands up and down. Although, she was not hitting any bass notes, her facial expression was very serious and determined.

I could tell by the tone of her voice, the swift choppy movements of her hands, and the expression on the owner's face that she was not just whistling *"Dixie"*. The shock came when she introduced me as "Capt. Ray."

Now, I realized the reason why she did not want me to wear my sergeant stripes. I had just been promoted! When she saw the shocked look on my face, she scowled at me and sternly spoke, "Shhh . . . Come! We inspect laundry. Act like you know what you do!" I followed along not understanding a word that was being said.

Her message must have been strong, because our laundry was delivered on time after that meeting. Their delivery system looked like a peddled motorcycle with a sidecar. Usually one of the employees delivered the laundry, but for some reason, the owner delivered one day. It just so happened that I was in our information center when he came in.

This guy totally went berserk! As his face turned beet red, he shouted in his staccato dialect and pointed at me. All I could understand was when he pointed at my arms and screamed, *"Sergento! Sergento!"* Then, he pointed at my arms and collar and continued to scream, "Capitan! Capitan!"

Well, we had excellent service until the owner made *that* delivery and then, things begin to get really dirty! In all probability, he was an officer in the Japanese army based on the attire that he was wearing the day we had inspected his business.

Things got back to normal, and once again, our residents were back to wearing stinky outer clothes. At least there was one bright spot. Along with cleaning the rooms and making the beds, the maids had additional duties. They hand-washed all of the female residents' lingerie. If it had been up to the regular laundry, the women might have started mooning people, because they would not have had any underwear.

Baby San

*He was always alone, and he usually looked
like he had been eating sour pickles.*

Do Not Disturb

I do not know what the stateside women who were living at the Surugadai had been promised, but I do know they expected to be put up in a Hilton Hotel as equal in quality to one in Washington, D.C. The Army only had three hotels available at that time for women, and half of our diverse mixture of guests were civil service workers from our nation's capitol.

Involved in the War Crime Trials, most of them were serving as lawyers, typists, and court reporters. Two of the court's security guards, who were ex-Wacs, were residing at the hotel. Their duties were to search the Japanese women who attended the trials. The other Surugadai guests consisted mainly of former military personnel. Most had come up through the war and had taken a civil service job in lieu of going home immediately.

Being crowded at times was only one of the problems. Having a private room was nonexistent among most of this group, and some rooms housed as many as seven women. For the most part, only community baths and toilets were available.

Oh, how the women hated the drinking water! Lister bags filled with tap water and treated with chlorine were placed on each floor level, which was the only place to get a drink other than the dining room. When one of the women needed water to brush her teeth, she would fill her cup to take with her to the bathroom.

One problem was getting the bags cleaned weekly and refilled properly with fresh water and chlorine. Cleaning, changing the water and adding the chlorine was a big job. The 40-gallon bags, which were made out of waterproof material, resembled a barrel when filled. Then, a five-foot frame was used to support the bags. There were four water faucets near the bottom of each bag that the women used to draw water.

Unless I was present to supervise the job, the Japanese help would just add water and the full amount of chlorine as if they had changed *all* the water. This was potent stuff!

Although the water situation was a bit of a challenge, the Surugadia was known for serving the best food in Tokyo. Each hotel guest was allowed to invite two friends per day to dinner. In addition to the guests, the hotel staff always had a number of friends that came plus the Japanese help was fed after closing time. It was not unusual to have a total of five hundred people dining at the Surugadai during the evening meal.

With all the contacts our guests made with the military personnel daily thru their work, dates, or friends dining at the hotel, a trend for unnecessary inspections evolved. For instance, the women from D. C. were prone to complain about their wretched living conditions and the military regulations that were most difficult for them to swallow.

One of the guests, who was a D.C. lawyer, did not like the Army's way of making up her bed! She would get her little Japanese maid and say, "Honey, let me show you how I want my bed made up from now on," and she would remove the GI blankets from her bed. Next, she would take one of her beautiful patchwork quilts and spread it across the bed, while instructing the maid never to tuck the quilt under the mattress. Then, she would give the maid some chocolate candy, just to help things along.

These types of situations seemed to occur daily, and I did not have the option of making exceptions. Carrying out Army regulations was non-negotiable. The quilt had to be removed, and the bed had to be made Army style. The maids were not pleased, and behind my back, they would stick up both their index fingers behind their heads and wiggle them—indicating *Ray San's a devil!*

Why did the beds and rooms have to be done a certain way? After all, these women were civilians. Since they were living in a military billet, they were also subject to military law; but, this also included having the same privileges as officers.

If the guest knew the right officer, she would ask him to intercede sometimes. Of course, the officer knew he could not change Army regulations. However, he would have an inspection, merely to pacify his friend.

I am not sure how I became the one to lead most of the inspections, but I suppose that Phillips might have made that call. Many times, the inspection team would pop-in. If an inspection team showed up unannounced at one of the other two hotels, we would receive a phone call, to *warn* us that an inspection was in progress. Naturally, we always returned the favor. This system worked well unless the team started with the Surugadai. In either case, I would be contacted and told to meet with the team.

It was unusual to have the same inspectors on a regular basis, and the number of inspectors varied each time. This is the procedure we followed: If the team consisted of more than one, the highest-ranking member would be in charge and first in line. When I arrived at the main office, saluting the team and stating my rank and name was the first order of business.

Phillips was in charge of the three hotels. In some cases, she would be at one of the other hotels and would need to be contacted. The team always waited for her. Her position was at the end of the line. By this time, the leader of the team would have informed me about what they wanted to inspect. The priorities were the living quarters, the kitchen and the dining room.

The mess sergeant was responsible for the kitchen and the dining room. When he was available, he would lead the team in this area. However, the inspection of the dining room and kitchen always came last. My job was to lead the team in all the other areas as requested.

Inspections! Inspections! And, *more* inspections! How were we supposed to have 157 beds ready for inspections by 10 o'clock each morning in addition to all the other things in the room? Let's not forget the dreaded white glove procedure. Any dirt or dust detected on the gloves would get us into trouble. To make the situation even more challenging, all the work was done by maids that had never been in the Army.

First, we hired four middle-aged Japanese women and assigned one to each floor. Each woman was given the rank of captain, and each captain had several maids to do the work. Next, I worked with Baby San and the captains to teach them what was necessary for the rooms to pass an Army inspection.

Sometimes I used the carrot, and sometimes I used the stick. And, sometimes I used the stick when I should have used the carrot. Sometimes I used the carrot when I needed to use the stick. I suppose at times, I deserved the display of index fingers sticking up behind heads, meaning—*Ray San's a devil!*

Some of our occupants worked the night shift and slept during the day. In order not to interrupt their sleep, I asked the general contractor, who worked full time at the hotel, to carve wooden signs. He then painted and lettered them in both English and Japanese—*Do Not Disturb-Women Sleeping.* I was so pleased with the quality of his work that I had him to make a double order.

One particular morning, the inspection team was about to arrive, and I had no idea where Baby San was. I was starting to panic! I didn't know what I would do without her. A slick operator who had saved my hide many times, Baby San was smart, with a mind that could think a hundred miles an hour! She knew the ins and outs of how to get things done. If she were ever afraid of anything or anyone, I never detected it.

The moment the team arrived, Baby San quietly and calmly entered the elevator and pushed number five. I asked the first question as I usually did, "Sir, do you have any preference where you would like to start?" While they were trying to decide, I would then say, "We could ride the elevator to the fifth floor and walk down instead of startin' on the second floor and climbin' the stairs." The answer was always, "Carry on, Sergeant." This was exactly what I needed to hear.

While I was doing the preliminaries, Baby San would be jumping off the elevator on the fifth floor. She would grab a hand full of those *off limit* signs, check each room and if it needed more cleaning, she would shut the door and hang a sign on it. By the time we reached the fifth floor, Baby San would be down on the fourth floor working her magic.

She would continue working the third and second floors. When my part of the inspection was completed, we would enter the dining room. There, I would introduce the mess sergeant, and he would finish the inspection. By the time I would get to my office, Baby San would be in there and give me *that* look like, "What took you so long!"

This procedure worked well and never failed, but it came *close* with a first lieutenant one day. I don't know where this guy came from. He just started showing up out of nowhere and wanted to inspect the living quarters.

He was always alone, and he usually looked like he had been eating sour pickles. It seemed like he had some kind of agenda, but I never could get a handle on it. I do not recall his finding anything wrong, but I always wondered if he was authorized to inspect our billet or not. It was odd that Phillips did not question him.

I will never forget the last time he inspected. When we got off the elevator on the fifth floor, his face turned red and he blurted out, "Sergeant, you think you're really smart, don't you!"

Startled, I replied, "I don't know what you are talkin' about, Sir."

"You know *exactly* what I mean!" he snapped.

"No sir. Please explain," I answered.

"You know *precisely* what I mean! Do you think I'm some kind of a fool?" he asked as his voice became sharper and more hostile.

Cautiously, I said, "I would never think an officer in the Army was a fool, but you need to explain what you're talkin' about."

"Okay! Those *cute* little signs hanging on the doors! I know and you *know* that there is not a person sleeping in each of those rooms!" he snarled as he glared at me and clenched his fists.

I was starting to get nervous and was thinking, "Boy, oh boy! This conversation is gettin' a little touchy. We are gettin' down to the nitty-gritty."

I was starting to wonder just how wonderful are those little signs? And, I was beginning to wonder just how far will *Lt. Sourface* go and if I will be able to fake him out.

"Sir, if you'll accept the responsibility, just tell me which doors to open, and it'll be done," I offered.

This guy was so hot that I thought he might set the place on fire! He was definitely one angry lieutenant. As he stood there speechless, his face turned ten shades of red. It soon became obvious that he was not going to pursue his objective any further. Without saying another word, either to Phillips or to me, he pivoted around, stomped off, got onto the elevator and left in a huff.

I never saw him again. If he is still alive, I wonder if he still remembers this incident. My guess would be, *definitely.*

Well, those magic signs worked once more. The only thing left to do was to tell Baby San to stop hanging them on so many doors!

Surugadai' Maids All in a Row and Sgt. Ray

*Whether you like it or not, you will be
spying on these people!*

Life at the Surugadai

During 1946, the *International Military Tribunal, Far East* was in session. Twenty-six defendants were on trial starting with Prime Minister/War Minister Hideki Tojo plus twenty-five of the highest-ranking military officers and government officials who were all being tried for War Crimes. The *Tribunal* consisted of eleven sitting judges whose names and countries are as follows:

Jaranilla (Philippines)
Northcroft (New Zealand)
Bernard (France)
Zaryanov (U.S.S.R.)
Mei (China)
Webb (Australia)
Higgins (U.S.A.)
Patrick (Great Britain)
McDougall (Canada)
Roling (Netherlands)
Pal (India)

It was extremely difficult to get a pass to observe the trial. Most of the military personnel stationed in and around Tokyo did not get the opportunity to see Prime Minister Tojo and his comrades. However, I was able to attend about anytime I wanted, because two of the female security guards who worked for the court, happened to live at the Surugadai. Sometimes the prosecutors would show films or pictures of war atrocities committed by the Japanese military. If my friends knew when the pictures were to be shown, they would pass the information to me. Then, I would just show up, and they would let me go inside to observe the proceedings.

The same number of Japanese as Americans was permitted inside to watch the trial. The Japanese were examined very carefully before they were allowed inside, and the two guards whom I knew, were responsible for the security checks of all the Japanese women before they could enter. I do not know if everyone who entered were searched or not. Since I did not have a pass and did not enter through the front door, I just walked up and the guards waved me by.

The courtroom was large, and we were required to sit near the back; each seat was equipped with a headset. It was very slow, really dull and difficult to follow, because everything had to be translated. One day of listening to translators was enough for me. I only attended whenever movies or pictures were being shown.

The times I watched the trial, the defendants showed no emotions whatsoever. Prime Minister Tojo, a short, balding man, who wore thick, horn-rimmed glasses, was on trial for atrocities committed under his command against American prisoners-of-war including torture, starvation, and cannibalism. Although he attempted to commit suicide by shooting himself, he was caught before his mission was accomplished, and was kept alive by American doctors.

The *Stars & Stripes* reported that a blood transfusion was given to Tojo by a sergeant, who was directly hooked up to him, in order to save his life. When most of us read about it, our anger shot up like "Old Faithful" in Yellowstone National Park. We were furious! However, we learned later the reason they wanted to keep Tojo alive.

If Tojo had been able to commit suicide successfully, he would have died an honorable death in the eyes of the Japanese. If Tojo had been put before a firing squad, that would have been considered a normal death for a military man who was convicted of crimes that carried the death penalty. However, hanging a military man is a dishonorable death. Tojo was convicted and executed by hanging.

During the trials, which were conducted near General Douglas MacArthur's Headquarters in the Dai Ichi Building, I would sometimes see MacArthur entering or leaving his office. Other times I would see him when I went with my buddies on our way to Ginza Street in downtown Tokyo to shop.

The times I observed MacArthur and the honor guards escorting him, I was thankful that I had been assigned to the Service Battalion instead. There was always a detachment of honor guards closely leading and following MacArthur's staff car. Whenever the entourage arrived, the guards would dismount first to clear and cordoned the street for security reasons and for crowd control, until the tall, flamboyant, media-loving, pipe-smoking MacArthur was safely escorted inside.

In a perfect world, we would not need law enforcement personnel. Since we do not live in a perfect world, we have international, federal, state, and local laws to bring the lawbreakers to justice. People choose to break the law for numerous reasons. Even in Tokyo, some Americans were breaching the law.

Early one morning, I was sitting in my office when two American civilians walked into the hotel. I could hear them ask the clerk, "Where can we find Staff Sergeant Dave Rosenberg and Sergeant Ronold Ray?" The clerk pointed to my office, and they barged right in!

One of the men, Sam was pint-sized with a baby-face—blue eyes, blond hair, and a fair complexion. He looked so innocent that he wouldn't even swat a fly. However, his looks were very deceiving. Sam was as cold and as hard as a steel ball. The other guy, Wilfred, was a large, tough-looking guy with a pro-truding chin, a ruddy complexion and a scar on his left cheek. I cannot remember his ever uttering a word.

But, the first words that erupted from Sam's mouth were, "Send for Rosenberg and get him here on the double!" I decided right then and there that I did not like Sam, and I certainly did not want to tangle with Wilfred. Being second in command has its advantages, and this is one time I was happy to let my boss, Rosenberg, deal with these two characters.

I sent a runner for Rosenberg and when he appeared, Sam took over the show. "We need to talk to you in private. Let's go in your office." As we did, Sam closed the door behind us. We had no problem in talking with them, but we sure did not like Sam's arrogance. Sam and Wilfred both flashed their credentials. Sam curtly announced, "We're FBI Agents."

Our attitudes were, "What the heck . . . what is this . . . we are in the Army." Well, Sam quickly pulled out a list of names from his briefcase, which included about a dozen of the women who were living at the Surugadai. "Do you know all these people?" He asked both of us. We knew most of them.

Next, he showed us a list of officers. "Do you know them?" Since we both had worked at the information desk as clerks before we had been promoted to management and all guests were required to sign-in, we knew most of the officers, too.

"Well, you need to memorize the names of every person on these lists and be able to recognize them," he informed us. "Your additional responsibilities effective *immediately* are to spy on them."

That is when good ol' even-tempered Rosenberg came unglued. He told them right to their faces, "We are *not* about to become stool pigeons!"

"Sure, you are," Sam smugly stated. I knew right then my gut feeling about Sam was justified. Rosenberg and I were in a Service Battalion and on detached service. Capt. Joyce Phillips, the officer in charge at the Surugadai, was not in at the time.

One heck of a discussion broke out between Sam and us. Tempers were flying off the wall! Wilfred stood silently and expressionless with his arms crossed as he blocked the doorway. Baby-faced Sam raised his voice, "Whether you like it or not, you *will* be spying on these people! You actually have no say in the matter."

Rosenberg decided to call our commanding officer, Major Lance Hudson at GHQ to report what was going on. Sam smirked and tossed his head. "Good. I thought you never would."

As he made the call, Sam whipped out his lighter and lit up a cigarette. After he sat down, he leaned back in the chair, propped his feet on Rosenberg's desk, and deeply inhaled before releasing a smoke ring the size of his head. To our dismay, Hudson told us that we would have to take orders from Sam. As much as we hated the idea of becoming stool pigeons, we fully understood the consequences of disobeying an order. We both wanted to end our Army careers with honorable discharges.

My career as a *stoolie* lasted about two months. I was not briefed on any of the results and have often wondered if the information that I had collected had helped or had hurt someone. In a way, I am glad I was never told.

Working at the Surugadai came with strict rules and was always a challenge, which is why I considered it the best job in Tokyo. Our occupants were all American women, who were civil service employees hired by the U.S. Government. Each civilian worker had the same privileges as a military officer. However, they were also subject to military law.

If they were billeted in a military hotel, inspections of their rooms were routine. One of the rules that applied to the eight to ten soldiers that were assigned to work at the hotel had to do with no fraternization. This rule was strictly enforced. We were not even allowed to eat in the same dining room with the occupants. Instead, we had our own private little dining room.

This rule proved to be a very good thing for us; we just told the Japanese chefs what we wanted and *pronto*, smothered steaks, with all the trimmings would be served! In addition, we could eat anytime between 5:00 a.m. and 9:30 p.m. What a deal! There was no more having to wait in long lines, having to eat an early breakfast, or eating only when the main dining room was opened.

The kitchen staff consisted of an Army mess sergeant, one cook and a baker, plus two Japanese chefs. With worldly experience, both chefs had worked at some of the finest hotels in Europe before the war and their daily cuisine was a mouth-watering delight. There were also many Japanese boys and girls working as waiters and waitresses, kitchen help, dishwashers, or whatever was needed to get the job done.

Since each person living in the hotel was allowed to invite as many as two guests for the evening meals, reservations were required two days in advance; the chefs needed to know how much food to prepare. The Surugadai not only prided itself on the finest food in Tokyo, but the invited guests were served in a huge, spotless dining room with a view of Mt. Fuji on a clear day, as well.

This was one place where both enlisted men and commissioned officers all dined together in the same room. I witnessed privates and generals sitting next to each other around the tables and all seemed to enjoy their meals and their girlfriends, of course.

In our private little dining room, we had as many guests as we wanted. Regulars were motor pool sergeants, sergeants of the guard, delivery guys, swimming pool inspectors, and people with whom we needed to maintain a good working relationship. In addition to the regulars, our close friends were welcomed.

The hotel received special rations in order to take care of visitors, so we were always fully stocked with food. Even the kitchen help was given complimentary meals. That was a real plus for them, since most of the Japanese were living on limited rations.

How did the no fraternization rule work? There were only two of us that were authorized to go above the first floor. The living quarters were located on the second thru the fifth floors. If I ever needed help for some task, it was permissible for me to take a clerk.

Now this rule did not mean we could not talk in the line of duty with the occupants. Of course, this happened every day. However, if we wanted to continue to work at the Surugadai, standing around visiting was a sure way to get a new assignment.

Regarding Sam, I realized he was just doing his job. Using such high-handed methods did not enhance his standing with us, but I think he enjoyed feeling important. So, why was he at the Surugadai and what was the problem?

Stateside newspapers were printing stories about the War Crime Trials that had not even been released by the military. The problem was to find out *who* was providing the information and *how* it was being transmitted. The people on the list of names that Sam had provided were all under investigation. Both lists were like a two-way street. It could be an officer having the information and his girlfriend as the recipient or vice versa. This is where my career as a stoolie came in.

Even with the rule of no fraternization, it was impossible not to have some sort of feeling for the people we were around everyday. We were all together occupying Japan and had been united in winning the war. I wanted the best for all of us, but I was not cut out for this kind of job. I hated everything about what I was required to do!

Just what were our orders? Well, Rosenberg or Ray would have to be present at the information center each day, starting at the beginning of the evening meal and remaining until the last woman was tucked into bed figuratively speaking. For recreation, the hotel offered movies, swimming in the Olympic-sized heated pool, dancing and a bar. If the women on our list stayed inside the hotel, our job was fairly easy. However, most of the time, the women went out on the town, and we were lucky if they all returned by midnight.

Rosenberg and I alternated nights unless one of us had something else to do. We never had a serious disagreement in the time we worked together, and trading nights was not a problem. We were given detailed instructions on how to fill out the nightly report which included keeping detailed records of their comings and goings and how the people on the lists interacted with each other. Then, we deposited the report into a lock box.

Determining how the suspects interacted with each other was the hardest part. Did he have his arms around her? Did she kiss him when she came down?

Did they have eyes only for each other? Did you hear any conversation? When did they leave?

Now when they returned to the hotel, we had to complete the list for that day. What time did they get back? What about alcohol consumption? Were they loop-legged? Were they overly happy or loud? Were they sick from too much drinking? How affectionate were they compared to when they left? If they were talking louder than usual, we were supposed to move near them and record their conversation. This really got to be a degrading job. I felt guilty every time I talked to one of these women.

In addition, we were ordered to rifle thru their rooms during the daytime for some sort of radio that could transmit a message, either code or voice. If we happened to see something suspicious looking, we were supposed to report it. After searching the occupied rooms, we then searched the unoccupied floors and even the roof.

Now Sam did not leave anything to chance. He provided us with an excuse in case we were suspected of searching rooms. "Put the blame on the Japanese maid and fire her immediately," Sam told us if there was a slip-up.

After about two months of snooping, Sam told us we could go back to normal duty. He did thank us for our cooperation. The extra hours we worked were bad enough, but the problems it caused among the staff were even worse. We were not allowed to tell anyone what we were doing, but spending so much time at the information center was highly unusual for us. This was very upsetting to the clerks. We lost a friend or two, but that was life.

I know they must have thought we were checking up on them. In more modern terms, it would be called micromanagement. Sometimes when things became really tense, I would tell the clerk to take a couple of hours off and the stress would go away. When the snooping was over, we were instructed not to tell anyone what we had been doing.

On one hand, I wanted to tell the clerks. On the other hand, I did not want the twenty to twenty-five people on Sam's list to know anything about it. Now when I look back, I suppose this was part of Sam's plan; he was protecting us. Out of a dozen irate women, at least one of them would have snatched us bald, not to mention the ten high-ranking officers that might have planned ways to retaliate.

The Occupation

Longing for Texas

Information Center 24-7

A new war was emerging, and my mind was becoming the battlefield.
Two opposing views were slugging it out,
and I could not stop the fighting.

Movie Madness

This story originates in Spearman, Texas in the late summer of 1944 while I worked in the wheat harvest. The story ends in Tokyo after the war.

Driving a tractor for Sam from sunrise to sunset was better than walking across a field of overgrown Johnson grass and stumbling over a big, juicy watermelon. I couldn't imagine anything better and considered myself very fortunate to have this job.

At five dollars a day, I was raking in the dough! Sam's mother even fed me dinner at noon. What great pay for that day and time! At least I thought so until a couple of my good friends, Gerald and Milton, went up to Spearman, Texas and were hired out for ten dollars a day plus room and board.

When I received word that I could double my pay by joining them in the wheat harvest, I was ready to catch the next bus to Spearman. Well, Dad had *something* to say about that. "Son, when you finish your job with Sam, you can take a job in the wheat harvest. But, you *have* given him your word," he reminded me.

So much for that idea! By the time I finished plowing for Sam, the wheat harvest was over, and I did not get the opportunity to make the big bucks. Gerald and Milton came home near the end of the harvest after a heavy rain. Milton decided not to return, so I went back with Gerald and worked for the same farmer in Spearman for eight dollars plus room and board per day. There, we scooped wheat out of one pile for twenty-one days and then, we plowed acres of land starting before sunrise until after sundown.

We were certainly in shape for the Army—our destination. I cannot remember if we received our notice to report for duty while in Spearman, or if we already knew the date at that time. Eventually, Gerald returned home, but I stayed for awhile longer. Stormy weather rolled in, and the fields were too wet for plowing; so, I had some free time. I decided to mosey into town and treat myself to a nice, cold, chocolate malt and check out the new movie. Although the sky had cleared, it was still sweltering at six o'clock that evening as I headed into town to see, *The Spiral Staircase*—a murder mystery, starring Dorothy McGuire.

In those days, most theaters showed advertisements, a cartoon, and the war news before the main attraction. As I sat in the theater waiting for the movie to begin, it occurred to me—this is probably the first time in my life I have ever felt totally alone. Well, *The Spiral Staircase* was about a serial killer who took advantage of women with afflictions, and one night the killer struck during a horrible thunderstorm. The movie was *spooky, spooky, spooky!*

This show scared the heck out of me, and that was just the beginning of what was to come. When I walked out of the theater, a severe electrical storm was in progress. The sky was now pitch black with cold rain pouring down and flooding the streets. Violent winds whipped trees around, and gigantic thunderbolts crashed to the ground. Of all nights to be wearing a short-sleeved shirt! Being caught out in the open in a North Texas storm is more than frightening. Although, it was only a mile back to the house, it seemed more like ten. I ran fast and furious to escape the electrically charged enemy. However, this was not my number one concern.

I was working for the Gibner brothers and was staying at the house of the brother who was a banker. Now it just so happened that Mr. Gibner and his family had left town for the weekend. His house was a large white-framed house with a basement, which is where my room was located.

The room was cozy with a comfortable bed, and there were some small windows just above ground level. Since the Gibners were gone, they left the backdoor unlocked so I could come and go as I pleased. And believe me, *go* was exactly what I wanted to do. But, where could I go?

Huge cedar trees overlapped the small back porch and when I finally got to the house, the violent wind was thrashing the tree limbs all over the place. I could sense *something* was waiting for the right moment to jump out and grab me! There was no porch light, and the inside light switch was positioned to where I had to come inside the house first, and close the door in order to reach around to flip on the hall light switch.

I was thinking, "If I manage to get past the trees, surely *something* has found the backdoor unlocked and will definitely be waitin' inside the house. And, it might wait until I go to bed and come down to the basement to get me!" An uncontrolled mind can certainly twist up one's thinking, especially at age eighteen. Well, it was one long night and daylight never looked better. What a relief when the Gibners finally came home!

Fast Forwarding to Tokyo

In 1945, when I was put on detached service working in Tokyo at the YWCA (Surugadai), I liked to have a little fun from time to time. My Commanding Officer, Captain Joyce Phillips was among the best in the Army Air Corps. Tall, and slender with light brown hair and a fair complexion, she had a pleasant demeanor and appearance as she wore her freshly ironed uniform each day. Phillips had been an old maid schoolteacher from Akron, Ohio and carried herself well with a quiet confidence. We generally got along great—that is, until I pulled one of my pranks. She just did not understand my sense of humor.

We were short staffed for a few months, so we had to work eight or more hours a day and seven days a week. In time, we received more equipment, more supplies, and more people. We even got GHQ to come and show a movie three times a week.

Major Lance Hudson from GHQ thought it was a waste of time to send a man out to run the projector. He thought it would be better to train a projectionist from the personnel who was already living in the hotel. Well, Phillips did not like the idea, but agreed to see if someone would take on the extra job. It just was not a good idea to say *no*.

Therefore, Phillips called her favorite and jack-of-all-trades—*me*. She suggested that I sit in the balcony for a week with the projectionist, and after a week, I could quietly decide if it would be too much of a burden to add another job to my busy schedule; some action was needed to satisfy the major.

There were many Japanese boys and girls, who were working at the hotel, and most of them were about my age. They were allowed to view the show only from the balcony and as long as they were not seen entering or leaving the auditorium. There was a passage from the basement to the balcony that they could use discreetly.

I never did figure out why the Japanese wanted to see the shows, because they could not understand the language. However, the balcony was always jam-packed, and the only American was the projectionist. I had never watched the shows from the upper floor, so this was a new experience for me.

Not needing another job, I paid more attention to how the Japanese were reacting to the different shows than actually learning how to run the projector. On the last night that I was going to be in the balcony, *The Spiral Staircase* was showing.

In the opening scene, there is an opened book on a table in an empty room. Very slowly the pages start to turn for no apparent reason. Then, there's this cat that suddenly arches its back with its tail in the air. All the hair on that tail is standing straight up and quickly, the cat lets out a bloodcurdling scream that sounds like a woman who is being strangled to death! When similar scenes appeared, there was a *shudder* throughout the audience.

The whole auditorium of people seemed to shiver or quiver or *something* like that. Now and then, the movie would just start whirling and rotating real fast, and all at once; an *eyeball* would jump right out at you! Unless you had already seen the movie, I guarantee this whirling eyeball would get anyone's attention! This scene caused more than a shiver or a quiver! I think a state of fear or fright might best describe it, and the music that sounded like a funeral dirge did not help matters.

All at once, this thought popped into my head! Why don't I have some fun out of this show? Why don't I run to my room real fast, and grab that ugly rubber mask that I purchased in downtown Tokyo? Without question, it was the face of the devil—red and black with two horns sticking up. Then, I can snatch a white sheet from the supply room, turn off some of the lights in the basement and wait inside a closet until the show ends.

Well, the show was about to be over, and the balcony moviegoers would be coming thru that hall in the basement very soon. I did not have a minute to waste and would have to hook-it to get this all set up; However, I barely made it in time! I fixed the lights, wrapped the sheet around me, put on that face and eagerly hid in the closet. I waited until some of the people were walking by, and all at once, I just walked out. I didn't say a word or anything like that.

I never dreamed this little prank would have the effect that it did; *Pandemonium broke out!* Of all the screaming and hollering taking place! I had never heard the like. They were running, and pushing, and falling down and others were running over them! You name it. It was happening!

Well, we had a tall, burly Japanese guard posted at the exit, which was used by the employees. So, here he came! He wanted to see what on earth was going on! By that time, I had jumped back inside the closet. All at once, I wondered what would happen if I walked out of the closet? How would he react? After all, he had *not* seen the show.

I knew the guard did not have a gun, and it was just too good not to try. I would give myself enough room to get the mask off if needed. So, I walked out of that closet and when he saw me, he dropped his billy club and ran like a jackrabbit!

I really missed the chance to put this one over the top. I could have returned the sheet to the closet, stashed the ugly face in my room, climbed up the backstairs and very quietly, slipped into my office. No one would have ever been able to figure out who was wearing the mask. And, the *Surugadai Ghost* could have been flittering around the hotel for years.

I knew the guards would be investigating, and I waited for them to come on down as they did routinely. I was thinking, "We'll have a big laugh when they see my costume and hear what had happened." Oh, we had a good laugh all right . . . until I heard the reason they were really there.

Then my amusement turned into, "Oops! Should've done the disappearin' act!" The sergeant, who was a good friend, told me that the people upstairs had heard the screaming and hollering while the changing of the guards had been in progress. Now, I was suddenly shaking in my boots when I learned that Phillips had been at the show and had sent the sergeant of the guard, with a couple of soldiers, to investigate what was happening in the basement and to report back to her immediately.

When Phillips found out who pulled such a stunt, she did not send for me. Instead, she retired to her hotel for the evening. I was not motivated to go upstairs just yet, so I turned in for the night. Well, the devil must have been after me! My dreams turned into nightmares as they were constantly inter-rupted by ghost and goblins floating by, pointing and yelling and making weird faces at me.

I would wake up and start visualizing my new assignment. Of course my new job would be standing guard at some lonely, out-of-the-way, scary guard post for the rest of my Army career. What a night! What would be my lot after this little escapade?

Early the next morning, Phillips requested my presence in her office. When I reported, I was also trying to read her mood. As usual, she was calm and in control, and her expression never betrayed her state-of-mind. She peered over her glasses at me and didn't say anything for a moment.

I was convinced that her clear blue eyes could see clear inside my brain, and she could always tell what I was thinking. She was a no-nonsense-kind-of-person, but unlike most of the officers, she was friendly. We felt at ease around her. That was one of the reasons I respected Phillips so much. She was comfortable with herself and wasn't trying to prove anything. She was not a stickler for the "spit and polish" stuff like most infantry officers were.

Phillips followed the standard pattern of building me up before getting down to brass tacks. "Sgt. Ray, you are among the best that I have ever com-manded, but for the life of me, I will *never* understand why you are always pulling pranks!" she began.

Phillips very firmly and quietly lectured me, "It's time for you to grow up and to stop acting like a teenager." (But, I *was* a teenager.) She did say some *other* things, too.

She pointed out that some of those things that I pulled were a reflection on her. The hardest part for me was knowing that I had worked hard and had been very loyal to Phillips; not only had I let her down, but I had let myself down as well. Causing her problems was the last thing I wanted to do.

It was, indeed, time for me to turn over a new leaf. For me, the war was over, and I was just waiting to catch a boat home. I would get up every morn-ing thinking about how wonderful it would be when I returned home to my family and friends. What great anticipation! I was going to have a normal life again.

During the sleepless night following the prank that had gone awry and had spiraled out of control, my head was cluttered with so many different thoughts and ideas. My mind was floating around like the white gulf clouds in which I had become so accustomed. I kept reliving and seeing our emaciated American prisoners-of-war as our trains pulled away from the depot, and I was reliving Okinawa again.

An unfamiliar thought kept surfacing—one that I kept trying to avoid. I was beginning to wonder about the future of the young Japanese boys and girls that I had known for almost a year. One girl had survived the bombing of Hiroshima; many of them had lost their fathers and brothers during the war, and the food rations for their families were meager.

A new war was emerging, and my mind was becoming the battlefield. Two opposing views were slugging it out, and I could not stop the fighting. The Japanese were becoming human beings in spite of the horrific images etched in my brain.

The township of Tokyo was so devastated from the bombings that it looked impossible to restore. However, most American civilians and military personnel were not very sympathetic, because the Japanese government had brought this down on their own heads. The sneak attack on Pearl Harbor and the atrocities committed against our POWs during the *Bataan Death March* were still fresh in our memories.

Knowing how the Japanese soldiers beat our sick, starved and wounded soldiers as they struggled to march the sixty-five mile course until it was impossible for them to go any further . . . until they collapsed, and how the Japanese would shoot, bayonet, dismember, behead . . . and even eat our soldiers, brought no sympathy from the Americans for the living conditions of the Japanese population. It was common talk that the Japanese were so barbaric that they ate the livers of American pilots. *Intense hatred* now occupied Japan.

Citizens poured into the Tokyo train station with hardly anything but the clothes on their backs, and with no place to go when they arrived. It was not uncommon to see children with swollen bellies caused from malnutrition. Nor was it unusual for some of the travelers to expire during the night. The future looked mighty bleak for Japan.

The people were not only frightened that night in the basement, but the bombings and burnings that had destroyed eighty-five percent of Tokyo was their reality. They were living in a personal hell, and here I was, dressed like the devil! For them, facing what appeared to be an impossible task of rebuilding their war-ravaged country, was a never-ending nightmare.

Sally came out of the office crying,
and we could see four fingerprints across her cheek.

And, Then Along Came Sally

When I met Sally Townsen, she seemed to be an easy-going person. A vibrant, attractive young woman with brunette hair and dark brown eyes, she was always friendly and had a pretty smile. She never caused problems for the staff and did not ask for any special favors. Sally, a veteran of the WAC (Women's Army Corps), had been overseas for two years and had been based on various islands in the Pacific.

As our military secured another island, the WAC would move forward as needed. When the war ended, Sally decided to take a civil service job, in lieu of returning to the United States. She was sent to Tokyo and was one of the first occupants to be housed at the (YWCA) Surugadai hotel.

Japan was in shambles, food was scarce and the water was polluted and unsafe to drink. One could not just run down to the corner drugstore for a hamburger and a coke or a much-needed item. However, some of the needs and services were available in the hotel. Receiving the occupants' laundry and returning it to them on time was one service and taking their beer requests and whiskey rations, requisitioning it and getting it to them was another. These were merely a couple of the many services we rendered.

Of course, most purchases were made at the PX (Post Exchange), but there was not one close by and taxis were non-existent. Free rides were available on Army buses that stopped by every half hour. Knowing which bus to get on or to get off and when to change buses could be fun, if you liked that kind of fun. In time, we got a small PX inside the hotel, which was a big plus. With all the interaction between the staff and guests, we got to know quite a lot about them.

One of the things that I learned was most of the residents always signed up for the beer and whiskey allotments; however, there were a few that did not. The ones that did not drink were usually approached by friends to sign up for their allotment and then sell it to them. This was the case with Sally. Her best friend, Wannita Sutton was a nondrinker, so she gave her alcoholic beverages to Sally. Sally managed her liquor just fine, went to work every day and never caused any problems until she received some unexpected news.

One day, Sally told me why she had taken the civil service job; she was very much in love with First Sergeant Clyde Teague. All of us on the staff already knew about their long-term relationship. Clyde was a friendly guy and came in almost every evening and dined with Sally. After the meal, they would go out or spend their time together at the hotel and take advantage of the activities offered there—swimming, dancing, watching a movie, or playing cards.

Clyde's plan was to take a civil service job, stay in Tokyo and marry Sally. She was floating on clouds most of the time. He was so devoted to her that he rarely missed more than one day without seeing her. And, whenever he strutted in with his wavy black hair, her face lit up like a Christmas tree.

However, there was a time that Clyde didn't show up for three consecutive days. Sally was so worried, she asked me to assist her in calling Clyde's company. All calls were free, but long distance calling required knowing the numbers of the different exchanges and the procedure.

After I was able to connect with his company, I handed the phone to Sally and vacated the office, so they could have a private conversation. Shortly there afterward, I could hear Sally sobbing uncontrollably. I walked back into the office to see what had happened.

My first thoughts were that Clyde had been involved in an accident, or maybe even killed. Sally was seated with her head on the desk and her arms around her head. She was devastated. Sally had just received word that Clyde had boarded a ship and was on his way back to the United States.

He had left a message with one of his friends to relay to Sally. "Clyde wanted me to tell you that he doesn't want you to *ever* try to contact him," he said. There was no explanation and no way to find him. Sally's world came crashing down around her, and she was unable to cope.

Her solution to the problem was the bottle. She began to miss work and was hospitalized several times. Her best friend Wannita stood by her thru thick and thin. Sally became very bitter and started giving the staff all kinds of problems. The change in her was almost unbelievable, and the problems she caused where many.

As the days and weeks passed, Sally became more and more distraught. Nothing seemed to matter to her anymore. She stopped eating regular meals and increased her drinking. The staff received the brunt of her anger, although we did our best to help her.

Sally knew about the *no fraternization* rule under which the staff served, and she knew that one little slip-up could get one or more of the staff demoted and transferred to some undesirable job within GHQ. I think she must have had this in mind when she pulled the following little incident.

During the evening meal, the dining room was crowded with people—perhaps, as many as three hundred at the time, which included the residents plus their invited guests. This was the busiest time of the day for the staff. Orders were for the manager and assistant manager to be present just in case we were needed.

I was visiting with Rosenberg when the telephone rang, and he answered. The caller, a resident living on the fifth floor, was in a panic, "Sally is headed downstairs to the dining room!"

"Well, what's wrong with that?" Rosenberg asked.

The caller answered, "The suit she's wearing."

He wanted to know, "So, what's wrong with her suit?"

"Uhhhhh . . . She's wearing her birthday suit!" the caller nervously replied.

Rosenberg called for Gloria, and we jumped onto the elevator! By the time we reached the fifth floor, Sally was headed downstairs to the fourth floor. Gloria was one of our interpreters. Her grandfather had been a British diplomat to Japan years before the war. His daughter married a high-ranking Japanese military officer. They had two children, and Gloria was the oldest.

When we caught up with Sally, Rosenberg's eyes bugged-out as he looked at me. I returned the look. He frantically said, "Well, do something!" I shot back, "The Army didn't teach me how to handle this. Besides, you've got one more stripe. *You* should know what to do!"

We tried to talk some sense into her as we jumped in front of her and blocked the stairway. However, nothing worked. Neither one of us wanted to make physical contact, and she continued to wobble past us down the stairs.

Soon, we were down to the fourth floor. We knew that we had to stop her from going into the dining room. We were both chickens, and didn't know how to handle the situation.

And, to tell you the truth, I was glad Rosenberg was the boss. Words were not working, and we had reached the third floor. If she got to the second floor and started downstairs, she would be in full view of all those people in the lobby!

I don't know what happened to our minds that day; we just couldn't think! Later, a friend asked me why we hadn't jerked a blanket off a bed, so we could have each grabbed an end, wrapped her up and taken her back to her room? What a simple solution to the problem. I wished I had thought of that.

In the meantime, Gloria had disappeared without saying a word. We thought that maybe it was too embarrassing for her to stick around. Wrong! She returned with a wet, rolled-up bath towel and was holding both ends of the towel in her right hand. With pure determination written all over her face, thru her clenched jaws, Gloria hissed, "Sally Townsen . . . Go back to your room this instant!"

Sally gave her a good cussin' and screamed, "I'm not taking orders from any low-down Japanese!"

She continued weaving and teetering down the stairs. What happened next was really shocking. Without saying another word, Gloria smacked Sally right across her face with the wet towel! Sally fell backwards and landed spread eagle on the floor.

Sally tried to get her balance, then slowly stood up and swayed for a moment. She started screaming every despicable name she could think of to Gloria. With daggers shooting from her eyes, Gloria popped her again!

Sally fell backwards for another hard landing. However, this time she decided to escape to her room. Gloria probably didn't weigh much more than a hundred pounds, but she had a *wicked* right arm. And, I know two soldiers who found out that she was very powerful with words. She did not use foul language, nor did she mince words in telling us what *pantywaists* we were.

It might seem strange to some that we allowed Gloria or Baby San the leeway to speak their minds, even when directed toward us. The fact is, we had to use an interpreter every single day; we needed to know why, where, what, when and how to deal with the Japanese employees. Their culture was so different from ours; we needed someone who understood why we were failing to get the desired results in certain areas.

In other words, we needed a teacher and an interpreter all rolled into one person. Therefore, we allowed them the freedom to say what was on their mind. It was about learning to trust each other. Of the several interpreters employed by the hotel, Gloria and Baby San were the only ones in which I was able to develop this kind of relationship.

In the Japanese culture, the women did not speak their mind to the men. Even when the words were mine, it took a lot of courage for Gloria or Baby San to speak the words. Although, I sometimes asked them to speak frankly, they were not used to talking to men in that manner.

How was Sally doing? Not so well. By this time, Sally was so deep inside the bottle that it looked impossible for her to climb out. She had lost so much weight that her clothes just hung on her. Her personal hygiene had slipped to an all time low. It didn't look as if she ever bathed or washed her hair anymore. And, her hair hung in greasy strands around her face.

She no longer wore her make-up. Her bloodshot eyes, with the dark circles underneath, looked so sad— as if she didn't have a friend in the world. When I allowed myself to think about how Sally had been so attractive with a vivacious personality compared to the condition she was presently in—it was beyond my comprehension. I had never been around anyone with such a serious drinking problem.

It must have been around midnight when I heard a frantic knock on my bedroom door and a voice, "Sgt. Ray, you're needed on fifth floor. They're fighting up there!" I quickly jumped into my uniform and ran to the elevator. I was not told which room, but that was not needed.

I knew Sally was on the rampage again. By the time I arrived, the fight was over. Sally's best friend, Wannita, was holding her by the arm and the other party in the fight was only interested in protecting herself.

Sally's drinking problem had become so great that she was always running out of liquor. She would beg others for a drink, but was running short of friends who would share. Her next method was to steal it.

One of her friends, Edie, had caught her appropriating her booze and told her if she did not stop, she would be reported. In Sally's mind, Edie was wrong for not giving her a drink, and she was justified in taking it. At the time, I needed some help in understanding this kind of *twisted* thinking.

In her mixed-up mind, Sally allowed herself to keep brooding about the imagined injustice in which her friend had threatened her. Edie was a small woman with long, shiny, blonde hair. Sometime during the night, Sally decided to get even with her. She waited until her roommates were sound asleep before she made her move. Quite as a mouse, she crept to Edie's bed. Very carefully, she wrapped those long locks of blonde hair around her hands. Edie must have been a heavy sleeper, because she did not wake up.

All at once, Sally jerked her out of bed by her hair! When Edie hit the floor, Sally began kicking her and anything else she could do. What a shocking experience for Edie! I am sure she thought that someone was trying to kill her. How could she have thought of anything besides trying to save her life? Well, Edie fought back like a tiger! Sally, in her condition, was easily over powered. When Edie realized that her attacker was Sally, she ended the fight.

Now, it fell my lot to deal with the aftermath of the storm. I sent two messages down to the night clerk. First, I instructed the clerk to call the sergeant of the guard and request that an extra guard be sent to the hotel immediately. Second, I instructed the clerk to call an ambulance.

Next, I talked to Sally and her roommates and told them that it would be up to an hour before the ambulance would arrive. Since this was not an emergency, we would just have to wait our turn. The part about Sally staying in the room did not go over well with her roommates.

They wanted me to take Sally down to the office to wait there for the ambulance. My mind kept flashing back to the day Sally decided to come down to the dining room wearing nothing but trouble. I was not able to cope with that situation, and I sure did not want Sally running around the hotel now in her thin, tattered, blue nightgown! Within minutes, the sergeant of the guard arrived with the extra guard. When I explained the situation to the sergeant, he ordered the guard to secure the door.

If I was ever going to feel sorry for a young soldier, this was the time. Most of the rooms on the fifth floor shared the community bathroom, so it was necessary for the resident to leave her room if she needed to go. Well, Sally decided she needed to use the toilet. This young guard kept looking at me, and I kept shaking my head, meaning, *no, no, no!*

Sally really knew how to put a guilt trip on this young guard. He finally stopped looking at me and started looking at the sergeant of the guard for relief. But, the sergeant told him to continue securing the door. Sally continued to beg, plead, and throw a fit until the ambulance driver arrived. The young guard was so flustered that he looked as if he might break down and cry.

After I explained the situation to the ambulance driver, he wanted to talk with Sally. The guard gladly opened the door, and I introduced Sally. By that time, she had changed her tactics. She was stretched out on her bed and didn't want to talk. When the ambulance driver told her that he was taking her to the hospital, she reacted violently.

Extremely upset, she kept telling us the hospital was the last place in the world that she wanted to be. Later that morning, I understood the reason why. The ambulance driver continued talking to her, and she kept saying she would not go. The driver indicated that he wanted to talk to me in private, so we moved outside the room.

"Sgt. Ray, I can't transport Sally to the hospital unless you go with me. You see, the lock is busted on the back door of the ambulance. So, I need you to go to restrain her in case she tries to jump out," he explained.

It was at that moment that I stopped feeling sorry for the young guard and started feeling sorry for myself. I said, "I won't be able to go with you." Then, I saw the frustrated and confused look on his face.

I am thinking, "What will I do with Sally if he doesn't haul her off? I will *still* have to deal with her." I was caught between a rock and a hard place. Then, I realized I did have an alternative. "Give me a few minutes. Let me see if I can get someone else to go with you," I said. "I'll be right back!" I asked the guard to let me back into Sally's room, so I could talk with Wannita.

"Wannita, the ambulance driver needs someone to go with Sally to try and keep her calm. I was wonderin' . . . since she's your best friend if you'd be willin' to ride in the ambulance with her. He's concerned that she might try to jump out."

Wannita panicked, "No! I can't believe you would even ask me to do that! I mean, Sally *is* my friend . . . and I know she needs help. But, what happens if she is admitted into the hospital? Then, I would have to come back all alone with an ambulance driver that I don't even know! And, that . . . well, that hospital is clear across Tokyo. No! I just wouldn't feel safe, Sgt. Ray!"

I sat there feeling ashamed of myself as I thought about what Wannita had just told me. "Now, don't get me wrong. I do want to help Sally. I'm very concerned about her," she added.

Things got quiet as we both were trying to think of a solution. I was really feeling like a jerk. I had been thinking only about getting Sally to the hospital, and I was asking someone else to do something I was unwilling to do. On top of that, I was asking her to compromise her safety. Thankfully, she didn't hold it against me.

"I know! Maybe you could go, too. That way, I could be there for her and then, you would be with me when we come back. I would feel much safer that way," Wannita suggested. "Would that work?"

Wannita had gone to the hospital with Sally before, and had already gotten out of bed and gotten dressed to go this time. She just wasn't expecting to go alone in the middle of the night. So, we decided that it would be best if we both went.

The ambulance driver was an impatient man. He acted as if he had ants in his pants. He growled, "Come on. We're runnin' late. Let's get this show on the road!" He positioned the stretcher along the side of the bed. "Come on Sally. Get on."

She screeched loud enough to wake the dead, "You *know* where you can go! I'm not about to leave this bed, and I'm not going to any stinkin' hospital!"

It was a repeat performance, both ways. His voice level increased and Sally's vocabulary decreased. The next verse was, *"Sally, either get on the stretcher, or we'll put you on it! "* He barked.

No response from Sally. She crossed her arms and her body stiffened.

"Sally, we're going to put you on the stretcher, and if you get off, we'll wrap you in a blanket and strap you down!" The driver yelled like a drill sergeant.

No response from Sally.

"Sgt. Ray, grab Sally by the hands, while I grab her by the heels—we'll just swing her off the bed and onto the stretcher. We need to get crackin'."

Mission accomplished! I was relieved when Sally stayed on the stretcher. I just could not see myself helping the guy roll her up in a blanket. We carried her down four flights of stairs without a mishap, and were soon loaded and on our way to the hospital.

Sally did not have much to say during the forty-five minute ride. Wannita kept her fairly calm as she talked to her. After, we carried her into the lobby, the driver firmly said, "Stay on the stretcher until the doctor calls for you."

When Dr. Fenton came out of his office, he asked, "Sally, are you able to walk?" She stood up, but was a bit tipsy. "Come into the office with me then. Let's talk and see what we can do." We were seated nearby and could hear the conversation. The doctor was asking Sally some questions, but she wasn't cooperating.

She wanted to tell the doctor about what had happened to her on the way to the hospital. Her story went something like this —"I just can't figure out what happened to me on my way to the hospital. When I left my room, I was wearing a beautiful, pink negligee. Now, look at this ratty, old gown I'm wearing. Doctor, do you have any idea how this could have happened?"

When Fenton asked her another question, she did not answer. She kept going on about her beautiful, pink negligee and kept wondering why she was wearing an ugly, blue nightgown. We heard a sharp slap. Fenton said, "Sally, I am not going to listen to any more of your stories! Now get back on the stretcher."

Sally staggered out of the office crying, and we could see four finger-prints across her cheek. I didn't think the slap was called for, and Wannita was clearly upset. I could see the tears in her eyes.

My mind flashed back to the Sally I once knew as she got onto the stretcher. I think I was getting a taste of what the real world could be like. I knew that war was hell, but I had never imagined how a life could crumble so quickly! I could not, readily, shake the two images that raced across my mind.

Sally got back on the stretcher. Fenton looked at the driver and me and said, "I need you to carry her inside." He had several keys on a ring and used one to open and close the first door. This procedure continued. For some reason, I just did not like the idea of being locked-in.

When we reached the fourth door, I asked, "Dr. Fenton, why are you locking all the doors behind us?"

He replied, "This is the Psyche Ward."

We left Sally in a small cell about six-by-eight feet with a concrete floor which was located toward the center of the room. The only thing in the room was a small, thin mattress. It reminded me more of a cage; there was no privacy and bars were on all sides with a door on one end. I didn't see a toilet anyplace.

Fenton explained, "Sgt. Ray, the reason we lock the doors is for security purposes. In case one of the patients manages to get out into the hallway, the patient would be contained to a small area."

I felt like I could finally breathe again when we got back to his office. Before I could leave, Fenton scratched his head and said, "Look, I realize it is getting late, but I really need to talk to you." Although he was a doctor, he was also an Army captain. Therefore, we went into his office, and I listened.

Fenton said, "Sgt. Ray, I need to discuss a couple of things with you. The first, of course is about Sally. Here's the deal. The Army doesn't have a suitable place in Tokyo for a patient like her. She shouldn't be kept in a Psyche Ward." He reminded me, "Sally has been in the hospital several times as you are aware, and really all I can do for her is to sober her up, release her and send her back to the hotel."

Fenton continued, "She's losing ground each time, and if she hasn't hit bottom by now, she is close. Sally desperately needs help, but the kind of help she needs is only available in the United States. I cannot stand by and watch Sally go down the tubes when help is available."

"But, I have a plan. The plan depends on Sally and you."

I sat there puzzled with what he was suggesting. I could not imagine what I had to do with his plan. I tried not to yawn.

"First, Sally is a civilian, and she will have to agree to the plan. But, even if she doesn't, we need to do what we can to give her a chance. The first problem is her civil service job. She has not worked for weeks, but apparently her boss does not want to take any kind of action. My understanding is Sally has a government contract."

"If we can break her contract, then she will be sent back to the United States. Since she is an Army veteran, she is eligible to receive treatment at an Army Rehabilitation Center. And, I can arrange it for her. All she has to do is agree to go."

"Dr. Fenton. That sounds great, but I don't understand what this has to do with me," I inquired.

"Now the other thing I need to discuss with you, Sgt. Ray, will involve your participation. There have been some very explosive situations with Sally at that hotel. So far, you have been fortunate, but eventually your luck will run out. Believe me . . . the staff, Capt. Phillips and you will be in serious trouble if something bad happens. And, you also have a responsibility to protect them and yourself."

I still was not sure what he was getting at. I couldn't control Sally. No one could. What was I supposed to do?

I defended the staff and myself, "Well, Dr. Fenton, we've been doin' the best we can for Sally."

However, Fenton shook his head. "Sgt. Ray, I couldn't disagree more. You and the staff are failing to do the *right* thing for Sally, and you are failing to protect yourselves."

"What more can we do?"

"Send Sally back to the United States for treatment. All you need to do is sign an affidavit which will be needed to break her contract." "Now wait a minute, Doc! I'm only the assistant manager. You need to talk to the manager," I insisted, while doubting I had the authority, and at the same time, wanting to dodge the bullet.

"I will check it out and see if you have the authority. Capt. Phillips has already talked with the manager, and he doesn't want to get involved."

"I don't understand. Why not?"

"Because Sally will know who signs the affidavit and will be entitled to a hearing if she chooses. She will also be able to ask questions, and have the right to face her accusers in an open hearing."

"Who else will be signing the affidavit?"

"Capt. Phillips and I will be signing."

I wanted to know more details. How long would Sally be in the hospital? When would she be sent home? Where would she be in the meantime? How long would she spend in the cell where we left her?

Fenton was very patient in answering my questions. He said, "I will hold her in the hospital for about twenty-one days. That's about how long it will take to arrange her transportation. Right now, Sally is physically and mentally, stressed to the limit. I would like to see her improve in both areas before releasing her to go home. As soon as she sobers up, she will be moved to a cell with a bed and toilet, but she will remain locked-in. She will receive a special diet, and I will do my best to counsel her."

After he answered my questions, Fenton asked, "Now, will you sign the affidavit if you are authorized?"

Squeamishly, I replied, "I want to think about it, and talk with Capt. Phillips first."

Fenton told me, "I understand. I don't want you to sign unless you believe it's the right thing to do."

By this time, the only things moving around outside were the hoot owls. On the trip back to the hotel, Wannita wanted to talk with me. She had heard snatches of the conversation between Fenton and me. She wanted me to fill her in on all the details. "Sgt. Ray, I want you to know what a good friend Sally is, and I only want the very best for her. If I need to, I will get down on my knees and beg you to sign that affidavit right now, so Sally will be sent back home where she can receive the proper treatment. Please tell me you will sign it," she pleaded.

"I need to find out some more details first, Wannita," I replied.

After getting back to the hotel, I crawled back into bed, slept a few hours, got up, showered, and had a big breakfast of sausage, eggs, toast and jelly with a large glass of milk. Phillips was already in her office.

She had an open-door policy, but it was always best to ask. "Capt. Phillips, I need to talk with you."

"Come on in, Sgt. Ray. Have a seat. I have already heard about Sally being admitted to the hospital."

She sighed and shook her head. Then, she took a sip of her coffee. "I have a copy of the affidavit on my desk. I've already spoken to Sgt. Rosenberg, but he doesn't want to get involved," she said.

I hesitated, "I'm not sure I want to either. What do you recommend?"

"Well, let me go over the affidavit with you first, so you will have a better understanding of what Dr. Fenton is asking you to do," she calmly said. As the schoolteacher emerged from within Capt. Phillips, she thoroughly explained all the parts in detail. I felt better educated on the matter at hand, and even felt like I could've passed a test with flying colors.

After she answered all my questions, it was time to make the decision. I asked for a pen and the affidavit. After I signed, Phillips confidently said, "I know it probably feels distasteful to do this, but something has to be done. This really is the best decision for Sally."

I started feeling nervous about having to face Sally in an open hearing and having to answer her questions. It became a constant worry and my first thought each morning was, "Will this be the day?" However, I was never called to appear. My best guess is that the doctor convinced Sally to sign some papers and forget about a hearing.

Sally showed up right on schedule. Her days in the hospital must have been good, because her appearance had dramatically improved. Her schedule was to spend two nights with her friends, get her personal things packed and ship out on the third day. She had agreed to refrain from drinking any alcoholic beverages until after she shipped. According to Wannita, she kept her promise.

On the third day, the bellboy moved her suitcases down to the lobby, and Sally began to tell the staff and the Japanese help 'good-bye'. She asked Wannita to go to my office and see if she could arrange a time when she could come down and talk with me. She had lost her chance by not having the hearing.

The time was set and Sally came down mid-afternoon. I closed the office door, we sat down and I listened. She was angry, but in control of her emotions. I think she had rehearsed over and over in her mind what she wanted to say.

I listened, never interrupted, and allowed her all the time she wanted. It was not a pleasant experience. The last words she said to me in her parting shot, "Of *all* the ones working here, I thought you would've been the *last* one to do what you have done!"

I got out of the chair feeling a sigh of relief and the weight of the world lifted from my shoulders. As I opened the door for Sally, I said from the bottom of my heart, "Sally, I hope things work out well for you."

The impact of Sally's story was my beginning in understanding that there is more than one kind of war going on in the world and society. I had been trained in the arts of military warfare where people face each other on the battlefield, but I had never been exposed to the kind of war that goes on inside a person's head. I was learning, at the age of twenty, that different people and Sally being one of them, were fighting a war just as much a reality to them, as the war in which I had been involved on the front line in Okinawa.

The war had changed us both forever,
yet we were still the same.

No More Lying

Keeping a seven-story hotel clean enough to pass an Army inspection proved to be a full-time job, but getting enough Japanese workers was not a problem. In addition to the military staff, we had a Japanese manager and his staff working full time. Having been a high-ranking officer in the Japanese army with difficulty of admitting defeat, the Japanese manager at the Surugadai was unfriendly, yet very efficient.

He was responsible for the hiring and firing, the Japanese payroll and all things related to the Japanese government. After the unconditional surrender, the United States put Japan under military law, but used the existing government to help administer the process.

The needs were the same as before the war; mayors, fire chiefs, policemen, city managers, and the usual people were still needed to provide services to the citizens. In addition, someone or an agency had to keep track of what our military confiscated. Items had to be invoiced, payments had to be made and accurate records had to be kept.

The Japanese manager at the Surugadai took care of those things for us. When we picked up items from a Japanese business, a requisition form was issued. Then, we filed a copy with the Japanese manager, and he took care of the rest.

One challenge was teaching the workers how to do things the Army's way. One of the problem areas was the large auditorium which had a balcony; it was used for church services on Sunday and for picture shows two or three times a week. The rest of the time, it was used as a lounge; so we moved the furnishings frequently. On Saturdays, the lounge was open until midnight. After that, the furniture and rugs had to be removed from the auditorium, the room had to be cleaned and the chairs had to be setup for church.

Capt. Phillips agreed to allow church services to be conducted in the auditorium if the chaplain could get a volunteer to rearrange the room. In a *weak* moment, I agreed. With the help of twelve young men, who were about my age, we could finish the job in about an hour. Soon after church services, we had to change the room back into a lounge. One good thing was we never had inspections at night or on Sundays.

The mess sergeant was responsible for keeping the kitchen and dining room clean. The gymnasium, which had been converted into a bar and dance hall, was managed by a crew who did not even live at the hotel. Opening, closing, collecting the money, and ordering the liquor was their responsibility. Since there was a shortage of liquor, the bar was closed part of the time.

The swimming pool and hot tubs, the basement plus most of the first and all of the second, third, fourth, and fifth floors were the staffs' responsibility. The cleaning crew for the pool, hot tubs, showers, restrooms, our part of the first floor and basement consisted of mature men and women. At first, I thought these crews would not need much supervision, but I was wrong. In fact, they were less eager to do things the Army's way than the maids and bell-boys were.

One morning, when the auditorium was setup as a lounge, the cleaning crew was sitting around doing *nothing*. When I asked *why,* they told me that they had finished cleaning. I had been having some problems with this particular crew, and I had a gut feeling that something was going on. Things looked fine on the surface, but they had not been working long enough to clean the room.

When I reached down and lifted up a rug, sure enough, dirt had been swept underneath. Well, this was one too many cover-ups for me! I decided to teach them a little lesson—one that I had learned in basic training. I told them to move the furniture and rugs against the walls. Then, I told them to get soap, water and government-issued brushes and scrub the floor on their knees.It was around 11:00 a.m. when Phillips came in and noticed that the room was not ready for inspection. She suggested that I meet her in her office at once. "Why?" was her first word. I explained the situation to her of how I had been having trouble with this particular crew and what they had done. I told her that I had, had enough and wanted to *show* them.

"What would happen if an inspection team came by and looked under the rug? Is it better to be in the process of cleaning a room or take a chance of someone finding filth?" I asked.

Phillips calmly and quietly informed me, "There *is* another option. Clean only under the rugs and be ready for the inspection." However, she did agree that teaching the crew a better technique was also important. And, they did improve after the dust settled that day.

The pool, hot tubs, and bathrooms were practically covered with ceramic tile. With so many people using the bathrooms, it was difficult to keep the showers, commodes and floors spotless. I do not recall ever leading an inspection team that failed to inspect the bathrooms, and it was a *cardinal sin* to be written up for a bathroom violation.

Now keeping the showers, commodes and floors clean required a lot of elbow grease. I was always trying to think of a better and easier way. I got to thinking about home and how we butchered the hogs in the fall, rendered the lard and made lye soap out of the cracklings. It was that lye soap that we used to wash the dirtiest things around the farm.

Then, I had a great idea! What we needed was some *lye*! I was excited, because I knew lye was the answer. We could fill a bucket with water, soap and lye and our cleaning time would actually become a pleasure. What a deal! I could just visualize the results even prior to requisitioning it.

When I heard it had to be ordered from the United States and would take about a month to arrive, I was disappointed. Nevertheless, thirty-days later a full case of twenty-four cans of lye was delivered. Thank goodness, it was the same kind we had at home. I could tell by the *skull and cross bones* logo on the label, and I could not wait to get started.

The next morning, I was waiting for Baby San when she arrived. It was time to demonstrate to the cleaning crew just how easy those little cans of lye were going to make their job. I had already rounded-up some long handles to screw into the cleaning brushes. I had the bucket, soap, and lye ready, but the first thing I needed to do was to warn and teach the workers the basics about using lye.

Of course, the number one thing I stressed to them was, "Do not get it on yourselves." I spent ample time *slowly* repeating, "Be very careful and do *not* get it on your skin or in your eyes." Then, I demonstrated how to use the stuff by cleaning a couple of bathrooms.

As I scrubbed, Baby San continued to tell them what to do and what not to do. When I finished cleaning and rinsing, the bathrooms sparkled. I was so pleased with the results that I told them to start using the lye the following morning.

While I was busy checking the fifth floor early the next day, a runner dashed upstairs and frantically told me that I was needed immediately in the lobby. Baby San was my interpreter for the day. We jumped on the elevator and rode it down to the bottom floor, stopped and asked the clerk on duty why he had sent for me. He directed us to one of the restrooms. When we entered, I could not believe my eyes. Talk about a shock! This was something that was totally unexpected.

Five men and women with bare hands and feet were down on the floor scrubbing the tile with lye water. Their hands and feet were on fire and blood red! I grabbed a couple of clean buckets, filled them with water and started rinsing their feet and hands. I think it was pure luck that things turned out as well as it did.

None of the workers' skin was seriously damaged, but they were so pitiful looking and did not understand that they needed to get out of the lye water. I could not understand what they were saying, but their body language said it all. In their eyes, I had done them wrong, and they had no redress.

One of the clerks had some knowledge of first aid, and was a big help in this situation. After awhile, the burning stopped and their skin returned to normal color. I checked the can and could tell that very little lye had been used, but the solution was still hot enough to fry eggs.

Later, Baby San informed me that the crew was going to find another job if I insisted on their using *that* stuff again. When it was time for me to leave Tokyo and return home, I went by the supply room to check on my precious supply of lye. Yep! Twenty-three and a half cans were safe and secure.

After that incident, I was very cautious about communicating instructions to the Japanese help even when they said that they understood. I learned that talking and communicating are two different things. I also learned how difficult it is to communicate with people of a different language and culture even when using an interpreter and to make allowances for misunderstandings. Foreigners, who study English, are seldom versed in the colloquial sayings that are so prevalent in the United States. My Texas way of talking created some problems for the interpreters, and it was necessary for me to keep that in mind.

At times, I was slow to realize some of the things that were happening to me. The hatred I had felt for the Japanese people was slowly fading. I was beginning to see them as individuals with needs and feelings like everyone else. My reflex in getting the workers out of the lye water and rinsing their hands and feet was somewhat of a shock to me. Why was I concerned with their hurts and problems!

Working closely with the Japanese for almost a year, helped me deal with the bitterness that had built-up during the Battle of Okinawa. Most combat veterans did not have such an opportunity. Sometimes, I get to thinking about all the decisions I had to make, and I wonder what percentage were good ones?

I did serve under a great captain who was more than twice my age and who was gifted with a lot of common sense. Being a schoolteacher prior to the war, Phillips was pretty good at keeping score. However, I never did ask to see my report card.

More Lying

One afternoon, I was in the midst of writing the daily reports in my office when someone knocked on my door. "Come in," I hollered, and low and behold, I dang near fell out of my chair when none other than Frank Sartor, my old high school buddy, came walking right thru that door!

How great to see him and to know he had *survived* the war. I jumped up from behind my desk. "Oh, my gosh! Speak of the devil! I can't believe it! What are you doin', Frank? Where on earth have you been? I've been wonderin' what happened to you after we left San Antonio. Thank goodness you're alive!" Although I was overjoyed, I thought *surely* I must be hallucinating.

However, Frank was very real. We shook hands. "It's great to see you, too, Ronold. Man! You look like *something* the dog dragged up and the cat couldn't cover up!"

We laughed and gave each other a couple of friendly slugs.

"So, where ya been, Frank?"

"Oh, I've been around. Okinawa. Cebu in the Philippines. Now I'm here in Japan for occupation duty. What's going on with Milton and Gerald? Have you heard anything from them?"

"Yeah. As a matter of fact I have. Ol' Milton got shot in the Philippines and was discharged. He's okay. Gerald was over there, too. After the war, he was sent to Seoul. While he was there, his Dad got really sick...some life-threatening health problem—not sure what it was. They sent Gerald home."

Frank said, "Well, what a relief to hear that Gerald and Milton are okay. How's Mr. Henson?"

"I believe he's doin' fine. Sure hope so. He's a good man."

Frank nodded. "Yeah, he certainly is."

"Hey, I was about to go eat. Are you hungry? If you've got time, we could go tie on the ol' feed bag and catch up." I suggested.

"Runt, you know me. Always ready to fill up these long legs!"

Since it was about time for supper, I took him into the staffs' dining room, so we could better visit and order about anything we wanted. When the chef came in and personally took our orders, Frank's eyes about popped out of his head.

"Holy smoke, Ronold! Y'all sure live high in the cotton here!" Frank exclaimed.

"Yep. I bet I could even requisition some c-rations for you!" I fired back. There were not many soldiers who were living the lifestyle as we were with their very own chefs, and I didn't want Frank to leave Japan without having at least one good meal.

The war had changed us both forever, yet we were still the same. After our steaks were served, it was time to get down to the meat of the matter. However, when I asked Frank about his war experiences, it was obvious to me by his uncomfortable demeanor as his body stiffened that he was not ready to talk about it. Normally, Frank was not an emotional person, but the painful expression on his face and the haunted look in his eyes came across loud and clear. This was not the time.

On a lighter note, we began to reminisce about our high school days and how I remembered the many basketballs that our tall, lanky center, Frank, bounced-off the heads of those shorty-shooters, and all those trophies the Novice Hornets brought home that year.

How on earth could we ever forget our Senior Class trip to San Antonio after our graduation and the night Milton, Frank and I spent in the overflow tank with all those winos, drunken soldiers and the puke! And, that awful soggy toast soaked in the oatmeal that was served to us the following morning in that stench! We decided to do our good deeds for the day by donating our breakfasts to the chowhounds.

The day before, our class had been shopping in San Antonio and one of the guys had lifted an item from the sporting good store. He was caught by a sales clerk in front of the store and the rest of us split! Out of concern, Frank, Milton and I decided to return to the store to check on our buddy, and the police had just arrived. They hauled us in as material witnesses for further investigation.

The Senior Class girls even came down to the police station to plead and cry for our release, but to no avail. After our night behind bars, the store was less interested in pressing charges than they were in *teaching* us a lesson.

However, that wasn't enough to get us off the hook. Our biggest worry was having to face our high school superintendent. He had a way of making you want to dig a hole to crawl in and pull in the dirt behind you. But, to our amazement, he called our class together for a meeting and told us, "What is done is done, and you are adults now. Both good and bad things happen in life, but the important thing is for you to learn and grow from your experiences. Just remember *you* will be the one to suffer the consequences of your actions. So, go ahead with your senior trip and try to enjoy each other, because it will probably be the last time you will all be together."

While we are enjoying our scrumptious steak, it brought to my mind a jersey bull that Dad had on the farm. "Frank, remember the time I got even with ol' Bully?" I asked. Frank died out laughing and said, "Oh, my gosh! Man, he was mean! Yeah, I will never forget how Milton slapped that mean ol' Bully right on his rump!"

No lying, it happened like this! In high school, it was a requirement for the boys to take three years of agriculture, and we were all members of the FFA (Future Farmers of America). About half of the course consisted of classroom study and the other half consisted of field trips.

One day Frank, Milton, a couple of our classmates and I went on a field trip with the agriculture teacher, Henry Green in his 1940 model Ford, so he could give us a demonstration of what we had been studying—grafting and pruning fruit trees. When we finished our pruning lesson, Green drove me home first since my house was the closest to where we had been having our class.

As we arrived, my devoted companion, Ruff, a German Shepard mix, came running up wagging his tail to greet me. I noticed that Mom and Dad were not there, but good ol' Bully was! When I saw him, I thought, "This is my chance to fix ol' Bully for good!" Before Green could drive off, I told him that my Dad wanted us to dehorn the beast sometime.

I piped-up, "Mr. Green, since we have the dehorners in the trunk of the car and there are five of us and you . . . and we all have experience, couldn't we just do it now?" I tried my best to stay calm while knowing my Dad had *never* even mentioned it and could show-up at any moment.

Green agreed, and I high-tailed it to the horse lot to make sure the gate was secured before Bully escaped. I was scared to death of that brute! Although he was a young bull and only weighed about eight hundred pounds, he was one mean sucker. Just his threatening looks at me were enough torture in itself.

He was number one in the pecking order and whenever I fed livestock each night, I always took my *Heinz 57* security team, brothers Ruff and Rowdy. They nipped at Bully's heels and kept him away from me long enough for me to do my job. Bully would manage to gobble his share, and then he would charge the animal that had the biggest pile of hay left! After he sent all the animals into flight, he scarfed down the chosen one's food with hopes of snatching a third helping.

Sometimes he would lower and start shaking his head sideways as if he were about to charge me, so I always took both dogs and tried to keep a fence between Bully and me. I certainly did not have any reservations about altering Bully's attitude. Jersey bulls are noted for being dangerous and are prone to fight and kill other animals and people.

The first thing we had to decide was *who* was going to take the bull by the horns? I went inside the barn and got three ropes. Our plan was to lasso him around the neck with two of the ropes. Milton and Frank tightly held and pulled one rope to the right and the other two guys firmly held and pulled the other rope to the left. This way they could safely maneuver Bully to the large oak tree which was inside the lot.

There they crisscrossed the rope around the tree and Bully violently resisted as he began to buck and bawl. He began shaking his head and did not want any part of my little plan! The guys hung on for dear life and managed to hold the ropes taut. Naturally, Ruff and Rowdy were on stand by to *sic* Bully as needed.

I ran the loose end of the third rope around his neck and pulled it tightly thru the *honda* (the ring at the end of the rope). Then, I looped it again just behind his front legs. Once more, I looped it in front of his hind legs. After all the looping, Green and I pulled the third rope as tightly as we could. Then, the other four guys slacked up slightly on the crisscrossed ropes around the tree to allow Bully just enough room to fall.

Green and I pulled hard on the third rope, and Bully struggled and bellowed and finally lay down on the ground and bellowed some more. When ol' Bully bit the dust, Milton ran down to help Green hold the rope while Frank and I jumped on Bully's head and placed the heavy-duty 36-inch long-handled dehorners over his right horn. Quick as a flash, we whacked it off! Bully wailed and the blood began to spurt.

Bully bawled and struggled to break away. Instantly, we placed the dehorners over his left horn and squeezed the handles together once more right down to the hair on his head. And, *presto* . . . project accomplished! Here we had a raging bull minus two horns on our hands and enough blood spewing from his head to paint the barn red. However, three ropes still remained around his neck.

"Okay, Ronold! We'll see ya later! Just wait until we get outside the lot before you remove the ropes!" Milton smarted-off.

"Has anyone got a pistol?" I retorted.

Frank said, "Well, if you were planning to shoot him, then why'd we make this bloody mess in the first place?"

I yelled, "Who said anything about shootin' the bull!"

Green said, "Now, boys . . . let's think about this. There's always a solution to every problem. Y'all keep the bull secured close to the tree."

Then he pointed to me. "Ronold, take the third rope off the bull and slip the end under the ropes around his neck. Then, run it thru the honda, and pull it all the way."

When I released the rope, Bully jumped to his feet and started to paw. He was ready to kick up the dust among other things. However, once again, the guys pulled him tightly against the tree and against his will as Ruff and Rowdy eagerly barked and nipped at his heels.

That's when I saw bristling Bully's protruding eyeballs and his hair standing up on his back. I sensed that he might have been sending me a message like, "You might've won this battle, but you'd better watch your back, Bucko!"

Green continued, "Y'all hang onto the ropes around the tree, and slowly back your way to the end of the rope toward the fence. When Ronold shouts, 'Lets go,' then get out of here!"

"Back your way to the end of the rope to the other side of the lot, Ronold. When you're ready, let us know when to drop the ropes. Then, yank your rope to release the other two from around his neck. After he's free, run for your life before Bully helps you over that fence!" Green warned. Bully snorted as if he could hardly wait!

Once Bully was released, I skedaddled over the fence faster than greased lightning, and when I turned around, ol' Bully did not look nearly as dangerous as he had a few minutes earlier. The job was complete, and it was time for Green and the other guys to get home.

I opened the gate to let Bully do his thing. As he trotted out *yowling* with blood dripping down his head, he flared his nostrils and glared at me as if he were thinking, "I'm gonna get even with you. I can *still* knock you for a row of stumps!"

Quickly, I put the ropes away in the barn to hide the evidence and wondered what Dad was going to do whenever he discovered his *humiliated, hornless, has-been*! Within minutes, Mom and Dad came puttin' up the road in the green two-door 1936 Plymouth, and I was worried that I might soon be feeling a little pain myself.

I ran and hid in the post oak thicket before they saw me, and I decided I would not say anything to my Dad hoping he would not notice. It was getting time to feed the livestock, and from the bushes, I watched Dad head to the barn. All at once he stopped near the oak tree. I knew right then, the fat was in the fire! No one had to tell me that he noticed a little blood on the ground.

Then, I saw him turn around and walk back toward the gate; it looked like he was following *something*. Perhaps, it was a little stream of blood. Well, he continued to walk slowly along the road with his eyes to the ground. I wondered, "What could he possibly be lookin' at!"

However, it did occur to me that maybe he was following Bully's bloody trail. It didn't take Dad long to track down Bully, who was also hiding in the bushes. While he was busy inspecting Bully, I nonchalantly walked inside the house as if I had just gotten home from school.

Then, I peeked out the front window and saw Dad heading up to the house. And, I knew my little escapade was fixin' to catch up with me. When he opened the screen door, he saw the blood on my clothes. There was no way of getting out of this one. "Son, what happened to Bully?" He asked.

"Well . . . uh . . . He ran into that big oak tree and knocked his horns plum off!"

Dad stared a hole thru me for what seemed like hours and didn't say a word. It seemed to me like he might be in shock. Dead silence filled the room as he stood there and waited to hear the truth.

I could feel the heat creeping up my face. A huge lump formed inside my throat. I thought I might never swallow again given the look on his face. Sweatin' bullets, I cleared my throat a couple of times. "Dad, I've been afraid of that bull for several months. Well, the opportunity showed up today, so I took advantage of it. I am sorry that I didn't ask for your permission," I nervously confessed.

Dad just shook his head and walked off. Perhaps, he was having a flashback of the time he was driving cattle and another jersey bull suddenly turned around, charged and gored his favorite horse, the one he was riding that day—Roany, a red roan gelding. Roany was severely injured, and Dad had to hand-feed and water him to keep him alive.

It took poor Roany three entire weeks to walk three hundred yards to the pond as he suffered and struggled every step of the way. After he reached it, it took him even longer to be able to bend his head down low enough to drink the water. Maybe that is the reason Dad didn't have any harsh words or punishment for me; he understood my fear and did not want anyone else to get hurt by another vicious attack.

The only blood I suffered was trying to get Bully's blood out of my clothing. Frank mentioned that his Mother was not too happy when he came home that day wearing his best school clothes spattered with blood.

Frank and I had so much catching up to do and shared a lot of laughs reminiscing old times. We were both looking forward to the day of leaving Japan and returning to the beautiful rolling hills of Central Texas. With Frank's intelligence, he was probably one of the top five who ever graduated from Novice High School. He told me that he was planning to attend a major university as soon as he returned.

After we finished our dessert, I realized that even the best-prepared food could never compare to the fellowship of a special friend.

*Frank
Sartor
in
Tokyo*

What Happened to Bully?
Dad gives "the look" as he stands beside Lester's Hotrod.

Unfortunately, some are never able to forgive, and the hatred and anger grows inside them like a cancer. Many who fought for freedom will never be completely free in their minds.

Two Unyielding Women

If I had to move *another* woman into their room, she would no doubt, become so intimidated that she would leave within a week! Two of the most obnoxious women in the entire city of Tokyo claimed this room, Lotte and Ulla—both ex-Wacs. Both must have been left behind the door the day good looks and manners were passed out. And, both were very verbal about not obeying rules or tolerating another person living with them.

The Surugadai had only a few single rooms and some of the rooms housed as many as seven people. One room contained three beds and three wardrobes—Lotte's and Ulla's room.

After running off each new roommate, they would toss out one bed and one closet into the entrance hall like yesterday's garbage. Each time we would find the bed and wardrobe outside the room, we would move the furniture back inside. We could count on it as we could the sun rising and the sun setting.

Both tall with large bone structures, these women were meaner than junkyard dogs. Trying to work with them was impossible. My concern was the inspection team. I did not like the idea of being asked "why the bed and portable closet had been removed."

Lotte wanted her bed made one way and Ulla wanted hers made another. They knew the only choice we had was to follow Army regulations, but that did not stop them from harping about it. This was merely one of the many things of which they complained.

Eventually, I realized that getting them to change was a lost cause. They were now civilians and were not inclined to live by military rules. In desperation, I asked them to move to another hotel. They told me that they *liked* their room, did not plan to change their stance, and they certainly were not going to move. About the only thing left for me to do was to talk with Capt. Phillips and find out what she suggested.

Phillips conferred with Major Hudson to see if we had any options. He told her that we could not make any changes. Phillips asked for permission to put the bed and closet into storage and move them back if needed. Hudson pointed out that this would be like opening up a can of worms, and if word spread around, we could have many more problems.

For instance, when a person moved, the other roommates might think they could just put the extra bed and closet out in the entrance hall ready to be stored. If we put the beds and closets in storage, we would not have rooms ready in case unexpected guests arrived. This would be a real problem at nighttime when all the help had gone home. Of course, I was not privy to the discussion, but I think the major agreed *unofficially* to let us store the bed and closet with hopes that nothing happened.

Phillips told me to have the bellboys move the bed and closet into storage. I suppose I could have said, "Mark one up for the other side." However, we still had another problem.

The Army was opening other hotels at the rate of two or three a month for women civil service workers. Pressure was on the government to bring the troops home, and recruiting civil service workers was one way to lessen the need for military personnel and to allow soldiers to go home.

When the women arrived in Tokyo, they were farmed-out into temporary quarters. The downtown office made the permanent assignments to the different hotels. However, I made the temporary room assignments to the ones sent to the Surugadai. For instance, if the Surugadai showed a vacancy of fifteen, we would normally get fifteen new women. This meant a trip back to the storage room for a bed, mattress, sheets, blankets and a wardrobe.

Lotte and Ulla figured they had won. They did not even fuss when I had to put the bed back into their room. Believe me; it was just for one night. They warned me *every* time I assigned a new person to their room to *never ever*, put a **Nesi** (American of Japanese descent) in with them. The military was actively recruiting interpreters from the Hawaiian Islands, and we were receiving several interpreters almost weekly who opted to stay at the Surugadai.

I talked to the two women and promised I would never put a Nesi in their room if I could avoid it. I also warned them that the time might come when there was no other choice. Well, they continued to tell me not to even think about doing it. I tried to explain to them that the downtown office sent the women according to the vacancies listed by each hotel, and that some day, it could happen that all the women sent to the Surugadai would be of Japanese descent. I told them that in that situation, I would have no choice.

That day arrived when we were sent several women and all were Japanese. The number of women received matched the number of vacancies listed on our biweekly report. We usually received advanced notice and a roster of all the women assigned to the Surugadai. Sometimes, there would be a request to have food prepared for them. This group would be arriving late, which would give us plenty of time to get the bed and closet moved back, and have the maids to prepare the bed.

After the room was ready, I went up to talk with the two barracudas. My message did not go over well. They were very adamant about not having a Nesi in their room. Well, I had it up to my ears with them and said, "Perhaps, we need to stop the Japanese maids from cleanin' your room and washin' your dirty underclothin'!"

This really set them off, and Ulla retorted, "Well, we are at work when the room is cleaned and having a Japanese servant is okay. But, living with one is a different story."

I finally told them, "The new woman has as much right to the room as you do, so get over it!"

When the women arrived, they were all very young and probably very close to my age—barely out of high school. I had waited to make the room assignments, because I was hoping one might be a judo expert. *No such luck!* While they were eating, I finished the room assignments. Bellboys were on standby to help with their luggage. After finishing their meals, it was time for the women to move into their rooms.

I went upstairs to introduce the new roommate, *Sakura*, to Lotte and Ulla. I could not believe my eyes. Both women acted normal and even friendly. I hung around until all the new women were situated in their rooms. After that, I went down to the front desk and talked to the night clerk for a few minutes before going to my room for the evening.

A couple of hours later while I was playing my new guitar, a hotel runner knocked on my door to tell me that the night clerk needed me. There was a problem upstairs. After riding the elevator up, I walked out into the entrance hall and saw the clutter. Suitcases, clothing, shoes, make-up, a bed and mattress, blankets and sheets, and a portable closet had been hurled out into the hallway! There sitting on one of the suitcases was Sakura, the young Japanese woman shaking like a leaf in the wind with tears streaming down her face. Scared half to death, she did not have the foggiest idea of what to do.

She sobbed as she gasped for breath, "I . . . want . . . to . . . go home. I . . . want . . . (*sniff-sniff*) my . . . *mooooo. . .*ther," she wailed, punctuated with a little snort.

I was thinking, "How in the world am I gonna handle this situation?" First, I needed to get her to calm down. I assured her that we could find a way out of this jam and that she was no longer in any danger. I don't recall much of the conversation or how long we talked, but in time she settled down. Then, she told me what had happened.

She started out by saying that after I left, both women turned their eyes toward the floor and did not say a word: not to her or to each other. Each time she tried to engage them in a conversation, they continued looking at the floor, as if they were in a trance or something. She said they would not answer her questions, or even utter a word to each other. Instead, they both continued to stare down, which made the suspense almost unbearable.

Sakura said she did not know what to do. She did not know anyone in Tokyo to call, and she did not have another place to stay. So, she began to unpack and put up the stuff she needed for the night. This treatment continued for at least an hour and a half. Then, the silence was broken.

Lotte, stared at the floor and said, "Ulla! Do you see *that*?" Ulla looked at the floor, "No. What are you talking about, Lotte?"

"I'm talking about that *thing* crawling on the floor!"

"What *thing*? I can't see it."

"The thing that's crawling toward your bed!"

"Tell me! What are you seeing?"

"Looks like a Japanese cootie."

"Oh, my gosh! I see it! There's some others crawling this way, too!"

"What should we do?"

"Kill them! Kill them! Kill them!"

Both women jumped up and grabbed their machetes from their closets. They began jumping around the room, banging and clanging the backside of their machetes on the floor and shouting, "Down with Japanese cooties! Down with Japanese cooties!"

Sakura told me that she ran for the door and into the entrance hall. As soon as she was out of the room, the two women started slinging her stuff out! When they finished, they slammed the door and turned off the light.

After hearing her story, I still needed to find her a place to spend the night; there were no vacancies in the hotel. However, I remembered that seven Japanese women were living in one of our larger rooms. Perhaps, they would take her in for the night. I could scoot the mattress inside the room for her to sleep on, and lock her luggage in the supply room.

However, I was also thinking that I couldn't afford to be knocking on bedroom doors in the middle of the night; I liked my job and wanted to keep it until I earned enough points to go home with an honorable discharge. I took the safe way out and let Sakura do the knocking and talking. I instructed her to speak in the Japanese language, hoping this would help.

The problem was resolved. I scooted the mattress in, and she gathered the things she needed for the night and a change of clothing for the next day. The rest of her stuff was moved down to the supply room and secured for the night.

The next morning, Sakura came down to my office to tell me how grateful she was for my help. She said that the Japanese women had been very helpful and had given her some good advice. She indicated that she would like to live at the Surugadai, but did not think she could stand to eat in the same dining room, live in the same hotel, or swim in the same swimming pool with the two women who had treated her so badly. She also went on to say that she would never forget the first night she spent in Tokyo.

Perhaps, I have been too harsh on Lotte and Ulla, for they also have a story to tell. I never had the opportunity to hear it, and because of our relationship with each other, I probably would not have listened. However, I think I know the basic things.

It all started on December 7, 1941, when the Japanese made a sneak attack on Pearl Harbor. During the following forty-five months, the war continued. Many battles were fought: Battles for Saipan, Okinawa, Iwo Jima, and the Philippines, is the short list. In addition, there was the *Bataan Death March* and the barbaric acts committed by the Japanese.

The American people had every reason in the world to hate the Japanese. Some people had the same attitude about rattlesnakes and the Japanese, "The only good snake is a dead snake." Does it seem a little bit too harsh? Before judging, consider this.

Did you lose a husband, a brother, a sister, a father, a mother, a close relative, friends, or a sweetheart? How did the war affect you? Did you feel it? What did it cost you? Regardless of who you are, if you were deeply involved in the war, your life could never be the same again.

Attitudes are shaped in war, and they can be very difficult to change. Memories of friends who made the ultimate sacrifice and others who gave a limb or eye are not forgotten when the shooting stops. Unfortunately, some are never able to forgive, and the hatred and anger grows inside them like a cancer. Many who fought for freedom will never be completely free in their minds.

Following is a composite view of what I think Lotte and Ulla probably felt:

We were in Tokyo shortly after the surrender of Japan. Fighting the Japanese one day and embracing them when the shooting stopped was most difficult! Lotte and Ulla were not ready to fraternize with a person of Japanese descent. Expecting them to embrace a Nesi roommate would be like putting a wildcat and dog in a barrel and expecting them to get along. It was not going to happen. Time has a healing element, and perhaps, Lotte and Ulla were successful in dealing with their problems.

The occupation of Japan was extremely difficult, stressful and painful for everyone serving in the American Military Forces, but even more so for the combat veterans. When I was serving in the 27th Infantry Division, our fatigue jackets had "Tokyo Express" stenciled on the back in red letters. We had strong feelings about wanting to march into Tokyo and black a few eyes and bloody a few noses!

On the other side of the coin were the Japanese people. Think of the extreme anxiety and suffering they must have felt when the atomic bombs landed on two different cities in the mainland. How distressing it must have been for them to hear their Emperor Hirohito announce in a radio broadcast that Japan was bowing to the demands of the United States and the surrender would be unconditional! He also informed the people that he was not a *supernatural person* and should not be worshiped.

What a shock it must have been for the once proud, arrogant Japanese military to accept defeat and occupation of their beloved country by a foreign power! How can soldiers be in war one day and turn it off like a switch the next day and live together in peace?

What an intriguing question.

. . . You do know that I won't be goin' down any more holes with you!

Mirror, O' Mirror

The shortage of mirrors was a constant complaint at the hotel. In fact, some of the women considered it an out and out crisis. It was a madhouse during the daily morning rush hour as they tried to get ready to meet the day and waited in line for the shower or the bathroom. The tempers flared regularly!

Before coming down to breakfast or boarding a bus for work, most of the women just naturally wanted to apply their make-up and fix their hair first. However, the straw that broke the camel's back for most of the occupants, was trying to comb their hair and put on their make-up without a decent mirror. The staff was *frantic* to get some!

We were not able to just go out and buy them or to requisition them from the United States. We did not have the authority to order them through our supply system, particularly since the war had just ended. Many other things with much higher priority were needed, and mirrors would have to wait.

There were several reasons why we could not buy them locally; Japanese currency was almost worthless, and the merchants with mirrors kept them out of sight. In fact, it was difficult to locate or buy any of the popular items. The Japanese were very shrewd business people, and hiding the highly sought after merchandise was common.

This was the way they protected their inventory from being confiscated by the U. S. Army. An entity like the Surugadai had the authority to requisition anything that was needed for the hotel if we found it in a business. However, we could not requisition things that belonged to a private citizen. If we found items that were small enough to be carried in the jeep, we would fill-out a requisition form, and give the owner a couple of copies. Then, we would take the items and head back to the Surugadai. I never requisitioned things that I could not take with me.

Well, the Japanese merchants despised this way of doing business. The price, in which they were being paid, had been negotiated and agreed on by some governing body which was far below black market prices. On top of that, the merchants preferred to exchange goods and services rather than accept the inflated yen. Therefore, bartering would usually get them an item they needed if they had a sought after item.

For example, if a farmer brought his produce to town in the wintertime, his greatest need might be wool blankets and warm clothing. If the farmer accepted the inflated yen for his produce, he might not be successful in buying a blanket to keep his children warm. Instead, he would spend time hooking-up with a family that would need food. If they were to have an extra blanket or warm clothing, a trade would benefit both families. When money becomes practically worthless, regardless of what country, bartering becomes a way of surviving.

One morning, Baby San was grinning as if she had never seen a bad day in her life when she came into my office. I had seen *that* expression before. Waiting her out was the best approach. It was obvious that she was going to hold me in suspense for a while. She certainly loved to play her little games.

Out of the clear blue, she blurted out, "Mirror, o' mirror hidden away, we go rescue you today!" Then, she rolled her eyes.

"Baby San, what in the heck are you talkin' about? You're not makin' any sense!" I said.

"Oh yes, Ray San! I find where mirror hidden." Animated with that familiar impish twinkle in her eyes, she was bursting at the seams. She then began to jump up and down with excitement. "Come, Ray San . . . crank jeep . . . we go!" she squealed.

"Baby San, what on earth has come over you? I've never seen you so excited. How'd you find out? How accurate is your information? Where're these mirrors located?" I was full of questions.

"At shop . . . hear people talk. I hear *mirror…* my ear perk," she said as she shifted her eyes. "They talk about place have mirror. I get close . . . *listen* for place. Outskirts Tokyo. Hurry! Time wasting!" She quickly said.

"Baby San, what if we can't locate the place or find the mirrors? All we have to go on is some loose talk you heard while shoppin'. This is pretty flimsy stuff." I was skeptical.

"Make no difference. We go. Wild goose chase. We go see," she persisted.

Capt. Phillips was in her office, so I decided to ask her what we should do. She said that we needed mirrors in the worst way, and to go and check it out. So, we jumped into the jeep and were off to the races! While I was driving, Baby San was directing.

She must have had the map of Tokyo etched in her brain! After we had been driving thru the charred rubble and debris for more than an hour, I was getting ready to turn around and head back to the Surugadai. Baby San kept insisting that she knew how to find the place. I did not know how anyone could have recognized anything in this war-ravaged city. Finally, when we were almost out of town, she eagerly pointed to a shop and squealed, "That's it! That's it!"

An uneasy feeling engulfed me, as we entered the building. Four pairs of eyes were riveted on me. It was obvious the Japanese people resented my very presence in their store. I glanced at Baby San, and even though she was small, her stance and attitude was that of a samurai warrior. She was poised and ready for battle!

When Baby San told the three men and a woman that we had come for their mirrors, it was as if a bomb had exploded! Their tempers flared and the sparks flew from their dark eyes. Angry and harsh tones erupted from their mouths as they flailed their arms in the air. I noticed one of the men had his fists clenched and the veins were bulging in his neck.

Although I could not understand the spoken words, there was no doubt in my mind by their body language, things were a bit tense. Since I did not know what was being said, I was no help to Baby San. Whatever they were saying, she firmly stood her ground and never flinched. However, I was thinking it might be a good idea to grab her and run to the jeep.

The war of words became more intense! Baby San was pointing at my GHQ shoulder patch, my sergeant stripes, and frequently saying, "MacArthur, MacArthur, MacArthur!" I think she was saying that MacArthur had given us the authority to take their mirrors, and in one sense, this was true.

As the shouting match wound down, I noticed that the man with the clenched fists had relaxed his hands. I was more than surprised when one of the men walked over and moved a chair from the middle of the room and set it against the wall. I was sure hoping he was not making room for hand-to-hand combat.

Next, he removed the rug on which the chair was setting. The rug was concealing a trapdoor. Another man reluctantly walked over and opened the trapdoor. I observed a wooden stairway leading into a basement. He started down and motioned for Baby San to follow. She said, "Ray San, come."

I must admit that I was not eager to go down into that hole, but I needed to support Baby San. As I followed her down the creaky stairs, one of the other guys was right behind me. Memories of the war flashed across my mind. I was still somewhat skittish about getting myself in a corner, and I was watching the trapdoor to see if the other guy closed it. I could just imagine him locking us in and standing on top while the two guys in the basement worked us over.

A good soldier always reconnoiters the lay of the land, and I was observing everything in sight. I was also thinking, "Why in the heck did I allow us to get into this situation!" The only light was a naked bulb dangling from the ceiling, typical Japanese lighting. The trapdoor remained open. The walls of the basement were concrete which served as the foundation for the building. The floor was dirt, and it smelled musty like a typical basement.

To tell you the truth, the basement was very well-kept. Shelving was plentiful and orderly. The merchandise was in excellent condition. All the mirrors were in perfect condition and consisted of three or four different sizes. What an experience! We had hit pay dirt! Finding so many mirrors in one place was as if we had struck gold.

It was only when the two guys started carrying the mirrors upstairs and loading them into the jeep that I realized Baby San had won the war. If you have lived around the Japanese, you might have noticed how stoic the men can be. At the same time, a close observation of their body movements can sometimes reveal what they are feeling.

When we first had entered the store, the animosity that I sensed from them was not normal. This suggested that they were perhaps, members of the old Imperial army and were fighting and winning the war with China when Japan surrendered to the United States. The attitude of the Japanese soldiers that had been fighting in China was different from the soldiers that had fought the Americans; they had not been defeated and were very hostile to American military personnel.

At the same time, they were very faithful to the Emperor of Japan, Hirohito. The emperor had instructed the people to obey the terms of the surrender and not to resist the occupational forces. I had a strong feeling that we were sitting on a keg of blasting powder and one wrong move could set it off.

The only thing left to do was for me to fill out the requisition forms, which authorized the owner of the business to get reimbursed for the mirrors that we were taking. He would need two copies: one to keep for his records and one to turn in with his invoice for payment. His claim would then be administered by the Japanese government. I completed the paperwork in record time, and *bang*, I was out of there like a shot fired from a rifle!

Baby San was mentally drained by the time we headed back to the Surugadai. I did not press her for details about the war of words. She did tell me that the only real problem was getting them to admit that they did have mirrors. I asked her, "Why were they so angry?"

"They want some mirror. I tell them, we take *all* mirror," Baby San replied trying not to smile.

As we were driving back, I started thinking about Baby San and the unbreakable spirit she possessed. So small in stature, yet she was such a courageous and remarkable little woman! "Now, Baby San," I said, "you *do* know that I won't be goin' down anymore holes with you!" She laughed, and it became our little joke. I teased her about it from time to time. However, I was not kidding.

Black marketing was rampant in Tokyo. Since the mirrors would have been worth much more on the street, I understood why the shop owner was so angry about the price he received for his merchandise. His predicament reminded me of a saying I had learned earlier during the war, 'Loose lips sink ships!'

Someone had let the cat out of the bag, and Baby San just happened to be at the right place at the right time. Sometimes things just fall in your lap. On this occasion, that is exactly what happened.

We rescued the bright, shiny mirrors from a secret life hidden in a dark, damp and drab Japanese dungeon. The women living at the Surugadai were so excited to meet their newfound friends, and the maids just loved to care for and clean them each day. But best of all, each time someone looked into one of the rescued mirrors and laughed, the mirrors thanked them by laughing back.

Technically, I had not disobeyed an order; the room was never actually entered, but I had been close enough to fall inside the doorway.

Mysterious Marcelle

Marcelle was one *weird* woman. She was a loner, and I think it would be fair to say that she was a borderline recluse. We would only see her when she left for work, when she returned, and as she was entering and leaving the dining room. I do not recall her ever having a dinner guest.

I do know that she had been an Army Air Corps officer. The fact that she had one of the best private rooms in the hotel, suggested she probably held the rank of captain or higher. A small, slender, brunette with olive skin, Marcelle rarely stopped at the front desk; when she did, it was usually for a second. She was definitely our mystery woman!

I was never privy as to why only four or five occupants had a lock on their door, but Marcelle kept hers locked. I had been instructed *never* to enter her room. However, I shared responsibility in seeing that all the rooms were ready for inspection by ten o' clock each morning, and this was definitely a sore spot with me. How could I tell if her room was ready if the maids were forbidden to clean it, and I was not allowed to enter?

One day, a maid told Baby San that a horrible smell was seeping out from under Marcelle's door. This called for a quick investigation! Sure enough, her room was stinking to high heaven! Capt. Phillips was not in her office and could not be reached by phone. Therefore, the only thing that made sense to me was to open the door and find out what was causing the odor.

I decided to go ahead and *spit in the churn* thinking I was doing the right thing before the inspection team sniffed out the Limburger cheese aroma flowing from *Room 504*. After grabbing the key out of the safe, I was on a mission and headed-up to Marcelle's room!

When I opened the door, the full force of the odor hit me, and I thought I was going to upchuck. What I saw inside the room was revolting. The portable closet and bed were missing; a mattress was located on the floor; and the sheets and pillow-cases were filthy. It appeared that all of her underwear and clothing were in a humongous pile and there was no telling what was underneath it. It sort of reminded me of a haystack, but it certainly did not smell as fresh as one. No, Marcelle's room smelled more like a day gone bad—*really bad* on the farm with sour milk and rotten eggs with a little pig slop thrown in!

My reaction was, "Where's the dang pitchfork! We're gonna move a bed and closet back in here, scrub this dump from top to bottom, wash and iron all her clothing and shine this place like a new penny." We had plenty of time and plenty of help to get it all done before Marcelle returned from work. Knowing full well that I was not suppose to enter the room, I went right ahead and made this my priority for the day—a decision I soon regretted.

When Marcelle came home from work and entered her room, "surprise, surprise, surprise!" All her clothing had been washed, ironed, and was hanging neatly in the closet. Her undergarments had been washed, folded and neatly put away. She now had a new bed and mattress, new pillows, clean sheets and pillowcases; the bed, which was made up Army style, would have passed the toughest of inspections. One thing for certain, if she chose to take a bath the next morning and change clothes, Marcelle would be one clean lady for perhaps, the first time in weeks.

Most of the time Phillips dined at the Surugadai. After the meal that evening, I noticed her and Marcelle going into her office. They were inside for quite a long time. I always thought that they had served together in the Army Air Corps.

When Phillips noticed that I was in my office, she stopped by and ordered me to report to her early the next morning. I could tell that Marcelle was not very appreciative of all the hard work we had done for her. She might have thought she had died and gone to hell and that her punishment was having to keep both herself and her room clean and actually sleep in a bed.

I knew that I had tread on a slippery slope, but at the same time, I believed the right action had been taken. I kept telling myself that if I was going to be held responsible for seeing that the rooms were cleaned, then I needed the authority to make decisions on the spot. However, I also realized that if a five-star general had to take orders from President Harry S. Truman, then I best take orders from Capt. Phillips.

Well, the crux of the problem was the fact that I had been instructed never to enter Marcelle's room, and I had disobeyed. The circumstances, under which I entered, did not trump her orders. And, I was warned not to go into her room a second time. The message was loud and clear! I vowed *never* to do it again. At the same time, I had this gut feeling that eventually, an inspection team would want to open the door and the fat would be in the fire. It did not seem fair that I would have to share the blame for something in which I had no control.

After leaving Phillip's office, I went upstairs to check and see how the maids were coming along on cleaning the rooms. Marcelle's new bed and closet had been moved out into the hall. Putting them back into Marcelle's room was off limits, and my only option was to return them to storage in the basement.

After a few weeks, that familiar stench was *oozing* out from under Marcelle's door again. As the days passed, the rancid smell only became stronger. Well, now I'm thinking, "The order was to never enter Marcelle's room, but nothing was said about *opening* the door." Of course, I was soon thinking, "Why not get the key and take a gander?" Very soon I found myself heading to the safe for the key.

One glance showed me a mess equal to the first time. Should I take any action? I decided not to. Instead, I decided to wait a couple of more weeks so her room would really be ripe. We might see some *things* crawling out from under the door by then! I was just hoping that the problem could be resolved before any varmints took up residence and an inspection team noticed.

I was rolling around different ideas inside of my head of how to handle this situation. It soon became an *obsession.* Despite having tried, I continued to feel as if a bomb was fixin' to explode, and someone needed to defuse it to avoid this potential disaster. I did not want it to happen on my walk.

One morning before Phillips came into the Surugadai, I lifted Marcelle's room key from the safe and slipped it inside of my pocket. When Phillips entered her office, I told her that there were a few little things upstairs in which I needed her advice. This was not an unusual request since she was my supervisor.

We rode the elevator up to the fifth floor, and I began to ask her about this and that. I could tell she was becoming annoyed at me with the trivial things that I was showing her. It was time for me to show her the real reason we were up there. It was now or never.

That is when I slipped Marcelle's key out of my pocket, walked over to her room, inserted the key, turned it and flung the door open! All the time I was thinking, "Is this going to be my last day at the Surugadai?" Technically, I had not disobeyed an order; the room was never actually entered, but I had been close enough to fall inside the doorway.

Phillips was simply stunned for a moment, and was temporarily unable to react. Her tone was as sharp as the crease in her pants. "Lock the door and meet me in my office in fifteen minutes." Well, that was a long fifteen minutes. I asked myself a hundred times, "Am I in trouble?"

The meeting was typical of Phillip's style—low-keyed, but authoritative. I sensed that this was a difficult problem for her in which to deal. I could tell that she was very disappointed in Marcelle. It would have been helpful if Phillips had shared some of the extenuating circumstances pertaining to Marcelle's strange behavior. I always wondered if Marcelle had been involved in or witnessed some tragic or violent event during the war and if Phillips had been touched by the same incident. There had to be a reason as to why Marcelle received such preferential treatment.

In the Army, there is a fine line drawn in the sand between regular soldiers and commissioned officers. Stepping over the line could be hazardous, and I was already in enough trouble. Although I wanted to, I did not dare ask any questions. I suppose the *whys and hows*, caused me a few problems during my Army career. The correct procedure was just to obey.

I was instructed to have the maids do a repeat performance on Marcelle's room. Phillips would counsel with Marcelle. From that day forward, we were not to make any exceptions to her room and to treat it like all the others and have it ready for inspection by ten o' clock each morning. Marcelle could take advantage of having the maids wash her personal clothing just as all the other guests did, and could continue to keep her door locked. However, it would be unlocked each morning for cleaning. Marcelle's days of living like a tramp were over.

The power in the spoken word is great and sometimes transforming. What a great time it would have been to be lurking in the shadows and to have heard the conversation between Phillips and Marcelle. Our mystery woman, certainly had her share of problems, but after that meeting and the changes were implemented, Marcelle also started taking pride in her appearance. And, the little stinker came out smelling like a rose.

The only reason I am in the Army is because a friend betrayed me.

Double-crossed

Ralph arrived as an unexpected addition to the Surugadai staff. Out of the clear blue, a call came from GHQ to announce that they were sending us another clerk. At the time, we were fully staffed, but one more clerk meant an extra eight hours off between shifts; no one was going to complain about that!

When Ralph arrived, we went out to meet him and to help him carry his gear into his quarters. Ralph was just an average looking GI—average height, light brown hair and blue eyes. However, we were very surprised that Ralph was about twice our age. He mentioned that he was from the Midwest and was being transferred from another Army billet located in Tokyo. Since he had been a clerk at the previous hotel, he said that he would not need additional training.

One of the staff members invited Ralph to join him and some of the guys in a penny ante poker game after the evening meal, but he declined the invitation. Normally after dinner, there would be a couple of penny ante poker games going on. One table was located in the lounge or the spacious hallway in the lobby. This game consisted mostly of hotel occupants and their guests. Sometimes the PX manager and some of the people in charge of the bar played. Since they did not live at the hotel, they were not subject to the no fraternization rule.

The staff used a very nice day room, which was located in the basement, where the other game was played. Many friends came to enjoy the scrumptious meals served each evening, and some stayed to play poker. Sometimes, a few guys showed-up just hoping for a chance to play.

One of the regulars was a civilian named Jackson. With a ready smile and firm handshake, Jackson was a guy's guy. He had rugged good looks—sandy hair and blue eyes. Although he was tall, he didn't exactly stand out in a crowd; he just blended in well and got along with almost everyone. Jackson was at the hotel so often that we thought of him as one of us. It was as if he had an addiction to gambling. The guys really liked him, not only because he was entertaining, but also because he was a lousy player. He certainly lost far more than he won.

The funny thing about Jackson—he had by far the best-looking gal living in the hotel. *Ruthie Mae Astor* looked as if she walked out of a bandbox every day with her hourglass figure, sparkling black eyes, curly black hair, flawless skin and perfectly straight pearly white teeth. She and Jackson were quite the item and were frequently seen together. However, it seemed as if he *never* passed up the chance to play poker.

We all liked Jackson, but we certainly did not understand his way of thinking. What was wrong with this guy! Was he out of his mind? Who would leave a gorgeous gal upstairs for some ol' penny ante poker game night after night? Especially when you never won! Ruthie Mae could have easily given Marilyn Monroe a run for her money. However, she was a bit snobbish unless you wore some brass.

The four clerks, who were already on staff, worked eight hours on and twenty-four hours off. With Ralph now in the rotation, the off time would change to thirty-two hours off. This was a far cry from when I worked as a clerk; we had worked eight hours each day with no days off.

The first shift started at midnight and ended at 8:00 a.m.; second shift, from 8:00 a.m. until 4:00 p.m.; and third shift, 4:00 p.m. until midnight. My hours were from 8:00 a.m. until 5:00 p.m., but if a clerk needed help, either Rosenberg or I was always on call.

I was a frequent visitor to the information center either to help out during the rush hours, give the clerks a break or just to visit during the late hours. It was just a natural thing for me to visit with Ralph when he came to work. It was evident that he certainly knew how to do his job. In fact, I found out that his occupation was actually hotel management. I was thinking, "The Army sure has some mighty strange ways. This guy has managed some huge hotels and here he is, working as a clerk with a country boy telling him how to do his job!" At least, we were doing it the Army's way.

From day one, Ralph was reserved, almost sullen, and did not interact with the other clerks. He never showed any anger toward me, but he did keep me at arm's length. His work was superb, but I could tell something was eating at his guts. Well, I figured he just had a good case of the *mully grubs,* or maybe he had just received a *Dear John Letter.* Surely, he would snap-out of it in a few days. But, he never did.

One evening when Ralph was working the third shift, he sent word that he needed to talk with me. I went to the office and asked him "Is there a problem?"

He boldly replied, "As a matter of fact, there is. It's important that I be relieved of duty for this one shift."

"Then, why don't you trade shifts with one of the other clerks?" I suggested.

"Well, to tell you the truth, my relationship is so bad with them that no one will trade," he answered.

Working the evening shift was no big deal to me. I had done it in the past for other clerks, so I told him. "Go ahead and take off, Ralph. I'll take care of it." Six days later, he was back on the evening shift and requested time off again. I reluctantly agreed to work in his place.

Soon after that, Rosenberg called a meeting. There was a soldier representing the clerks, and they were upset with Ralph and wanted him transferred. If they could not get him moved to another hotel, they wanted him moved out of their room.

They were angry, because he refused to play poker with them or to interact with them in any way. His very presence caused tension. They were also unhappy, because I had covered for him. I pointed out that neither Rosenberg nor I played poker with them and that I had also covered for them at various times.

The spokesman added that Ralph did not like Jews, and Rosenberg and one of the clerks were of Jewish descent. I knew that Ralph was a difficult person, but I had no idea that the animosity was so strong with the rest of the staff.

After the meeting, Rosenberg and I had a lengthy discussion about what to do. We looked at the facts; Ralph was difficult to get along with, but he was probably our best clerk; on the other hand, he did have the right not to interact with others; there was a storage room in the basement that we could offer him if he were willing to move down there; and, he would be shipping home within two months.

We decided that Ralph had not really done anything to justify a transfer, but a meeting with him was necessary. The circumstances almost dictated that I should be the one to talk with him. From that point on, the problem with Ralph seemed to take on a life of its own.

Rosenberg briefed Phillips about our meeting. It came as no surprise to her, because she had been told in advance about Ralph and the problems he had created. She was also aware that he had been shuffled around from one hotel to another. Her advice was for us to handle the problem and not to involve her unless it was absolutely necessary.

While Rosenberg and Phillips were meeting, I was in my office trying to figure-out what to say to Ralph. I was not looking forward to telling him the things that we had discussed and for sure, I wanted to be prepared and talking from my notes. I decided I would talk to Ralph sometime during the afternoon and put it off as long as I could.

While I was busy trying to finalize my little speech, in walks Ralph! "Sgt. Ray, I just wanted to save you the trouble of having to send for me. I know what's going on. I was just informed by one of the clerks about the meeting you had and how you are trying to get rid of me."

Well, so much for my speech! My preparation turned out to be a waste of time. Before I could say anything, Ralph started talking, and I became the listener. The things that he told me that day and the following weeks were very *intriguing*.

The first thing he said, "Ray, you might not know this, but I have already been kicked out of two hotels for being antisocial and for not being a team player. I have never had a friend in the Army, and I don't intend to have one. He paused a moment and bit his lip as his eyes scanned the room. Next, he grabbed a chair and sat down.

"The only reason I am in the Army is because a friend betrayed me," he continued. I did not have the slightest idea where we were headed, but I grabbed the bottom of my chair, and leaned forward. I was all ears!

Then, he kind of leaned back and said, "Ray, I'm a professional gambler, and high stakes poker is my specialty. I can read a person like a book. I have spent twenty years developing my skill, and I am one of the best."

"You know those two nights I asked off?" he asked. I nodded. "Well, I was actually out playing poker." After that, he jumped back to the problem at hand.

"Now, I will admit that I have a lot of resentment, and playing penny ante poker and being one of the boys, is not going to happen. I realize that has caused some bad feelings and problems, and I would not blame you the least bit if you went to Capt. Phillips and requested to have me transferred. However, I would really like to stay here until I receive my orders to ship home," Ralph added.

We then discussed how we could ease some of the tension at work, and he admitted that he could do better. "I was thinking about that storage room down in the basement, Ralph. Would you be willing to move down there? I know you'd be isolated, but it is a solution," I suggested.

"Actually, that would be perfect! I will even volunteer to stay out of the staff's dining room unless it's empty," he offered.

We talked about how he might be affected by being alone so much. He said, "Oh, don't worry about that, Ray. I am already isolated. You're really the only one who talks to me as it is."

I sat there not knowing what to say, since I could not imagine why someone would not want to be with others. Ralph sensed how I was thinking—that isolation would be punishment. He assured me, "Seriously, I'll be fine. This is a good idea."

Later, I had a long talk with Rosenberg. We both agreed that as long as Ralph did his job, we should not ask for a transfer. Rosenberg talked to the clerks and warned them not to make any trouble, and that was the last time we discussed it. The things Ralph told me the following weeks boggled my mind.

He had, indeed, managed a large hotel. However, his reason for doing so was for the purpose of running a gaming operation or high stake poker games, which were against the law. He had devised an elaborate alarm system, and did not worry about the police being able to spring a surprise visit.

Wealthy people from a five-state area were frequent weekend players, and each one had been screened before being invited. There were loosely connected games going on across the nation, and Ralph was involved in some of them. There were two regular local people who played at Ralph's game—the Judge and the Banker.

The Judge was Ralph's personal friend and was not much of a poker player, but he loved to play. He was not a target, but was a protected player; it was good for business to have him involved in this illegal operation. To say the least, it compromised his integrity and could prove helpful to Ralph in case of trouble. His winnings were meager, but over the long haul, he was allowed to win.

Now, the Banker was a prime target. The prime targets were selected for their wealth and vulnerability. The courting period could last for several years. When the prime target was ready for picking, a *ringer* would be sent in for the kill. Ralph was a ringer, and traveled often to San Angelo, Texas for another operator. His counterparts would reciprocate when he needed a ringer.

The courting period of the Banker lasted four years. The first night that he played, he was allowed to win big. Over the next four years, he was allowed to win more than he lost. He would win big, but most of it would be won back in the next game. The Banker was being programmed.

The Banker was winning larger amounts and consequently, was becoming willing to play for higher and higher stakes. He was also becoming hopelessly addicted to gambling. The signs were just right for a final game. This would be a game with no holds barred—a game with no limits set.

A ringer was called in, and several hands had been played before the Banker was dealt this fantastic hand. It was a hand that most poker players dream about, but never pick up. The odds were stacked in his favor. The chance of anyone having a better hand was nil.

His reaction was to *shoot the moon*, or go for the big money. Never mind that he was already the richest man in town, who owned office buildings, apartment complexes, farms, and just about anything you could think of—he owned it. However, this hand was too much to pass up!

The Banker made a huge bet and was called and raised. What a stroke of luck! Now the stakes were even higher. The betting and calling and raising continued, and the stakes shot up like a Roman candle. The climax of four years of programming was about to be realized. The ringer had set him up and naturally held the winning hand.

Ralph told me that collecting bets was not a problem, but he never explained whether the cash had to be laid on the table or not, if checks were accepted, or if real estate was transferred. He just said that welshing on a bet was not tolerated.

The following weekend, the out-of-state players had come to town and a big game was in process. Suddenly, the door swung open and several policemen barged in! The police chief ordered, "Don't anybody move! Put your hands on the table and no one gets hurt!" Everyone in the room was arrested and booked into jail. The players were charged with a misdemeanor and released the next morning. Their big embarrassment was spending the night in jail and having their names printed in the newspaper the following day.

Well, Ralph was not so fortunate. He was charged with a felony. The players were merely gambling, but Ralph was running a gambling house. After he was released on bond, he decided to go get advice from his friend, the Judge.

The Judge took Ralph back into his chambers for a private conversation. Ralph wanted to know what was best for him to do, and asked if he would need to hire a lawyer. The Judge advised him—since he had been caught red-handed, his best approach was to plead guilty and to let him handle the rest. He told Ralph that he had been expecting him and the document for pleading guilty had already been prepared. All Ralph needed to do was sign the plea form, and the Judge would set the sentence on the next court date.

Ralph closed his eyes briefly, shook his head and grimaced. "I *knew* I shouldn't have signed that plea! Something just didn't add up. And, the moment I signed it, a strange feeling swept over me—like I should've hired a lawyer." When Ralph went before the Judge for sentencing, he gave him the maximum fine and the maximum years in prison for the class of felony that he had committed. And, that is when Ralph realized he had been *rooky-dooed*.

"I was shocked clear to my toes! Then, I was offered a chance to escape a prison sentence. I was told that since we were at war, I did have another option—go into the Army and ship overseas. Well, now you know the *real* reason I am here, Ray. I guess you could say I'm *slightly* bitter." Ralph said.

What about his feelings of his betrayal by the Judge? This is another part of the story and some things that Ralph did not know about when his life was unraveling.

After the Banker got over the shock of his misfortune and realized that he had been setup, imagine his anger! The Banker was on a mission to get revenge on Ralph! In addition, he had some leverage on the Judge.

The Judge was a silent partner in a huge insurance agency, and the Banker was their biggest client. A cancellation of the entire Banker's insurance would be a tremendous loss to the insurance agency and would knock a huge hole in the Judge's pocket.

What did the Banker want? He merely wanted the Judge to inform the chief of police of how to breach the security of the hotel, so they could go in while a game was in progress. After they arrested Ralph, the Banker wanted the Judge to give Ralph the maximum sentence for his crime. Although the Banker never recovered his money, he did succeed in making life miserable for Ralph.

By the time I met Ralph, he was so obsessed with finding a way to get even with the Judge and the Banker that his life was a living hell. The evils of gambling have a way of eventually destroying many people and what a pathetic person Ralph had become.

Why were they bearing the brunt of a decision
made by a few military elitist to bomb Pearl Harbor?

A Sentimental Journey

"Captain Phillips needs you in her office immediately," one of the runners announced early that morning. Phillip's door was opened and before I entered, I could see that she had a solemn look on her face. Well, this called for my snappiest salute!

She waved me over to a chair. "Sit down, Sergeant. We have some things to discuss," she said. Oh, boy! The last time I had seen her looking so stern was the morning after I had wrapped myself in a sheet, put on that ugly, rubber face and scared the living daylights out of the Japanese help. I braced myself while trying to anticipate what was coming next.

Phillips took a deep breath and paused, which gave me more squirm time. She sniffed and pushed up her glasses. "Sergeant, the time has come for you to move on," she said in a deadpan voice. The silence that followed was frightening—more frightening than any words.

I was speechless. My first thought was, "What have I done *now* to bring this on?" Whatever it was, the flat tone of her voice told me that the decision was final. I sat there in shock.

After what seemed like forever, her countenance began to change. Phillips cupped her right hand over her mouth. It looked as if she were trying to keep from smiling. She took another deep breath.

Then, she even chuckled softly as if she were actually enjoying this moment. I didn't know what to do. My mind started racing with all kinds of random thoughts.

This was so *unlike* Phillips. I was getting more nervous and started thinking, "Man! This is terrible. She is really, *really* glad to get rid of me!"

Her next words were, "Sergeant, it's time for you to saddle up that Texas bronco and hit the trail . . . the trail back to those rolling hills of Coleman, Texas. I have your shipping orders on my desk."

Wow! What a difference a few moments can make. She really had me there for a minute. I believe that Phillips, who was always the teacher, had used our last meeting to try *one* more time to teach me a lesson about the dumb pranks I was prone to pull. Or perhaps, since this was the last time we would see each other, she was willing to set aside military protocol and let me know she did, indeed, have a real sense of humor.

We bid our *farewells* before leaving the office. Phillips stood straight and tall and extended her hand to me. As I had heard on more than one occasion, "Sgt. Ray, you are one of the best soldiers with whom I have ever had the honor of commanding, and I hope you will do as well in civilian life as you have done in the military." Her last words were not spoken as my commanding officer, but were spoken more as a friend or a relative; there was no doubt in my mind, about her sincerity in wishing me the best in life.

I was ecstatic about my shipping orders! In just a couple of days, I would be catching a boat. A little more than eighteen months overseas had seemed like a lifetime. Fantastic! What a high time in my life! I would soon be at home. So, I decided right then and there, that when the time came to board the ship, I would not complain about having to stand in line, even if the line was a mile long.

My mind was jumping around like lightning in a thunderstorm! So many things were popping into my head at once—one was the day I had met Phillips. Major Lance Hudson from GHQ had given me such a verbal beating for allowing something to happen that was humanly impossible to prevent and had told me to pack my bags and that I was being transferred. Phillips had intervened on my behalf and Hudson had yielded to her request.

I thought of how Phillips and her friend trusted me to keep their valuable jewelry and money so many times while they went swimming; we did not have lockboxes. Numerous things came into my mind about Phillips that morning. After all, she had been my commanding officer for almost half of my Army career.

I was thrilled to be shipping out, but saying *good-bye* was not so easy. In my heart, I knew that Phillips had been a blessing, and in my book, she was number one. I was able to communicate my feelings to her, and I could tell she was touched. Her parting words were, "Sergeant, it is time for you to get back home and find yourself a lifetime boss." Then, I caught a little twinkle in her blue eyes as she smiled and raised her brows.

I grabbed my shipping orders and took off to find Rosenberg and Weiss. When I showed them my orders, they rolled their eyes and Rosenberg said, "You lucky dog! Now you're going to dump all your work on me!"

"Yeah. Startin' right now. I'm outta here!" I chuckled.

The adage, "what goes up, must come down" had started kicking in. I was in hog heaven! This was the day for which I had been waiting. And yet, it was bittersweet. Most of the time, leaving good friends is sad or painful, and this was no exception. It is just a part of the human experience.

I had spent almost a year working with the hotel staff: the interpreters, especially Baby San, and Gloria, plus so many Japanese men, women, boys and girls. Now, just as I had done with so many friends in the past, it was time to say "so long" again.

It was beginning to dawn on me how interrelated people are. And, here I was—in the process of taking myself and duffel bag home. How great it was! But, at the same time, the experience of living in Japan and working with the people whom I had known for the past year would always live in my memories.

The soldiers with whom I had trained, the soldiers with whom I had shared a foxhole, and the soldiers with whom I had played in addition to my experiences while serving in the occupational forces, had all touched and changed my life. I would be taking home with me memories of the entire time I had spent in the military. For good or bad, my Army experiences would be a part of my life forever.

The next thing on my agenda was to pack and be ready to catch my ride at 2:00 p.m. the next day. My jeep ride would take me to Yokohama where I would board that long anticipated boat ride. One of the things I had learned in the Army was to always be punctual. Believe me, this was one time I planned to be early.

Decisions! Decisions! Should I take all my junk with me or travel light? I decided not to wrestle with any unnecessary baggage. Instead, I packed only the Army issued items and got rid of the others.

One thing I needed to decide about was a box full of Japanese currency that I had accumulated. What good was money if I couldn't buy anything with it? So, I added it in my discard box, along with the ugly, rubber, devil mask. When I finished packing, the discard box had more stuff in it than my duffel bag had. But, the Japanese staff made good use of the things I left behind.

The staff surprised me with a dinner party, and the two Japanese chefs whipped up a fantastic meal just for Ray San and his friends. What a meal it was! It was *my favorite*—smothered steak with all the trimmings and for dessert, freshly baked hot apple pie with vanilla ice cream heaped on top. What a way to spend my last night in Tokyo!

Of course, my friends needed to get in their last *licks*, and everyone took full advantage of the opportunity. They told me that Sippora Finkler wanted my address, so she could come for a visit! They asked me if I had packed my twenty-three and one-half cans of lye, so I could *impress* all my friends back home. What great Christmas gifts they would make! And, red was a perfect color for the holidays! They warned me to watch out for those naked women roaming the stairways. It was quite awhile before they ran out of material.

The party lasted for hours and the camaraderie was great. After the last story was told, and our "good-byes" were exchanged, it was way past bedtime. However, I was wound-up tighter than an eight-day-clock and spent most of the night tossing and turning before finally drifting off to sleep. Oh, what a day September 6, 1946 had been!

It had been such a day, that on September 7, I didn't wake up. The clerk on duty sent a runner down to my room to see if I was doing okay. I looked at my watch and could not believe my eyes! It was after 10:00 a.m. Holy cow! I had never slept that late since I had been inducted into the Army.

I jumped up, hit the bathroom, took a quick shower and was dressed in record time. All the things that I was leaving behind had already been distributed. I threw the clothes I had been wearing the day before into my bag along with my toilet articles and quickly headed for the office.

The clerks gave me a hard time, and did their best to convince me that I had already missed the boat. I suppose we did need one last laugh. It was lunch time and this gave me another opportunity to *thank* the two Japanese chefs for all the great meals they had specially prepared for me during my assignment at the Surugadai.

By the time I left the dining room, it was after 1:00 p.m. As I was waiting for my ride, I noticed that something unusual was going on. The lobby began to fill with the Japanese help, but no one was saying anything. People continued to assemble in the lobby. After a few minutes, one of the bellboys came over and told me, in his broken English, "We come tell Ray San bye-bye." I was very humbled.

When my ride arrived, I grabbed my bag and guitar and started walking through the lobby toward the door. I turned around and looked one last time. With one last smile, I waved to my special friends. All at once, the Japanese began to wave and cheer, "Sayonara! Sayonara! Ray San! Ray San!" As I rode away in the jeep, I could hear them chanting until we were out of earshot.

I was not in a talkative mood as we headed out for Yokohama to board the boat. Of course, I was fired-up and ready to leave, but my mind was going back over the past year. It was on September 7, 1945 that the 27th Infantry Division had been flown in from Okinawa and landed in Japan. I was thinking about my attitude, my feelings, and my conversations with my buddies, and how we had loaded our rifles and fixed our bayonets as the plane circled the landing strip and prepared to land just one year ago.

I must admit that my mind-set, along with my buddies's was, *"Let's kick a few butts!"* In my own way, I was trying to understand or reconcile my thinking or feelings of intense anger and hatred on the day I landed in Japan, with my present attitude of concern for the suffering that the average Japanese citizen was now feeling. Why were they bearing the brunt of a decision made by a *few* military elitist to bomb Pearl Harbor!

Got My Bag, Got My Reservation. . .

We made it to Yokohama about an hour before departure, and there was no waiting line. Most of the troops had already boarded the USS *Marine Serpent* (T-AP-202). When boarding, I was told to just grab the first bunk available, because the ship was carrying the maximum troops. I made it down to the first compartment where soldiers were billeted. I was told that there was only one bed available—the bottom bunk near the stairway.

I did not even bother to go down to a lower compartment in search for a better location. I considered myself lucky to have a place to sack out, with the other four soldiers who would be sleeping above me. Of course, we did have eighteen inches of breathing space between each bunk, unless there was a heavy guy sleeping directly above; this would certainly dip into the spacing. We were so tightly packed that guys with large noses had to sleep on their sides.

What an exciting moment when the *Serpent* opened her throttle, and we could hear the engines begin to whine, and we could feel the vibrations. And, when those propellers started turning and the ship began snaking its way out to open water, we knew we were homeward bound!

I had never seen so many happy soldiers in my life! To add icing to the cake, with courtesy of the Navy, "Sentimental Journey" by *Les Brown & his Band of Renown* sung by Doris Day flowed from the speakers. It was played over and over for at least two hours. Oh, how we loved that song and especially on this joyful occasion! We were certainly *revved-up* and could not have heard it played too many times.

I did not see anyone I knew . . . that is, until the third day. The chow line was on the top deck and the line wound around like an obstacle course. It seemed like you could meet yourself coming back. The line moved toward the front of the ship, looped around and headed back in the opposite direction. As I was moving toward the front, I noticed a soldier moving toward me. For a moment, I thought I recognized him.

He looked so much like Jackson—the tall, sandy-haired guy who had been a regular in the penny ante poker games played at the Surugadai. But, *this* guy was wearing an Army uniform, with three stripes up and two rockers down, and the name stenciled on his fatigue jacket was certainly not Jackson.

As the line moved, we came face-to-face, but I just passed by. I decided this guy was a look alike for Jackson, because Jackson was a civilian and this guy was clearly a soldier. He reached out, caught me by the arm and asked, "Hey! What's wrong, Ray? Are you not speaking to me anymore? "

Oops! How embarrassing! Jackson had been at the Surugadai practically every day for the past several months, but he was always dressed as a civilian and soldiers were required to be dressed in uniform. I was dumbfounded! How could he be in two places at the same time? In fact, he had attended my going away party a few days earlier.

Jackson went on to say, "Let me get in line with you, and after we have finished eating, I have *something* to tell you." I could not imagine what was on his mind. Although he was usually an easy-going, jolly fellow, it was obvious that he was very serious about wanting to talk.

My ears perked up! I was ready to hear his story. After we finished lunch, we found a good spot on the top deck to sit, and I patiently waited to hear what he had to say. It was almost like he was struggling within himself, and rethinking that maybe he should forget about talking and just let his intentions slide by.

After a few moments, he took a deep breath and asked me, "Ray, if I reveal some things to you, will you swear you won't write a word of what I say to your friends back at the Surugadai? If you betray my trust, I could get into some real trouble!"

I assured Jackson that I would never do that. He said, "You know, Ray . . . I know you *much* better than you realize. That's why I believe you'll keep your word."

Along about here, I was becoming very confused. What on earth was this soldier talking about! He *knows* me much better than I realize? He knows me *much* better than I realize! *What?*

It was becoming clear that Jackson had decided to go ahead and talk. In fact, he asked me to just listen until he had finished and if I had questions, he would answer them later. He mentioned a few things about his visits to the Surugadai and how he had enjoyed playing poker with the guys. He talked about the great meals that he had enjoyed. Then, he made some more small talk. It was like he did not know how to get into *the* subject. After pausing for a moment, he dropped one heck of a bomb!

Nervously, he cleared his throat. "Ray, I was attached to the CID (Criminal Investigation Division) and my job was to infiltrate the staff at the Surugadai. Part of my cover was to always be dressed as a civilian. I was a mole and spied on each one of you guys and your friends."

I listened, but did not like what I was hearing at all.

"I actually kept a dossier on each one of you and a select few of your friends. The CID provided me with poker money, but I was instructed to lose most of the time."

Oh, man! I didn't say anything, but I was thinking, "What a creep! *"*

He coughed a couple of times, cleared his throat and fidgeted with a button on his sleeve. Jackson was obviously overwhelmed with anxiety. "Worthless Japanese yens were being converted into American money and the U.S. government was trying to discover who was responsible for this illegal operation; I was part of the team doing the investigation," he said.

I loathed even touching her; except I wanted to put my hands around her neck and squeeze until those black eyes popped-out!

It was easy for an American soldier to get a sack full of Japanese yen, because the Japanese were constantly trying to buy American cigarettes, chocolate candy, watches, blankets, and just about anything a soldier had. I suppose if I had been willing to strip down to my underwear, they would have bought my clothing. Plus, they would have paid black market prices.

However, there was a catch! Finding something worthwhile for Americans to buy from them was almost impossible. I do not know if the Army had any regulations about selling cigarettes and candy to the Japanese. The hot items that we purchased at the Army PX were rationed items; so if we sold those things, we did without.

Payday came once a month, and we were paid in Japanese yen. So, for all practical reasons, we were being paid with worthless money. The method of paying had one major flaw; we could not convert the yen to American currency which created a real problem for the military personnel. But, it solved a problem for the government.

If the almost worthless yens could have been converted to dollars on demand, we would have all become millionaires overnight and Uncle Sam would have had to pick up the tab. A system was worked out to accommadate the military personnel and protect the U.S. government.

This is how the system worked. To convert the yen to American currency, we would ask the paymaster to issue an authorization slip in the amount of our pay. Then, we could go to an Army Post Office and buy a postal money order. Most of us had plenty of Japanese yen, and since we could not use American money in Japan, we would send our paycheck home. In my case, I mailed the money order home, and Mother deposited it in the bank for me.

There was a staff member that claimed to be playing the game, *Yens for Dollars,* and he was not bashful about trying to get other people to invest in his little scheme. He charged a small fee for his services. His deal looked to me like a slippery slope or twenty years in Leavenworth. In fact, I thought he was just blowing smoke, because he was always coming up with harebrained ideas.

Jackson continued with his story, "The CID knew that a penny ante player was operating from the Surugadai and their interest was for me to lead them to the next guy up the ladder and eventually to the top man. They thought it would definitely be a high-ranking officer in the Finance Department."

Jackson talked about the staff and our friends. He knew who was running the operation at the hotel and which ones were converting yens into dollars. He did, in fact, know more about me than I ever realized. For this ol' country boy, his story was mind-boggling.

As the time ticked away, he revealed how spying and collecting information on each one of us had affected his life. He had been a platoon sergeant during the war and had led and lost several members of his platoon in hand-to-hand combat during the Battle of Okinawa. He did not condone wrong doing, but instead, he had a soft place in his heart for combat veterans and remembered how we protected each other when the chips were down.

This guy was far from being a creep. By nature, Jackson was actually a very likeable person. However, being ordered to use his charming personality in a deceitful way, was eating at his guts.

All at once, I remembered how I hated spying for the FBI. We discussed how we disliked being ordered around by the FBI and the CID. We agreed that we would never take a job working as an undercover agent or spy.

Jackson told me at the beginning that I could ask questions after he had finished telling his experiences. I asked several, but there was one burning question I saved for the last. "How about your beautiful girlfriend, Ruthie Mae? Do you think she'll be true to you until she returns to the United States?"

His face flushed with anger, and he didn't answer immediately. In the meantime, I am thinking—"they must've had a lover's quarrel, split the blanket or *something* like that, and it was too painful for him to talk about."

It was out of character for me to ask such a personal question. However, his addiction to poker seemed to be more important to him than being with the most gorgeous gal at the hotel—a hot topic of discussion among the Surugadai staff. Of course, it was not any of our business, but we thought it was unusual.

Jackson pulled himself together. "Wow! I didn't expect *that* question. You sort of caught me off guard!" He blurted out.

"Oh, don't worry about it. You don't need to explain," I said.

"No, it's okay. It's really okay, Ray."

Ol' Jackson was full of surprises, and his reply was nothing less than astonishing. He sort of cringed, "Hmm. . .Ruthie Mae. Where do I begin? I can't stand that witch! How's that for starters? Just being in the same room with her grates on my nerves.

"My pet name for her is *Charming Ruthless*. She has the ability to charm a black widow spider out of her web and is ruthless enough to pull her legs off one at a time for sheer entertainment. From the first day I was assigned to the CID and she was introduced as my boss, my life has been nothing but miserable. She is the most despicable person I have ever known!" Jackson continued, "I was forced to dine with her, swim with her, dance with her and breathe with her!

"This was part of my cover and her way of spying on the hotel occupants. The thing I despised the most was dancing with her. Although we were both excellent dancers, I loathed even touching her; except I wanted to put my hands around her neck and squeeze until those black eyes popped-out!

"She had a list of suspects. Three nights a week, she rotated to different officers' clubs to socialize and dance with her unsuspecting friends. She would even encourage them to drink more than they normally would with hopes that the alcohol would loosen their tongues.

She lived and breathed her job, twenty-four hours a day and was always looking for a lead. What a relief it was when she wasn't around! I even requested to be relieved of my duty and to be transferred back to my regular outfit, but we were both firmly embedded at the Surugadai and the CID would not release me.

"I know what it must have looked like to you and the staff. You guys thought I had the world by the tail with a downhill pull. You thought I had quite a deal. . .having my girlfriend in Tokyo with me. . .couldn't beat that with a stick! But, remember, Ray . . . all that glitters is not always gold." Then Jackson asked me, "Did you ever suspect that I might be a spy?"

I answered, "Of course not! But, Jackson, you're right about one thing; We *did* think you were one of the luckiest guys in Tokyo. You were so friendly and seemed so calm . . . like you didn't have a worry in the world. There you were dinin' and dancin' with the beauty queen. Shucks! You were the talk around the office!"

Jackson said, "Yeah, you saw me as a calm person without any worries, while in reality, I was like a duck swimming on a pond. My feet were churning under water, but I was not allowed to let you see that. You know, I have so many things on my mind that I'm overwhelmed!"

"Well, do you wanna talk about it?" I asked. "What else are we gonna do?"

Jackson said, "Yeah. The main thing bothering me is what happened in the war. I led my platoon into battle and over half of my friends were killed, but somehow I managed to survive. I don't understand. Why did I live and why did so many of my men die? I want to just forget it ever happened! But, I keep seeing it and reliving it. It won't go away!

"Working with Charming Ruthless was a diversion for awhile, but now I'm back to square one. I think working for the CID will soon fade from my memory, but the war never will. Ray, you were there. How are you dealing with it?"

"Well, first of all, my combat duty was light compared to yours. I wasn't involved in hand-to-hand combat like your platoon was," I replied. "But, Jackson. . .you can't beat yourself up for what happened. It wasn't your fault. We lost a tremendous number of our best military personnel on Okinawa. And, yes . . . we need to find a way to cope with our feelings. And, we both know that it isn't gonna to be easy."

I continued, "I've come to the conclusion that I'll *never* be able to forget, so forgettin' isn't an option for me. The events of the past two years have become a part of me and will be with me for the rest of my life. Like you, I'm still havin' nightmares, but they're less frequent.

"I remember an old song, "Time Changes Everything". This song is about a guy who lost his girlfriend, but hopefully, the title will also apply to us. We cannot afford to sweep the problem under the rug and hope it'll go away. If we do, it'll surely come back to haunt us. Time is our ally, and each new day will bring new opportunities. Things will be different when we get home," I said.

"Before being inducted into the Army and until the end of the war, our future was on hold. Have you forgotten all the questions that we were grapplin' with back then? Would we be killed in action? Would we live through the war? And if we survived, would we come back with all our body parts?" I asked.

"Perhaps, for me, the greatest concern was comin' back so crippled that I wouldn't be able to function normally. . . physically, mentally, or both. Comin' back as a burden to my family or society was definitely one of my greatest fears.

"These questions have been answered, and for the *first* time in our lives, we now have a future; we have choices. Now, we can plan and make commitments. In a way, it's like our life has just begun. We can't change the past, but like a good Army scout, let's advance boldly and aggressively into our new life!

"Jackson, don't you agree that the dominant influence in our mind or our thinkin' will have to do with our future and the past will become less of a factor?" I asked.

Jackson exclaimed, "You're absolutely right! By golly, we're survivors! We conquered the Japanese army! We'll win our present and future battles." Jackson and I shook hands and never saw each other again.

Traveling almost five thousand miles on a troop ship was long and tiresome, but we were one excited bunch of soldiers, knowing our destination was home and our future was looming before us. This was my fourth time to ride the waves of the Pacific Ocean, but this voyage was smooth sailing with only small ripples.

The clouds floated by revealing the clear blue sky, and it felt as if the clouds had been lifted from me revealing a bright future. The ocean was a mirror image of the bluish cast from above and the salt water smelled so fresh and clean.We were jam-packed on the top deck to watch the sunset and what an amazing sight it was to see that enormous orange ball of fire slowly disappear into the Pacific.

After sunset, some of us started to leave when we heard a sailor shout, "Attention, everyone! Please remain on the top deck. You haven't seen anything yet!" Shortly after twilight, the stars began to twinkle. Growing up on a farm, I had spent hours on end gazing up at the stars, but I had never seen anything so spectacular. The darkness of the night, the clear sky and the reflection of the stars in the water was out of this world.

Words cannot describe the celestial beauty that so many of us witnessed on the fifth night out from Yokohama. What a brilliant display of God's creation! The sky, the sunset, the twilight, the stars, and the darkness of night that surrounded the ocean were reminders to us of our Maker's presence as he shared his magnificent handiwork—one that I would never forget.

We were totally surrounded by stars that appeared close enough to reach up and touch. The scene was so breathtaking that a hush fell over the troops. What an experience! What a blessing! It was like a good omen had been showered upon us. This scene was *unquestionably* the high point on my return to the states.

However, there was another event that was foremost in our minds—the sighting of the west coast and Seattle. Until that happened, someone had to do the cooking, cleaning, and serving for the three thousand soldiers aboard. I think most of us played the little game of *hide and seek*—actually it was more like *hide*.

An announcement was made over the PA system that everyone, regardless of rank, was subject to KP duty, and it had been eighteen months since I had pulled KP duty. I was not in the mood to participate. I got to thinking, "The only one on this ship that can identify me is Jackson, and he doesn't know where my bed is located."

In fact, we were not assigned beds, so how could anyone find me? It was obvious that a sergeant would be going around with a clipboard in his hand and would randomly select soldiers for duty. So, if he couldn't find me, he would just get someone else. The problem was the location of my bunk.

My bed was eight to ten inches above the floor and adjacent to the stairway. I would be shining like new money and would definitely be a KP candidate. Escaping was next to nil, but hope sprang eternal.

Just what I had dreaded, happened the first week. A sergeant came downstairs with the *trusty* old clipboard in his hand, looking for soldiers to pull KP. Since we were the first rack of beds, he did not look any further. He started from the top bunk and began to work his way down.

I still have trouble believing I actually did this, but the sergeant with the pencil had his elbows resting on the top bed where he could write and his legs were spread wide. It made it very convenient for me to crawl out between his legs and walk downstairs to the next deck. Well, troop ship fans can make a lot of noise as they force fresh air into each compartment. This proved to be a good cover that day for my escape!

The trip back to the United States was fairly low-keyed. Most of us were thinking about home, family and friends, starting our lives over, and in general, wondering what life was going to be like out of the military. We reached the Seattle Port of Embarkation at approximately 3:00 a.m. on September 17. A few soldiers spent the night on the top deck, waiting eagerly to spot the lights of the West Coast. About daylight, there was a mad rush to the top deck. We were estatic!

My stuff was on the second deck, and I was in the first group to disembark. I don't recall whether breakfast had been prepared that morning or not, but if it had been, the fish must have had Christmas in September! The important business at hand was walking down that gangplank. Who could think of eating at such a momentous time!

Early on, we began to disembark. We were transported by Army trucks to Fort Lewis and joined up with other troops that had arrived a couple of days earlier. Rush, rush, rush was the order of the day. Within seventy-two hours, we were processed, regrouped and shipped to our respective separation centers.

That night in the mess hall, I noticed a familiar face sitting a few tables away. "Hey, Ray! Let's go get a haircut!" he wised-off. "Oh, my gosh! When did they let you outta the brig?" I shot back. It had been almost a year since I had seen Red.

Later on that night after he had visited the PX and had a few beers under his belt, Red staggered back into the barrack where we were staying. I was playing my guitar. He made his presence known as he cleared his throat and stood on my guitar case as if it were a podium before making his big announcement—then, he belched loudly.

As the case caved in under his weight, he lost his balance and crashed to the floor. "Red, you're gonna need to get the chaplain to punch your TS card when I get thru with you!" I snapped.

He rolled over and looked up at me thru those familiar bloodshot eyes. It was apparent to me that he was having another one of his funny drunks as he grinned. "Rayz. . .. wouldz youz loanz mez somez moneyz. . . .forza lit...lit...tlez. ..hoo...(hic) hoo..hooch. . .(belch)." As I looked down at Red, I thought about stuffing him inside the case and throwing him in the baggage compartment the following day.

Countin' Every Mile of the Railroad Track. . .

Red didn't seem to be in any big hurry to get back to Georgia, but when I learned that my destination was San Antonio, I could hardly wait! Being back inTexas was a dream come true. If shoveling more coal into that firebox would have made the troop train glide down those rails any faster, I would have been the first to pitch in. However, I soon learned that troop trains *now* yielded to all other traffic since the war was over.

Stopping on the sidetracks and waiting became the norm, and getting off to stretch our legs was common. Some of the sidetracks were out in the boonies. It was during these times that we would jump off and examine the landscape.

On one afternoon, the train conked-out on us when one of the wheels developed a *hotbox*. We sat on a sidetrack for four hours before a crew came from *somewhere*. The repairs were made and soon we were moving again. One of the good things about the train were the Pullmans. Having a bed of our own was a luxury for which we were so grateful.

Although, it was a long and exhausting ride from Seattle to San Antonio, I met a couple of my old buddies from the 27th, besides Red. And, we had some long and interesting talks. We also made plans to have a night out on the town when we got to San Antonio, and we were sorely disappointed when things did not work out. Perhaps, I missed my last chance to see if Red could top our *Odawara fiasco* in the Alamo City.

Transportation had been prearranged and was waiting for us when we arrived in San Antonio. Our destination was the Separation Center. We were instructed that dinner would be served at the regular time and to find a bed for a good nights sleep. Early the next morning, we would start the process of becoming civilians. My stay in San Antonio was for a few days, but it was long enough to send a telegram to let my family know when to pick me up at the Novice Bus Station.

I was one of the soldiers that was getting a furlough, so more paper work was required than the ones that were receiving their discharges. My discharge papers would be mailed to me a couple of months later. I was still in the Army and on full pay—the best two months of my military career!

There was one thing that I insisted on doing before I left San Antonio. My younger brother, Lowell, was taking basic training near the Separation Center, and I simply was not going to leave until we had a visit. I had been able to get a message to him that I was in town and would be coming to see him.

It was around 4:00 p.m. when I received my orders and some money and instructions on when to catch my ride to the bus station the next morning. If I caught the first bus out, I would need to be up and ready by 9:00 a.m.

Next, I called a taxi and was soon at the Company Headquarters where Lowell was billeted. I asked a soldier for directions, and he was nice enough to take me to Lowell's barrack. Lowell was in the Medical Corps and their day of training had just ended. Several of the recruits, including Lowell, were sitting around on their beds waiting for chow time.

It was one of those great moments in life! He was the first one of my family, other than Lester, I had seen in almost two years. And, Lowell had been busy growing taller than me since I last saw him. I don't remember ever calling him little brother after that day.

He introduced me to his buddies, and they had plenty of questions. However, the old clock was ticking away. As soon as I could, without being rude, I said, "Lowell, hit the shower and jump into your Class A uniform! We're goin' to town and eatin' the biggest, juiciest ol' steaks we can wrap our jaws around!"

Some of the guys snickered. One blurted out, "He can't go. No one's allowed a pass."

"What's the name of the company commander?" I asked.

This really set these guys off. "Oh, there's no way you'll get past the corporal outside his office, let alone see the captain," another soldier said.

I looked at Lowell. "Be ready!"

Since getting by the corporal was not going to be easy, I needed a plan. I kept asking myself, "How's the best way to approach this? Do I need to be straight forward, or should I plant a *little* thought in his head that would cause him to be afraid of the consequences if he refuses to let me talk to the captain?"

Most of the corporals that I had known would never bend the rules, so I decided to try to *outfox* this guy. I walked up as if I were a long lost friend of the captain and requested permission to see him.

"What is your name and the nature of you business?" asked the corporal.

"Well now. . .I want to surprise the captain!" I replied.

"I have my orders. I need your name and the nature of your business," he insisted.

" Oh, sure. I understand. You see, I want to *surprise* the captain and the nature of my business is personal," I persisted.

"Orders are orders, and that's the way the Army works," he firmly said.

"I see. Well, I'll just be goin' on my way then. But, don't forget to tell the captain I was here," I added. At this point, I turned around and began walking slowly down the hall, and was not sure if my plan was working or not.

"Just a minute!" The corporal called out. "Let me talk to the captain before you leave."

Bingo! Things were looking up! The corporal ushered me into the captain's office.

There was no question in my mind how to approach the captain. It would be straight forward, and I would ask for a favor. My uniform would tell the captain that I had been overseas for at least eighteen months; my Combat Infantryman's Badge would tell him that I was a combat soldier and my shoulder patch would tell him that I had been assigned to GHQ in Tokyo.

When I walked up to the captain's desk, I gave him my best salute and stated my name, rank, and serial number, proper army protocol. "What's the nature of you business?" he asked.

"Sir, I just got back from eighteen months of overseas duty and have been given a two-month-furlough, after which I will be discharged. I will be catching a bus for home in the morning. I have a brother, Private Lowell O. Ray, who's assigned to your company and is taking his basic training."

"I have been told that no passes are being granted during this phase of their training. I understand Army rules and regulations, but sometimes I know that exceptions have been made. I'm here asking for an exception to be made in this case and to allow me to take my brother into San Antonio for dinner and to catch up on what has been going on in our family."

"If you can grant the pass, it will be greatly appreciated; if you can't, I will fully understand." I added.

The captain replied, "Sergeant, I will be happy to grant your request, but there will be stipulations. The pass will expire at midnight, and I will be holding you responsible to have Pvt. Ray back to the barracks on time. Wait in the outer office, and send the corporal in. He will bring you the pass."

When the corporal handed me the pass, it was obvious that he was not a happy camper. He knew that he had been manipulated, and there was nothing he could do about it. I was not ready for what I found when I returned to Lowell's barrack. He was *still* sitting on the bed just like he was when I left.

"Hey!" I growled at Lowell. "I thought I told you to be ready! We're goin' to town!"

"Well, *you* might be goin' to town, but I can't," he said.

"And, why the heck can't you go!" I snapped.

"Because we aren't allowed to go to town without a pass—we can't have one," he explained.

"Look, Lowell," as I shook the piece of paper at him, "I know you have *never* seen one, but this is called *a pass*. Your pass. It's good 'til midnight. Now, shake a leg! You're wastin' our time." I said. As Lowell looked at the pass, his mouth dropped open. And without saying a word, he was in the shower lickety-split!

While he was getting ready, his buddies asked me questions about my time in the service and the number one question was, "How'd you get that pass?" Of course, they wanted me to get them one.

I motioned for them to gather around in a huddle and lowered my voice to almost a whisper, "Well, you see. . .the secret is waitin' for the corporal to go to the restroom. Then, you can just walk right into the captain's office, and he will be mighty glad to grant your request!"

Lowell was ready to go by the time the taxi arrived. "Where to?" The driver asked. "Just take us to a good steak house," in unison we replied. We glanced at each other and chuckled.

The taxi driver transported us to a nice looking restaurant in San Antonio, and we spent three hours eating and talking. The steaks were good, but the apple pie topped off with vanilla ice cream, was excellent.

We had so many things to talk about. Lowell had more questions than a porcupine has quills. And, I wanted him to brief me on everything that had happened during the past two years. We were having a big old time enjoying each other and recalling some of our past history when suddenly, lightening blazed across the sky and violent thunder shook the building! The power went out in the restaurant. A voice in the pitch dark announced, "I heard on the news that we're under a severe weather alert. Heavy rain and flooding's expected."

I remembered what the captain had told me about getting Lowell back before midnight, and decided to call a taxi and cut our visit short. Some of the roads were being closed due to the high water. The rain was pelting down in sheets, but we were fortunate and made it back to Lowell's barracks on time.

Like a Child in Wild Anticipation. . .

The following morning, I was *Johnny on the spot* at 9:00 a.m. and so was my ride to the bus station. The agent informed me that there would be a delay due to the rising water. In fact, some of the basements in downtown buildings were flooded. Crews were using heavy equipment to pump out the water onto the street.

The delay was not much of a concern. I was closing in on the last 230 miles and had plenty of time to make it home before dark. I found a window seat and settled in for a pleasant afternoon. Central Texas never looked better. I could not even come close to estimating how many miles I had traveled in the past two years, but I do know that a lot of water had washed under the bridge. It would not be long before I had come full circle.

The sun was casting long shadows on the ground when we pulled into Coleman, and I wanted to bail out and run down Commercial Avenue, the heart of the town where I had spent so many carefree Saturday afternoons. The red cobble-stoned streets with the gaslights centered in the median would have cars lined-up on both sides—cars ranging from the early 1930 models to the early 1940 models.

Farmers and ranchers, typically decked-out in blue and white striped Oshkosh overalls and chambry shirts, and people from the surrounding rural communities, would pour into town to shop. And, the street would be bustling with energy! As soon as we hit Commercial Avenue, we would be greeted by the aroma of *Fattie's Hamburgers.*

The restaurant window opened onto the street, which made it easy to lure customers inside, once they got a whiff of those big, fat, juicy burgers cookin' on the grill. A Fattie Burger with a large coke, chips and a candy bar altogether was twenty-five cents. The farmers and ranchers especially liked Fattie's humongous bowl of homemade chili with tons of saltine crackers and a cup of coffee or a coke. All of that was only a quarter!

Coleman was the hub, and many would come into town to stock up on groceries, chicken feed and farming supplies. However, it seemed like the most popular item of the day was *chewin' the fat!* People could be seen standing around or sitting on sidewalk steps visiting with one another and catching up on the latest gossip and news.

J. C. Penney, F. W. Woolworth's Five-and-Dime and the catalog stores such as *Sears* and *Montgomery Ward* were popular. But, my favorite place to hangout was right on the corner! *Owl's Drugstore* was the place to meet friends and students from other schools. Sometimes, I would have a ten-cent cherry coke and a fifteen-cent burger, or I would splurge on a large chocolate malt for thirty-five cents. If I was short on change, then a five-cent coke without the cherry syrup would have to do. However, I really liked it when *Louise* was working behind the counter, because sometimes the coke was free!

One of those cokes with a lot of crunchy ice would've tasted good about now. With eighteen miles left to go before reaching Novice, I looked at my watch for the umpteenth time. We had just passed the *Dixie Pig*, a popular hangout for the younger crowd, on the outskirts of town. I asked the driver, "*How* much longer?" He laughed and said, "Soldier, give me twenty minutes."

What a great moment when my boots hit the ground in Novice! Mother, my youngest brother, Ed, and sister, Opal were all waiting to welcome me home. Dad was working out of town and was not able to get home until later that evening. I was so excited that I jumped off with my guitar and had completely forgotten about my bag. However, the bus driver hadn't.

It was apparent how relieved Mother was to see me home safe and sound. Having five sons in the service had taken its toll on her and Dad; I know it was the same for all families who had members in the military.

Not only was I on an emotional high, I was shocked out of my wits at the same time. I know that other soldiers returning home had this same kind of experience. Without realizing it, time had stood still in our minds. We had an illusion that things would be, more or less, like they were when we had left.

It might sound strange, but during combat, we needed an anchor; something to hold on to, and memories were about all we had. We were not around to see all the changes going on, so the world back home had stopped turning for us.

My first shock was seeing Opal and a couple of her girlfriends who were with her. When I had left for overseas, she and her friends were silly, little, giggly thirteen year old girls. But now, they had blossomed into beautiful young ladies. Lester had been back for awhile and was working in Del Rio. Alfred and Cecil had been discharged soon after the war and were working in Lubbock.

After I had been home a few days, things began to settle down. However, I was still officially in the Army. I decided I needed a car. Riding the stud was not going to cut it anymore. I asked Raymond, one of my older brothers, to take me to Abilene and help me select a good used car. I had already tried to purchase a new car, but the waiting list was eighteen months. I didn't want to wait until I was an old man to have a means of getting around!

Since the government had put a freeze on automobile production in order to conserve metal and further the war efforts, there were no late model cars available. After spending most of the day poking around motor companies and used car lots, I drove back home in my very first car! For $875.00, I was the proud owner of my first set of wheels—a black, four-door, 1940 Plymouth!

Sometimes strange things can happen without any rhyme or reason. Shortly after I was home, I woke up in the middle of the night to hear Capt. Phillips's parting words to me, "Sergeant, it's time for you to get back home and find yourself a lifetime boss." Well now, I was fixin' to get rid of one boss, and I wasn't all that eager to sign up for a lifetime. But, I had to admit that Phillips had never given me bad advice.

Gerald had been home for awhile and had already found some musicians to jam with, and it was just natural for me to join in. This morphed into playing for parties like old times, and of course, girls always showed up at parties.

Well, I decided I might ask one for a date, but she had to be at least eighteen years old. I was at a party, and did not know who was who. I noticed an attractive girl and was fixin' to ask her for a date. That is, until Gerald told me that she was only fifteen.

I soon realized that adjusting back to civilian life was going to be much more difficult than it was when I had to adjust to Army life. It was, indeed, time for me to take the advice I had dished-out to Jackson—build a new life and further my education. I had actually thought about making the Army my career, but after serious consideration, I decided my best bet was to return to school and build a new life in the private sector.

As Dad had said, "Things have a way of working out," and little did I know, that one of Opal's giggly, little girlfriends would eventually become my lifelong boss, and Opal would become Gerald's.

Sister Opal and friend check out my new wheels

Takin' a spin in the Plymouth
on twenty-five cents per gallon

Opal and Gerald's Wedding
August 20, 1949

Newly Weds
Ronold Ray and Wanda Woodard
July 31, 1948

Wanda Lou Woodard
The gal down the lane

Dating Daze

Rayunion

Home Sweet Home

The first Rayunion was on the second weekend of June 1947 and became an annual event for 60 more years. The last, was the weekend of Gerald's funeral, June 2007.

Standing beside our house are:
Front Row-Alfred, Grace, Vivian, Mother, Dad, Opal and Ed
Back Row-Ronold, Lowell, Lester, Raymond and Cecil

The Ray Brothers Serving in WW II

Corporal Cecil Ray entered the Army Air Corps October 27, 1943, and was honorably discharged February 19, 1946. He married Maude Tyson, and they made their home in Lubbock, Texas. Cecil was 94 years old in 2008.

Sergeant James Ray entered the U. S. Army January 19, 1942; served with the Medical Corps and was honorably discharged January 11, 1946. He married Ineva Pribble. Making their home in Lubbock, they had two daughters, Connie and Brenda. James was 88 years old in 2008.

Private First Class Lester Ray entered the Army Air Forces October 1, 1943, served with the Eighth Air Force and was honorably discharged February 12, 1946. He married Dorothy Coots, and they made their home in Carlsbad, New Mexico. They had two sons, Billy and Joe. Lester passed away in 2002 at age 79.

Sergeant Ronold Ray entered the U.S. Army September 7, 1944; sailed to the Pacific February 5, 1945; fought on Okinawa; served with 27th Division; served in Tokyo, Japan with the Occupational Forces; and was honorably discharged 1946.

Milton Terrell served in Company L, 27th Infantry in the 25th Division and was wounded on Luzon in the Philippines. He received his honorable discharge on October 31, 1945 and was awarded the Purple Heart.

When I first came home from the Army in 1946, I visited Milton in Sundown, Texas where he worked as a pumper in the oil field. I only saw him a couple of times after that. He married Lois Cook on January 15, 1947 and they had two sons and one daughter.

The last time I saw Milton was January 1957 at our friend Eddie Gotcher's funeral. Eddie was killed in a freak accident when he was adjusting an irrigation pump and was hit in the chest by a 36-inch pipe wrench.

Milton moved to Levelland, Texas in 1962 and continued on as a pumper. A few years later, he decided to leave the oil field and moved to Eastland, Texas. Attending school in Fort Worth, he earned his real estate license. He opened his own business and operated it until his death.

His wife, Lois told me that Milton just lived a normal life, but he would not talk about his war experiences. She did not press the issue, and never heard the story of how he earned his Purple Heart Award.

She also said that Milton enjoyed the small town atmosphere of Eastland, his church and church activities. He dearly loved to play Forty-two and dominoes with his friends and neighbors. It reminded me of how competitive Milton and I were as teenagers and how we used to partner up and challenge the gray hairs at their favorite game.

Another thing he enjoyed, was taking Lois for evening strolls. On March 1979 after their walk, Milton rested for the last time in his favorite chair in their den. Suddenly, he slumped over and died of a heart attack.

Sergeant Frank Sartor, served in the 77th Infantry Division as they landed on Ie Shima April 16, 1945. The 77th was instrumental in securing the island and encountered extremely heavy and fierce resistance and the fighting was fast and furious!

Departing Ie Shima on April 25, they relieved the 96th Division on Okinawa, April 28. It was on Okinawa that Frank was involved in the most vicious fighting of the campaign where so many American soldiers were killed or wounded.

After Okinawa surrendered, the 77th moved to Cebu, Philippine Islands. During October 1945, they moved to Japan for occupation duty.

Frank and I visited a couple of times after we got home from Japan and our trails never crossed again. After his honorable discharge, Frank attended Texas Tech University in Lubbock where he earned a Mechanical Engineering degree and graduated with honors. On September 14, 1946, he married Tena Medlock in Lubbock, Texas. They had two sons, Joe and Tom and one daughter, Cynthia who provided me with this information.

During the Cuban missile crisis, Frank was in charge of the mechanical systems for Atlas Missile sites at Abilene, Texas. He received numerous awards for his contributions at the Air Force Academy in Colorado Springs, where he was employed as the supervisory mechanical engineer from 1972 to 1983.

Frank was a family man and a deacon in his church. He never lost his passion for basketball and coached children's' basketball at his church. He partied, hunted, fished, played bridge, gardened, RV'd, and lived a full life.

It was not until his last days, at age 76, that Frank would finally talk about the war. It was only because he was trying to comfort his children by telling them that he had accepted his death as a young man decades before on the battlefield. After surviving the war, he considered his life a gift of extra time, because so many had sacrificed their lives. Frank won his last battle on September 16, 2002.

Gerald Henson and I remained close friends and continued to jam until we were both 81 years old. We cut a record in Arkansas when we were 18 and a CD when we were 80.

Gerald served in the 108th regiment of the 40th Infantry Division, and saw fierce action in the Philippines. He was in the mortar section and fought the Japanese on the Island of Luzon. Gerald earned the title of *Expert*, the highest level as a marksman in the military. Few recruits were able to shoot at that level.

During the Leyte Campaign, Gerald contracted acute lymphangitis which left untreated could have proved fatal. He had to walk alone two miles thru sniper-infested terrain and cross a raging river before reaching camp and reporting to sick call. He felt that he only made it thru *divine intervention* since no shots were fired and a group of soldiers met him at the river and helped him cross. The doctor hospitalized him immediately, and he spent twenty-one days where they lanced and scraped the infected areas.

After the war, he was sent to Seoul, Korea which was a far cry from the battlefield. He was assigned the task of trouble-shooting office equipment.

Soon, Gerald was called home on emergency due to his Dad's serious illness and was needed to run the family farm that they had recently purchased near Lawn, Texas. He received his honorable discharge June 7, 1946.

Mr. Henson eventually recovered and was back on his tractor plowing and doing the things he wanted to do and needed to do by the time I got back to the states. And, Gerald and I immediately started playing music and partying again like old times.

In the Fall of 1947, we moved to Abilene, Texas and shared an apartment as we both attended Draughon's Business College. Gerald completed his education at Hardin Simmons University, and I graduated from Draughon's.

On August 20, 1949, Gerald and my sister Opal were married in Lawn, Texas. His first job out of school was working as an accountant in Winters, Texas. In the Spring of 1955, my wife Wanda and I were excited when Gerald and Opal and their three children joined us and our two children in the middle of nowhere—-Monahans, Texas! There, we enjoyed many years raising our children and grandchildren together in this small West Texas town and shared many activities, outings, meals and holidays together.

Gerald and Opal had four children: Becky, Jerry, Karen and Tracy, all whom graduated from college and nine grandchildren.

Gerald worked as an accountant until his retirement. He enjoyed Little League baseball, hunting, woodworking and his children's activities in school and in church.

Although my good buddy, whom I met in first grade, and I spent over seven decades of friendship on a regular basis and talked about everything under the sun, he absolutely did not like to talk about the war. It was too painful and had a dramatic impact on his life.

I was with my lifelong friend right up until he passed away in his home on June 6, 2007. Thru seventy plus years of life's experiences, we managed to keep our jaws goin' and those strings burnin' as much as possible.

Ronold Ray

Returning to civilian life proved to be somewhat difficult for me. Being stationed halfway around the world, living and dealing with people of a different culture and the scarcity of news from the states, seemed to have caused time to stand still. And, I was not alone in this. My mind kept telling me that things would be basically the same as when I left.

The war had ended for civilians a year earlier, but for combat soldiers just returning from over seas duty, many of us needed time to adjust. Like most everyone, I had come out of battle. In addition, I had become accustomed to a very active, demanding and fast-paced way of life serving as the assistant manager of the *Surugadai*.

As I arrived home, it seemed everything had come to a screeching halt! It was peaceful and serene, but taking care of sheep, cattle and horses was nothing to get excited about anymore. Even ol' Bully seemed tame compared to what I had been through.

With most of my friends and family scattered, it was not the same. Milton was in Sundown and Frank was away studying at Texas Tech in Lubbock. I missed my brother, Lester, who was working in Del Rio and was not around to play for parties like old times. Of course, Lowell would be away in the service for a year or more. It seemed as if everyone had disappeared.

Thankfully, one thing hadn't changed—My buddy, Gerald, was still around. He and I started playing music together again and partying like old times. And, like before, meeting girls at parties hadn't changed either. Now partying was fun, but I needed to make a decision about my future, like getting a job or going to school.

It was during this time that my cousin, Glenn Mitchell and I had some serious talks about making a career out of the military. After much soul searching, I decided against it. Glenn was in the Navy during the war, but signed up for a hitch in the Army.

I did visit Tim Turner in Chillicothe, Texas once and met his wife and baby daughter. He was very happy with his decision to enlist in the regular Army for eighteen months.

I enrolled in Draughon's Business College, in Abilene, and made the 35-mile jaunt back home in my black 1940 model Plymouth on the weekends. However, it was not for the purpose of feeding the chickens. I realized that the girl living down the road on the next farm was becoming very important to me. I just couldn't seem to resist those dark eyes. Taking Wanda Woodard to the movie in Winters on a Friday night or to a party on Saturday night soon became the norm.

On July 31, 1948, we were married at the Novice Methodist parsonage with Gerald and my sister, Opal as our attendants. Then, Wanda and I made our first home in a garage apartment in Abilene while I continued my education. I graduated from Draughon's on March 4, 1949. Soon, Larry Don made his debut at Hendricks Memorial Hospital July 11, 1949.

Next, I studied electronics at Taylor County Vocational Radio School 25 hours a week while working seven hours a day in an upholstery shop learning another trade. I graduated December 31, 1950.

In January 1951, we three Rays came sliding and skidding down Highway 80 in the ol' Plymouth braving a severe ice storm as I clutched our life's savings of $35.00. Our reason for moving was because my oldest sister, Vivian, and brother-in-law, Francis Nail, made me an offer, which enabled me to start my own business in Monahans where they resided.

With their help, we rented a three-room shotgun house, and I was able to start my first business-*Auto Upholstery Shop*. On December 29, 1953, Gina was born.

After owning my business for seventeen years, I sold it to my employee. I wanted to try my hand at avionics and spent almost three years as a specialist working on automatic pilots and flight director systems in Midland, Texas. However, I decided I preferred to work for myself.

Over the years, my ideas changed with the times, and I opened an electronic and major appliances store, with service in 1971. In January of 1985, I was approached by a county commissioner and was asked to finish serving a term for one of the Justices of the Peace. I was always game for a new challenge and accepted the offer. Eventually, I liquidated *Professional Electronics.*

I was elected to office in 1986 and served for eighteen years as Justice of Peace in Precinct 2 Ward County, Texas and completed 480 clock hours at the Texas Justice Court Training Center.

Wanda and I and our two children, Larry and Gina, had a full life living in the small west Texas town of Monahans as we all were actively involved in the traditional activities of school, church and community. Larry completed his double degree in Math /Science at Sul Ross University in Alpine and made his home in Monahans with his wife Kathy where they had three children—- Eric, Ginger and Chad. I thank God that he gave us our super-charged, fun-loving, and charismatic son, Larry to love for 45 years before he was called home on September 24, 1994.

Gina, who completed her degree in Journalism/Photography at Texas Tech University, has one son, Brian and lives in Coppell, Texas. We stay in touch and get together often and enjoy our annual trip to Branson. Although writing this book together has been a thought-provoking and an emotional experience to relive, it has also been a great time to fellowship with my daughter.

In December of 2002, my life changed dramatically. After 54 years of marriage, Wanda passed away on Christmas Day, and I retired December 31 at the age of 77. Since then, I have stayed so busy that I don't know when I ever had time to work.

I have been traveling, playing the piano and my mandolin with various groups entertaining in small communities, churches, nursing homes and senior citizen centers around Texas and writing. I have continued to enjoy my grandchildren, family and friends and have remained active in The First United Methodist Church, roaring in the Lions' Club each Tuesday, playing bridge and letting the younger generation challenge *this* gray hair in dominoes!

Gina Ray

It has been an honor and a rewarding experience to write this memoir with my Dad. Most World War II veterans could not talk about their painful experiences. However, Dad has been talking about it for as long as I can remember. His unique situation, during the occupation of Japan, allowed him to get to know the Japanese personnel of the hotel in which he worked. In doing so, he was able to begin the healing process before he returned home.

Instead of dwelling on the tragic losses, he shares his stories of people he met and the many lessons he learned through those experiences which have carried him through life. As tragic as any war is, he has not forgotten the ultimate sacrifices that were made. Yet, he manages to find the positives in any given situation no matter how grim it might be.

All my life, I have witnessed his faith in God is strong and unwavering. He knows that no matter what the circumstances are, through Jesus Christ, life's battle has already been won. His life has been dedicated to service and leadership to this great country, and to his community, church and family.

For courageous men and women, who have fought for and defended our precious freedoms, I will forever be grateful. *Thanks, Dad.*

CPSIA information can be obtained
at www.ICGtesting.com
Printed in the USA
LVHW060502260119
605316LV00001B/1/P

9 781598 587067